DIRECTING THE
MARKETING EFFORT

Ray Willsmer is one of the very few men to have held Board appointments in manufacturing, media and advertising. He started his career as a university lecturer in economics and statistics until called up for service in the RAF. On his return to civilian life, he joined the marketing department of J. Walter Thompson, where he spent three years. For the next nine years he worked at J. Lyons & Company, where he progressed rapidly from Brand Manager to Marketing Director of the Tea, Coffee and Grocery Division. A return to advertising, with Ogilvy and Mather, followed, where he handled a large portfolio of blue-chip accounts. Until the early part of 1973 he was Marketing and Planning Director of the Thomson Organization. In September of 1973 he formed his own advertising agency, Ray Willsmer and Associates. Twice past Chairman of the Marketing Society, he is Chairman of the CAM Education Panel and External Examiner at the University of Strathclyde.

D1387548

Editorial Advisers
M. A. Pocock BSc(Econ), A. H. Taylor MC FCCA

Management Series

DIRECTING THE MARKETING EFFORT

RAY L. WILLSMER

Revised and slightly abridged for this edition

PAN BOOKS LTD
LONDON AND SYDNEY

First published 1971 by Staples Press Ltd
This revised edition published 1975 by Pan Books Ltd
Cavaye Place, London SW10 9PG

ISBN 0 330 24125 7

Printed in Great Britain by Cox & Wyman Ltd,
London, Reading and Fakenham

To the memory of my son, Dermot – 1960–1968

CONTENTS

INTRODUCTION

This book had its genesis in a series of one-day seminars I gave for the British Institute of Management under the title 'What Every Director Should Know About Marketing'. It became increasingly obvious that there was a demand not only to know what 'Marketing' is, but to know what to expect from the experts, how to organize Marketing departments where none existed and to what extent the techniques employed are applicable to different kinds and sizes of business and how reliable they are. At the same time, from other lectures given to Marketing men and experience in consultancy, it was clear that many aspiring Marketing Directors had no idea what they were heading for in managing a coordinated department and were thus unlikely to be of the greatest value to their Chief Executive. I have tried to draw these two elements together by aiming at:

1. Chief Executives who need to know more about Marketing, want to know how trustworthy the welter of pseudo-science is and how to extract the best from their Marketing department.
2. Newly appointed – or aspiring – Marketing Directors who will suddenly be faced with the special and unique problems of managing a complex, integrated Marketing department.
3. Existing Marketing Directors whose responsibilities are about to expand to take in more elements in the mix and/or those who wish to expand the sophistication of their department.

This book does not aim to be a highly technical treatise on specific topics nor does it pretend to be all-embracing. Rather, it is a personal distillation of practical experience of matters that are most frequently questioned, ignored or mishandled. Underlying all I have written is my firm conviction that the

Marketing concept is the only way to business success and that as a philosophy that concept is inherently simple. Unfortunately, it has been confused with the increasingly complex and often esoteric techniques of Marketing to produce a welter of mumbo-jumbo that has made Marketing another in the ever-increasing list of tyrant management cults.

To cover the needs of the different people to whom this book is addressed, I have divided it into three separate parts. In Part 1 I have tried to emphasize the essential underlying simplicity and appropriateness of the Marketing philosophy and to relate it to the everyday business problems of survival and growth. Part 2 provides a fairly elementary glossary of the more common 'techniques' and items in what is normally termed 'the Marketing mix'. Again, I have adopted a deliberately practical bias, for even the busy expert often overlooks the deficiencies and limitations of the tools he works with. Finally, Part 3 deals with the vital mechanics of planning, checking and achieving plans and the peculiar management problems of Marketing where, for many participants, the word 'manager' is a complete anachronism.

There are many excellent books on aspects of Marketing and I have tried to avoid duplication. Rather, I suggest further reading at the end of each chapter for those who may wish to follow up particular points. Please, however, beware of theories and systems, whether they be in this book or in any other. Marketing is a dynamic subject where facts change fast and buyers' behaviour is frequently completely irrational and totally unpredictable. It is the very essence of the Marketing approach to business that one is continually questioning and reappraising what one is trying to do, what one ought to be doing and how the company should be organized to do these things. It is unlikely that any business will ever have the ideal form of organization and if it did it would only be the ideal at a point in time. This is especially true of the Marketing function where the organization will depend upon changing circumstances, the people available and the way those people develop in their jobs. What may be a perfectly adequate form of organization under one set of conditions may become inappropriate to a new circumstance such as a takeover or entry into a new area of business expertise. We have few laws in Marketing and not many more generally applicable rules. Part of the purpose of this book is to examine the degree of reliance we can place on such rules.

This book is somewhat unusual in that I have deliberately refrained from asking any prominent person to read all through it. Only one chapter has had the benefit of outside comment and for that I must thank my colleagues John Williams and Alan Wolfe, and I especially thank Alan for the many fascinating discussions we have had during the two years we worked together. Whilst I have called this book largely a distillation of personal experience I must acknowledge the enormous contributions of my former colleagues at J. Lyons & Company Limited in helping – and sometimes forcing – me to arrive at certain conclusions. I am, too, immensely grateful to the many students and managers I have lectured to who have argued with me about the relevance of certain techniques to their particular business and thus given me a much more rounded outlook than I otherwise would have had. I think we have proved to each other – and I hope this book helps to reinforce the view – that the basic Marketing philosophy is applicable to all types and sizes of business and that only the items in the mix and the validity of certain techniques vary.

Finally, I want publicly to thank my wife and children for giving up so much during the writing of this book, for being so helpful and encouraging by keeping relatively quiet and turning the sound of the television down lower than they would have wished! I owe, too, an enormous debt of gratitude to Mrs Valerie King who had the unenviable task of deciphering mountains of my handwriting and typing the manuscript so accurately and with such charming cheerfulness.

Part 1

The Marketing Philosophy

Chapter 1

The Meaning of Marketing

'Would you tell me, please, which way I ought to go from here?'
'That depends a good deal on where you want to get to,' said the Cat.
'I don't much care where . . .' said Alice.
'Then it doesn't matter which way you go,' said the Cat.
'. . . so long as I get *somewhere*,' Alice added as an explanation.
'Oh, you're sure to do that,' said the Cat, 'if you only walk long enough.'
Alice felt that this could not be denied, so she tried another question.
'What sort of people live about here?'
'In *that* direction,' the Cat said, waving its right paw round, 'lives a Hatter: and in *that* direction,' waving the other paw, 'lives a March Hare. Visit either you like: they're both mad.'
'But I don't want to go among mad people,' Alice remarked.
'Oh, you can't help that,' said the Cat: 'we're all mad here. I'm mad. You're mad.'
'How do you know I'm mad?' said Alice.
'You must be,' said the Cat, 'or you wouldn't have come here.'

I would not like it to be thought that the world of Marketing is in any way like Alice's Wonderland or that one has to be mad to read on!

That quotation is so relevant because businesses – like Alice – are often more preoccupied with getting *somewhere* rather than ensuring that they are going in the right direction.

If there is any one thing that Marketing in the practical sense is concerned with it is making sure that the direction is right. And that direction will always be the one which leads the way the customer would choose for himself. Marketing is about customers, not producers; demand, not supply.

The whole subject has become a gigantic paradox. We have taken a simple statement of philosophy and so confused the issue with techniques, mystique and mumbo-jumbo that one part of the business world feels that Marketing is all too mysterious and expensive for them, a second part feels itself enmeshed in a new form of management science tyranny whilst a third, and most dangerous, section has adopted Marketing as one adopts the latest fashions – and may well discard it as readily.

The root cause of all this doubt is the confusion that we 'professionals' have created by our concentration upon the techniques of Marketing instead of hammering home the simple philosophy. What makes the subject a paradox is the fact that virtually all those who express the biggest doubts about Marketing would accept the basic tenets without question.

Put at its simplest, Marketing expresses the age-old philosophy 'the customer is always right'. To this, it adds the belief that a man who takes a business risk is entitled to make a profit as his reward. So we are basically concerned with making a profit by giving customers what they want.

Round these two simple ideas, we have developed a whole subject – part science, part art and, regrettably, part myth. Peripheral subjects (with their associated industries) have grown around this simple philosophical foundation like a host of satellite stars all designed, let me emphasize, to ensure that what we ultimately offer will be acceptable to the consumer and more desirable than our competitors are offering.

Inevitably, we must talk about definitions. There are literally thousands of them and most of their originators must bear heavy responsibility for creating the fear of Marketing that many businessmen experience. Definitions tend to be of two types: simple statements and omnibus attempts that try to get everybody into the act.

It is hard to say which is the more damaging. The simple statements too often confuse the philosophy with one of the techniques available. This leads to statements like 'Of course, Marketing is really only Selling'. The omnibus attempts often read like Acts of Parliament and frequently suffer the same fate of having a horse and cart driven through the loopholes. Many of these long definitions sound more like the job-statement of the Chief Executive of a small company.

One of the crosses that the Marketing man has to bear is the inability to describe simply what he does. We can, however, express the function of Marketing much more simply. I am going to give you three 'definitions'. The first two are almost clichés and are complementary.

Firstly, to describe the philosophy: *Marketing is selling goods (or services) that won't come back to customers who will!*

Secondly, to cover the techniques: *Marketing takes the guesswork out of hunch!*

Let us examine these two statements before trying to become more erudite. They are simple, they are memorable and they are true.

The test of any product is the amount of repeat purchases. If the customers keep on coming back and there is no dissatisfaction with your product you have passed the Marketing test. However, as we shall see later, you have passed the test only at that particular point of time. As time passes, attitudes change, new techniques are discovered and new competitors attack. At this stage, you will want information on which to base decisions.

Science alone has eliminated many bad products but it hasn't produced many good ones. It has improved innumerable ideas. This is perhaps the prime function of the more sophisticated techniques. They give you the chance to put the bright ideas to the test without committing vast amounts of capital, and to make sure that they stand up to that most vital of tests – consumer demand.

No one can really make much of a claim for originating any definition of Marketing; the basic ideas have been around too long. Sir Paul Chambers summed up what it is all about when he said: 'Productivity in the quantitative sense is irrelevant: productivity is for the purpose of meeting human needs, and unless you meet what people want there is no productivity. If you produce a lot of rubbish that nobody wants to buy, your productivity is nil, and to hell with statistics. That is the point, and it is not really understood.'

Two centuries earlier, Adam Smith was expanding the doctrine of 'the Sovereignty of the Consumer' (in *The Wealth of Nations*) and writing: 'Consumption is the sole end purpose of all production; and the interest of the producer ought to be attended to only so far as it may be necessary for promoting that of the consumer.'

Expressed in those forcible terms, Marketing has obviously always existed, albeit intuitively. Could anyone deny that Sir John Cohen (of Tesco fame) is a magnificent intuitive Marketeer who has recognized the need for satisfying consumer desires and has harnessed this to the entrepreneurial skill of taking risks on perceived opportunities? By the same token, Agatha Christie and Georges Simenon have 'marketed' their writing talents. Interestingly enough, jazz (and now 'pop') musicians have long summed up the 'Marketing' of their art – pandering to public taste – as 'going commercial'.

Where Marketing enters the realms of greatest difficulty is where one encounters the problems of growth. Businesses do not stand still for long: they grow or they die. To grow and go on growing, one is led increasingly towards sophistication in Management. Sophisticated Management cannot exist without acceptance of the basic philosophy of Marketing and its infiltration into every corner of the business.

Let me quote a wonderful example of this. The company was Petfoods Limited, a subsidiary of Mars. A colleague and I were talking to a machine operative who was describing how ingredients were fed into a machine, mixed, 'cooked' and then blown up to greater size. My colleague decided to play this man along a little. 'Surely you aren't doing the best for your company? Your job is to make that product at the lowest possible cost and here you are blowing it up to make it bigger. You're just adding cost.'

The operative came straight back with his reply: 'My job is to make the product the customers want at the lowest cost and I'm making it the way we know they want it.'

I was impressed not merely because a machine operative

could talk pure Marketing sense but because someone had taken the trouble to communicate this philosophy and information right the way down the line. It is no accident that this is one of the most successful businesses in the country with an enviable return on capital employed.

There is no business anywhere that will not be improved by understanding this simple message and by making sure that the Marketing concept is understood and applied by every part of the business.

As a counter to the Petfoods story, I must mention the (unnamed) company which had an abnormal number of complaints about one particular batch of product. So many, in fact, that it was forced to call in several weeks' production and destroy it at vast expense. The reason? A buyer had varied the recipe by using a special cheap job-lot of one ingredient which he felt sure no one could notice. After all, he and his assistant couldn't tell the difference.

A little earlier, I slipped in one word and one phrase and neither should pass without remark. The word was 'Management'. Marketing and Management cannot be separated, for unless the Marketing philosophy is accepted and practised, there is no business to Manage. It is effective Management that projects the Marketing philosophy into every nook and cranny of the business.

The phrase was 'return on capital employed'. We are all in business to make a profit. It is important, however, that we measure that profit against something. The 'something' may vary from business to business and from time to time. It will include such things as previous performance, relationship between final net profit and total assets employed, dividend performance and possibly others. This is not the place to question the wisdom of these various measures. It is the place to emphasize that the success of the Marketing philosophy must be measured in continuing profit and profit must be measured against some appropriate yardstick.

And so to a definition of Marketing which draws together the various threads of this chapter: *Marketing is the Management skill of identifying opportunities of satisfying customers'*

*requirements and, by so doing, maximizing the long-term profits
of the Company against an appropriate financial yardstick.*

Let us understand clearly the importance of the word 'skill'.
Marketing is not, and never will be, a science. There are too
many areas where irrefutable laws – the essence of science –
will not be possible. We use science where we can to eliminate
possibilities but we are almost invariably left with the exercise
of our own judgement. Even the computer is no panacea; it
merely allows us to look at more things more quickly but it
does not give answers.

Only people do that. One of the tasks of this book is to
suggest what questions we should be asking, outline some of
the techniques that can help and suggest how we can best
organize ourselves for success.

Suggestions for Further Reading

Almost every book on the subject begins with a chapter on
definitions. The best introduction, in my opinion, is to be found
in *Marketing in a Competitive Economy* by Leslie Rodger,
published by Hutchinson. In his first chapter he traces the
economic derivation of the subject and discusses the requirements of good Marketing theory.

Chapter 2

Marketing and the Size and Nature of the Business

Introduction

It is a rare experience for any speaker on Marketing addressing an audience of experienced businessmen to escape being told that Marketing is all very well for detergents and foodstuffs but has no place in the small business or industrial companies or service industries.

The message of the first chapter is that such statements are quite untrue. The Marketing attitude of mind is for every business and for every manager within it. It is only when one comes down to techniques and specific approaches to problems that the size and nature of the business become an important consideration. Indeed, in many instances, the so-called 'fast-moving consumer goods' are worse off than other types of business, and whilst the small business may lack people and financial resources to permit the use of the more sophisticated approaches it possesses a number of valuable advantages over its larger competitors.

This, relatively short, chapter is complementary to Chapter 1. Throughout the book we shall consider the special problems of various types of business and quote examples wherever appropriate. For the moment, let us just look at the main, very broad, types of business and examine the relevance of the Marketing philosophy to each and any key points of difference which may assume special significance when dealing with later topics.

'Fast-Moving Consumer Goods'

This has become such an accepted phrase that job advertisements frequently use the abbreviation 'fmcg'. Yet, ironically, many products included in this category are actually slower to sell than the products of some light industries. (For example, many supermarkets have discovered that electric light bulbs have a faster turnover than some foodstuffs.)

If there is any single definition of this category which is more meaningful than a long catalogue of products, it is that they are mass-market items with short, or relatively short, lives whose purchasers are private individuals. Thus, we include grocery and confectionery products, soap powders, detergents and cosmetic items in an incomplete list. Cosmetics represent a good example of the grey area where slow-moving items merge with fast-turnover products.

Those not in these markets tend to assume that, apart from a fiercely competitive environment, all is plain sailing in Marketing terms. In fact, the reason for high expenditures on research and the large staffs is a direct reflection of the complexity of operation. When the potential is so great the risk is enormous and the correct analysis and quantification of opportunities is absolutely critical. Because of these difficulties and because it is so vital to come up with the best possible answer, the majority of the Marketing techniques that are best known have been developed for goods in the 'fast-moving' category.

A distinguishing feature of products in this category is the importance of what might be termed socio-psychological motives in buying behaviour. This creates an emphasis on non-product attributes (such as packaging and value added by advertising), leading in turn to an armoury of techniques which are generally applicable only to this particular field. Nevertheless, it always remains true that no package however well constructed and designed and no advertisement however clever can continue to sell a product that does not come up to customers' expectations or which they don't want anyway.

Industrial Markets

For the moment, let us assume that we can talk about a single valid category under this heading. In fact, we should separate out capital goods, consumer durables, raw materials and so on. Later on, when it becomes necessary to the examination of specific techniques and approaches, we shall do so.

At any given time, the number of buyers is likely to be small and the value of the sale very much higher. The number of buyers for very heavy, specialized, machinery is small at any time. The market for furniture is theoretically some sixteen million homes but the number actually in the market for a three-piece suite at any time is quite small. In both cases, considerable shopping activity precedes purchase and alternative products are carefully evaluated for life, performance and price. Price is directly related to anticipated performance without the influence of socio-psychological overtones (except, to a limited degree, where fashion – as with some furniture – is an element influencing choice).

Over a large part of this area, the manufacturer or supplier is concerned with goods or services which are sold to buyers who in turn use them to produce something for other buyers. This can create often very serious problems of identifying the customer. Who is the customer who must be satisfied, the final user of the finished article, or the intermediary? In some product fields, there may be several possible buyers influencing the purchasing decision. For example, the manufacture of nylon must influence the maker-up, the retailer and the wearer of nylon garments.

Another characteristic of industrial Marketing, especially with the heavier industries, is that the financial implications of the buying decision are so much greater than with consumer goods. The buyer has to consider not just the capital cost but such items as the lost-opportunity cost of late delivery and poor after-sales service, the quality of components and other factors which all reflect upon the final price of the purchase and the costs of production with the plant purchased. Many of these considerations, of course, apply equally to consumer durables. For example, the attitude of Volkswagen, who will not expand in an overseas market until adequate servicing facilities exist, contrasts sharply with that of most British car manufacturers who have been spoiled by the fat years when demand exceeded supply. It still does for one or two makes: those with a high reputation for reliability, careful factory inspection and rapid after-sales service.

In industrial markets (using the term in the widest sense) adopting the Marketing philosophy frequently means providing facilities to look after the product until the end of its life. British industry on the whole compares unfavourably with overseas competitors in regarding after-sales service as part of the total product. This has created an impetus towards leasing in the industrial and office equipment fields and renting and hiring in the consumer durable field. (Research into television rental, for example, shows that prompt service at no extra cost is the main reason for renting.) The buyer in the industrial (and most consumer durable) markets likes to feel that he has a continuing discourse with the seller throughout the product's life even though he does not necessarily expect free service.

Service Industries

This is another category which covers a multitude of businesses. Advertising agencies, banks, computer bureaux, insurance companies, for example, all come under this heading. Because the field is so diverse, one can examine only a few generalizations and a couple of specific businesses at this juncture.

Speaking very generally, there seems to be a distinct difference in users' reactions, depending upon whether the user is a company or an individual. Where service industries are bad in consumer orientation it tends to be because they are not being sufficiently disciplined by the consumer or because the 'competing' companies all offer the same inadequate service. Here one must inevitably think of the banks who choose to do their business at times which cause the maximum inconvenience to working people. In the United States, banks have sought out the customer by late opening, making loans as easy as possible to obtain and competing on charges. One must have an enormous amount of sympathy with British bankers who, until quite recently, have been precluded by Government action from taking advantage of the enormous latent demand for credit. However, giving personalized cheque-book covers is only scratching the surface of a Marketing approach to banking.

Insurance has been a field where the persuasiveness of the salesman has been the traditional method of selling. In recent years the dual challenge of inflation and Unit Trusts with linked life assurance benefits has brought a new Marketing vigour to life assurance in particular which previously was open only to those who dealt through brokers. (Without wishing to enter into argument about the merits of using a broker against consulting one company, other things being equal, the customer will be presented with the best solution to his problem by a broker compared to the only answer any one company can offer.) Whilst it is clear that no insurance company can tailor schemes to individual customers (any more than one coffee roaster can tailor blends to pander to every conceivable taste), Marketing departments are now being established to create policies tailored to modern conditions. Psychologically, there is a growing tendency to concentrate upon the benefits received at maturity of the policy rather than the death benefits.

There is nothing so new about this. I knew a door-to-door insurance salesman who made a real 'killing' in the East End of London in the 1930s by using the simple approach 'If you pay me a penny a week, I'll bet you (naming the appropriate sum) you don't die before you are sixty-five! And you can't lose. My company will give you back all the money we've collected from you when you are sixty-five. We'll just be saving the money for you.' (No profits on this policy!) That man was an intuitive Marketing man. He had sized up his market, sold them an attractive proposition and addressed it to them in the buyers' own language.

What a contrast to those dreadful advertisements which emphasize death. Advertisements like the happy family scene where the devoted father has a cross marked over his heart and the copy says, in effect, 'What are they going to live on when you are dead and gone?' Or do you remember the series showing an empty office desk with the headline 'Who will go through your desk tomorrow?'

The very word 'service' should imply that consumer satisfaction is paramount, yet we are surrounded with evidence that this is not so. Transportation, catering, public utilities, garages – all these, and others, present numerous examples of lack of consumer orientation. There is perhaps greater opportunity for a real Marketing breakthrough in the service area than in any other kind of industry.

The Small Business

Whenever I am asked to speak or write about Marketing and the small business I am reminded of Maupassant and the man who had been speaking prose all his life without knowing it. The small business that doesn't totally satisfy its customers very rapidly ceases to be a business. If one examines those definitions of Marketing which list the tasks involved one finds something which reads suspiciously like the job description of the Chief Executive of a small business.

'Small', of course, can be relative. Definitions in common use tend to be expressed in terms of turnover limits, the number of senior executives involved in decision making, relative size (compared to the leader in the field) or some combination. There are merits and disadvantages in each of these. £500,000 of turnover may seem an adequate definition of a small business for most purposes but this would exclude, for example, a £2,000,000 company in the biscuit market: a market currently worth some £150,000,000 at retail prices. Such a company is certainly a small fish in this particular ocean. A small number of senior executives is certainly a characteristic of the really small business but, used alone, this would let in some highly efficient, very large companies. Relative size has the advantage of letting in the hypothetical biscuit company of my earlier example. Unfortunately, it sets different standards for different industries. If, for example, you define as 'small' any business with less than fifty per cent of the market you could include a biscuit company with a turnover of £50,000,000, yet a small business in a £1,000,000 total market would have a turnover of less than £500,000.

The small business has many problems peculiar to it. Perhaps the most basic are:

1. Priorities.
2. Why do people buy from a small company?
3. Problems of growth.

All these points will come up several times as we progress. Some brief comment is appropriate now, however. The small business is a classic example of the basic issues of pure economics: the allocation of scarce resources with alternative uses to competing ends. Capital, time and people are the scarcest resources of the small business and the degree of pressure on each of these will determine priority. Selling and service, for example, will normally occupy a much higher place and advertising a much lower place than in the large business.

When we come to consider a form of Marketing self-analysis, we shall see how important it is to identify reasons why you are in business. Why should a small business be able to withstand competition from the giants of industry? The reasons may well be to do with the allocation of priorities; prompt local delivery, for example, may score over the longer delivery dates of the larger company. Some companies actually prefer to deal with small companies, feeling that they are leaner and hungrier than their big competitors. If that is the reason why you sell, it is vital to stay keen.

The third special problem is that of growth. All kinds and sizes of business have this problem but in the small business it is often harder to recognize. This is especially true of those problems specifically relating to demand and which will be dealt with in the next chapter. But the small business has many advantages which allow it to harness its energies for growth.

The business is still basically in a totally controllable Marketing state. Because fewer people are involved in the decision process, reactions can be swift and decisions implemented rapidly. Not only has the top man the authority to act, he is always aware (or he should be) that those beneath him are waiting for him to act and this acts as an incentive to him.

International Marketing

'International Marketing' is an omnibus heading which covers the many ways of selling products outside their country of origin or the home of the parent company. In practical, everyday terms there are numerous differences between domestic and international Marketing. Reduced to the philosophical terms in which we have been dealing so far, there are three important considerations:

1. Can the domestic product be sold overseas without changes?
2. If not, what changes are needed and is the operation still viable?
3. Does the volume and/or profitability justify setting up plant overseas?

The first two questions highlight the essential demand aspect of international Marketing; the third really distinguishes between 'export' and 'international'.

As domestic markets shrink or the incremental cost of additional business reaches new heights, there is a strong temptation to look overseas for new markets. It is totally wrong to assume without question that a product which is successful at home will be successful overseas. Tastes change, preferences for colours differ, Government regulations may vary considerably. Names, selling slogans and advertising media differ and can significantly affect results.

There are many wildly diverse examples. The turkey industry in Spain is developing slowly, using British-bred stock. The Spaniards are great chicken-eaters and would appear to offer an enormous potential for turkey. However, the Spaniards are very fond of saffron-coloured food and the creamy-white meat that is to the British taste was not right for Spain, and special breeds have been introduced. Many British food products contain additives and colourings which are not permitted in the United States. Conversely, American regulations permit many preservatives to extend the life of food products which are not allowed in this country. Many brand names and sales messages literally do not translate and some which do produce unfortunate results. A colour signifying gaiety in this country may indicate mourning in another. A product requiring demonstration may fail in a country where there is no suitable medium like television or cinema.

All in all, international Marketing obeys the same basic rules as any other category and one should investigate a new overseas market just as one would examine a new product opportunity at home. If any qualification is necessary, it is that one should exercise extraordinary care. An operation conducted at a distance is always more difficult to control. Moreover, one is frequently confronted by very low levels of Marketing sophistication often associated with high levels of enthusiasm from local agents. Never, never be tempted to do your preliminary investigations on the cheap and do not make any major investment without visiting the market yourself and making sure that some Marketing-oriented, objective executive makes a thorough and unbiased study of conditions. There are many Government aids to exporters; there are numerous good consultants – at home and abroad – capable of carrying out thorough research and investigation. Before you sign the cheque, however, you must see for yourself: there is no substitute – as long as you go with an open mind.

Conclusion

Marketing is a philosophy aimed at satisfying the consumer profitably. It is part of every manager's job to practise this philosophy and it is equally applicable to any size or type of business. The job of a Marketing Director is to be (as Proctor and Gamble Ltd always put it) the consumer's representative within the company. He will guide the decisions of his Chief Executive by assessing and reducing the degree of risk inherent in the choice between alternative courses of action. It is only when it comes to the use of specific techniques and approaches that the type and size of the business make for significant differences.

Suggestions for Further Reading

The small business is better catered for than the industrial whilst the service industries are ignored in this country. I do not feel competent to recommend any book ostensibly dealing with industrial Marketing which varies by more than the odd chapter from any book dealing with large consumer goods companies. There are some good specific chapters, however, in *Industrial Marketing* by Lawrence Fisher, published by Business Books. John Winkler has written a most readable book called *Marketing for the Developing Company* published by Hutchinson Marketing Library, and Graeme Roe has written one entitled *Profitable Marketing for the Smaller Company* published by the Directors Bookshelf. Mention should also be made of the excellent courses run by the Institute of Marketing.

Chapter 3

Demand

The Nature of Demand

Marketing is concerned with demand, not supply. Demand exists only at the point where a transaction takes place. It is important to understand the difference between 'desire' and 'demand'. You may have a very strong desire to own a Rolls-Royce but, unless you are one of the very fortunate few, you will never actually buy one. So far as Rolls-Royce are concerned, you are not in the target market for their cars for there is no real prospect of your ever converting into action your desire to join that élite band. In the terms of the classical economists, demand exists only at a price.

The correct estimation of potential demand is the first task of the entrepreneur. A piece of consumer research (in the form of test-drives) of Rolls-Royce cars would undoubtedly produce a highly favourable result, with perhaps 100 per cent saying they would like to own one. Unless that response is analysed in terms of who can actually afford one, garage it, manage the high cost of keeping the car on the road, and so on, one would have a very false impression of the likely market for Rolls-Royce cars. This is a very obvious example, yet those of us who deal with many different product fields continually run into examples where a market has been interpreted in terms of desire rather than in terms of the number of people actually likely to buy and how frequently they will purchase. A quick-cooking rice earned exceptionally high ratings in product test against ordinary rice pudding and quite a satisfactory number of housewives said they would buy it. It failed in test market. Research carried out during the test showed that housewives normally only made conventional rice pudding when the oven was already in use (say, for a joint). Under these conditions, speed meant nothing. Although the product performance was all that could have been wished for, there was no real demand – willingness to buy – for such a product.

It is absolutely vital to identify as early as possible the real target market for the goods or services you are selling. It is no good saying, for example, that everyone should be insured or have a bank account. Identify the immediate prospects first: leave the problems until the last. Later, when we consider techniques, we shall touch on this problem again. We should always be seeking to maximize our profits: that will only come from tackling those whose basic desire for what we are selling can be quickly and economically converted into action. Demand occurs when money changes hand.

Recognizing Signs of Decline

One cannot seriously consider questions of demand without studying problems of when demand stops. Demand may cease for any one or combination of reasons. Every product has a life span and every industry is made up of competing products whose individual life spans will differ. This is the concept of the 'Product Life Cycle'. This is such an important subject, and one which is capable of so much greater use than most managers make of it, that it will be the subject of the next chapter. This section therefore deals only with a couple of very simple points.

Many businesses, especially developing ones, are carried away by steeply upward-sloping sales curves and fail to recognize the signs of impending decline. Every sales curve contains within it the seeds of its own decline. A straight-line graph represents sales which, whilst growing, are growing at a declining rate. For example:

Table 1: Sales v Percentage Increase

Year	Sales	Percentage Increase
1	10	—
2	20	100
3	30	50
4	40	33·33
5	50	25
6	60	20
7	70	16·66
8	80	14·3
9	90	12·5
10	100	11·1
11	110	10·0

It is very seldom that one sees a straight-line sales graph but the message is clear: examination of percentage increases is one way of looking for an eventual slow-down of growth. (Plotting sales figures on logarithmic paper automatically does this for you. One of the useful properties of this kind of graph paper is that the graph will advance by an equal increase in height for the same percentage increase. This makes it particularly valuable for comparing the relative progress of two brands or your trend against that of the market as a whole. There are, however, some peculiarities which need understanding and the reader who is unfamiliar with logarithmic paper is recommended to do a little further study as recommended at the end of this chapter.)

Another measure of future progress is the cost of each incremental increase in sales. As one begins to 'top out' on the sales curve, each increase in sales costs more to achieve and eventually one would reach the point where marginal revenue (the income from selling one more unit) is less than the marginal cost (the cost of making that one unit). In theory, one does not go beyond the point where marginal revenue equals marginal costs. However, there are often short-term situations where this policy is deliberately adopted, for example, where such strong pressure can be exerted that a competitor will lose share or be forced out of the market (thus changing the whole situation). More frequently, in multi-product companies, selling continues beyond the theoretical top point in order to increase the total cash value of the gross contribution to overheads (a point which will occur several times throughout this book).

It would, however, be dangerous to take the cost of additional sales as the sole measure of the likelihood of lower sales in the future. One must be certain that the total business is operating as efficiently as possible. The answer to marginal revenue exceeding marginal cost may well be additional or more efficient plant. Clearly an analysis of the cost of sales must be married to careful analysis of total target market demand and what share your own business can reasonably expect. If both are greater than they are now, one should examine ways of producing the desired volume economically. Costs do not rise smoothly. Fixed costs rise in a series of plateaux. In the early stages of any new plant, cost per unit is high unless a substantial volume is rapidly achieved.

How Good is 'Good'?

Many companies have been deceived either by failing to recognize that their own progress was not as good as the market in which they were operating, or by overestimating the share of the market they could achieve in the face of competition. The relatively short history of Marketing is full of examples to prove that share of market is more important than total volume sales in the long run. An obsession with one's own figures without regard to the rest of the market can be fatal.

Let us accept that the size of any market is limited. A competitor growing more rapidly than you is taking a larger share of the cake. As he gets larger, he will tend to have wider distribution through potential outlets, will occupy more space in warehouses, stockrooms and on shelves and counters and, generally, reinforce his image by greater recognition simply by being seen more often. (The same considerations apply to

more bank branches in High Streets, more shops, etc.)
Retailers tend to gravitate towards brand leaders for they draw
more shop traffic. In all businesses, people tend to lean
towards the biggest. It is vital, therefore, to check your
progress against the market as a whole and, wherever possible,
directly against your major competitors. The main methods
are considered in the section on techniques. Technical
industries and smaller markets tend to have very efficient trade
associations which collect total market statistics. These
businesses tend to be quite well served by Government
statistics too. Obviously, neither of these sources allows you to
identify your competitors directly. However, if your growth is
not matching the market, someone is growing at your expense
and steps need to be taken. Spending some money on research
may be one of them.

The answer to 'How good is "good"?' is that 'good' (or
'bad') is only relative and standards of comparison should be
part of the armoury of every Chief Executive and Marketing
man. (Witness the market research manager who, when asked
how his wife was, replied, 'Compared with who?')

Before we leave the important question of share of a market
let us briefly consider the deliberate tactic of operating on the
periphery of large markets and the tactics of declining markets.

One per cent of a very large market can be attractive in its
own right. Moreover, the business operating in such a small
way is unlikely to attract the attention of giants. Such an
operation may well be regional, confined to certain outlets or
possibly geared towards a sub-segment of the major target
market. Successful, deliberate, small-share operations have
been carried out (and still exist) in markets as diverse as pet
foods, cosmetics, cake mixes, banks and insurance companies.

Markets decline and it is seldom politic or profitable to
abandon a product once a turn-down has been reached. Indeed,
with the abandonment of advertising and special sales force
and management effort, often substantial short-term profits
can be made. We usually call this 'milking the brand': extract-
ing every scrap of profit for as long as the product will last.
However, a more profitable course may be to seek to stay in

the market longer by using whatever method is necessary to hold one's rate of decline to something at least no worse than that of the market as a whole. This will be a sound tactic where the product makes a significant contribution to general overheads and where there is no immediate successor to absorb the burden.

There are, as we have noted in passing, both economic and business theories as to when to cease the effort to expand. There are often overriding considerations which determine the need to carry on beyond the theoretical optimum. It is a fundamental maxim of Marketing that whatever course you take you must have a good reason why. Examination of relative brand-share position is vital to judging the success on the way up, the likely 'topping out' position and monitoring one's progress and performance on the way down – if one does carry on beyond the high-point of a brand's career.

Changing Reasons for Demand

There are innumerable reasons why demand for existing products may cease, including technical improvements to competing products, obsolescence, fashion, changes in taste and so on. Such changes bring in their wake new demands for new products or brands. However, a market may change or the demand for a single product may alter simply due to a change in the consumer's rationale for buying the product. More often, the market demand is for something other than what the manufacturer thought. Lyons Ready Brek was originally sold as an instant porridge and reached an early and rather unsatisfactory peak. Research showed that the correct positioning was as a hot instant breakfast competing with what are generally known as the variety breakfast cereals (Sugar Puffs, Rice Krispies, Sugar Ricicles, etc) and selling mainly as a product aimed at young children. Repositioned, it became highly successful and drew new competition in the form of imitative products. Johnson's Baby Oil finds considerable use as a general cosmetic cleansing oil and the same company now promotes its Baby Powder as an adult talcum. It is not only among fast-moving consumer products that such changes occur. A piece of machinery now widely used in the production of instant food products – the roller-drier – is based upon a machine originally designed for making cardboard! New uses are continually being discovered for existing products and the vast majority are initiated by customers, not manufacturers. A producer who fails to identify the real market he is satisfying is not making the most of his chances and may lose his place completely.

Of all the factors leading to changes in demand, the single most important one is time. Many of the other reasons – changes in fashion, product obsolescence and so on – are all functions of the passage of time. Just as every ascending sales curve carries the seed of its eventual decline, so every new product has begun to age. This leads us again to the concept of the product life cycle.

Suggestions for Further Reading

Chapter 2, 'Comparison of Data', of I. R. Vesselo's *How to Read Statistics*, published by Harrap, is a useful introduction in a very readable book. Chapter 3 of the Pelican Book *Facts from Figures* by M. J. Moroney deals with the same subject.

Chapter 4

The Product Life Cycle

The Basic Concept

'In the long run,' John Maynard Keynes is supposed to have said, 'we are all dead!' And so are our products. Like people, products are heading towards their ultimate demise from the day they are born. The concept of the product life cycle merely says that both volume sales and profits tend to follow a broadly similar pattern. It does not say that the shape of the curve will always be identical, that launching a new product invariably results in an initial period of investment (making a loss now to produce a profit later) or that the time span will be the same for all cases. The typical life-cycle curve is represented in Figure 1.

The most normal pattern for an industry or an individual product within an industry is one of gradually accelerating growth in volume, eventually reaching a plateau and finally falling into decline. Unless deliberate steps are taken to withdraw the product, purchases may continue – at a very low level – for a considerable time. For any product there always seems to be a sort of 'lunatic fringe' who go on buying the product long after it is outmoded. They may genuinely prefer it; it could just be habit (possibly related to age); it could have something to do with the use of old machinery: the demand for spares for obsolete machines often continues for an embarrassing length of time.

Before we consider the separate stages of the cycle, let us take note of the fact that the profit curve takes a different shape and reaches its maximum point before sales do. It is easy to work at a loss during the introductory stages and even easier to lose money when the product is in decline. What is not as readily realized is how much more expensive each additional sale is to obtain once a certain point has been reached. In Figure I, we have a clear example of the law of diminishing returns where the cost of reaching saturation level is less profitable than a position lower down the sales curve.

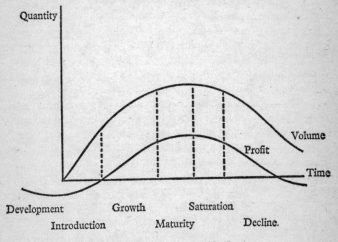

Figure I. The Product Life Cycle

In our representation of the product life cycle, the area designated 'development' is deliberately left blank. Clearly there are no sales during this period (test-market sales come into the introductory period) but costs are highly variable depending upon the complexity of the project and the speed with which success is attained. Examination of large numbers of new product development projects in this country, Canada and the United States shows an alarming tendency for this development period to be both longer and more costly than was planned or desirable. If a product is to enjoy a healthy and profitable life, this development stage must not be skimped: many of the large number of product failures could have been avoided if sufficient care and caution had been exercised earlier.

The introductory phase covers the whole period from initial test market or cautious national launch to the point where it is now a serious contender poised for growth. During most, if not all, of this period the product will be in an investment situation. This, together with the development expenditure, must be offset by future earnings or written off if the product either does not get beyond the development stage or fails very early in its life.

Nowadays, there are few companies who do not put a time limit on the 'pay-back period': that period of time during which profits must have recouped all previous investments. These will be:

1. Research and Development costs. (Many companies now regard these as a central charge to be absorbed by corporate profits and not the profits of a single product.)
2. Marketing investment. Research, advertising, promotion, discounts, deals and so on amounting to more than the revenue produced.
3. The backlog of contributions to specific expenses, depreciation and general overheads which cannot be made until the brand is in profit.
4. The backlog of forgone net profit whilst the product was in an investment situation.

Thereafter, the brand is in a true net profit situation, making the required contributions to total expenses and achieving its required rate of net profit or net contribution to total corporate profits. By now, the product should be well embarked upon the growth stage.

You will notice, in Figure 1, that the slope of sales in the growth phase is already steeper than that of profits. This again is a fairly typical picture. A growth brand will probably by now have settled down to an affordable level of promotional expenditure but it will almost certainly be subject to the full forces of market competition. Some of these competitors may still be spending at investment levels. Somewhere during this phase, the law of diminishing returns will set in and each increment of sales will cost more than the preceding one to obtain.

But there is another reason why sales rise more rapidly than profits. Early in the growth phase, Management reaches a crucial decision point: do we go for moderate turnover at high margins or low margins with high turnover? (The difference between the corner grocer and the High Street supermarket.) To most managements growth of cash profits is more important than percentage profits. In this case, the actions taken may be quite different. Prices may be slashed, advertising increased, distribution extended to lower potential outlets (or new shops or branches opened in less rewarding situations). There are clearly dangers in this situation and we have seen many companies fail by paying more attention to turnover than rate of profit. The sensible company aims for an acceptable return on capital employed (profit rate related to total assets) together with an acceptable growth in total profit.

Although there is general agreement about the general shape of the life-cycle curve, there is a good deal of difference of opinion about how many phases there are and what they should be called. 'Maturity', in Figure 1, refers to the point of maximum profit: sales are still growing. This merely elaborates the previous point; not only does the profit curve fall off before sales stop rising, profits actually start to fall whilst sales still increase.

This is another major point of decision. Does one cut back on sales effort in an attempt to maintain profits at peak level or does one press on until the market is saturated? This is a matter for careful calculation. Marketing is concerned with long-term profits: these can be achieved by the sum of many successive short-life products or by prolonging the profitable life of existing products or replacing them with new, long-life products.

The phase of sales saturation tends to be more of a plateau than a point and is generally a fairly flat, smooth curve. It is important to recognize that saturation level – the point where every possible buyer is buying as frequently as they wish – will arrive at different points for various products competing in the

same market. It is obvious that the saturation limit for a
particular model of Rolls-Royce will be reached long before
that of a Mini. It is perhaps less obvious that the peak sales
level for a certain brand of cigarette will be reached before the
ceiling for all cigarettes is arrived at. Things like tobacco taste
and strength come into it, filters or non-filters, small or
king-size, price, with or without coupons, as well as all the
additional psychological values created by packaging, presentation and advertising. Even with products where differences are
minimal (like similar blends of tea or sugar) company reputa-
tions, availability and many of those things mentioned for
cigarettes give one brand a higher ceiling than another.

Finally, inevitably, comes the decline. In our diagram, we
have a situation where an actual loss arises. This has been
chosen deliberately to illustrate a point. Products do frequently
remain on the market although profit is declining or even when
volume, too, is falling. This is perfectly sound if the profit
margin is acceptable. It is always better to have some profit
than no profit and it is seldom possible to turn back the clock
and deliberately sacrifice volume in order to achieve higher
profits: it is only too easy to slide back down the hill and make
even less profit. At least, when volume is going up you have a
strong platform from which to launch new products or product
improvements. There are, too, many pressures on a company
not to discontinue existing lines. Apart from the 'lunatic
fringe' mentioned earlier, salesmen believe that continuance of
A is necessary to the success of B; you can't save any salesmen
if you stop selling A and in any case you have no other use for
the plant which otherwise would become scrap.

There are no easy answers in Marketing. That catalogue of
points could be a series of excuses capable of leading the
company into bankruptcy, or perfectly valid reasons (in
combination or singly) for carrying on well into the decline
stage. Obviously, there is no possible excuse for operating (as
in the example) at a total loss in the decline stage of a product's
life cycle. However, there is often justification for operating at
an accounting net loss where the product still makes sufficient
gross profit to contribute handsomely to total company

expenses and overheads. Two examples will suffice, both concerning multi-product companies. The first had three newspapers all using the same plant. The largest circulation paper, a daily, made a net loss in the books of £30,000. The other two, an evening and a weekly, made £75,000 and £9,000 respectively. However, the costing was based upon *pro rata* use of the machinery. Although the daily lost £30,000, it made a contribution of almost £200,000 to total expenses. The other two made slightly less added together. Without the loss-making daily newspaper, the other two could not exist. A similar situation occurred in a confectionery company where the four largest brands all showed book net losses (only three were in decline) but between them paid the whole cost of the sales force. Looked at this way, the smaller brands were making excess profits.

One could argue with the accountancy that produces this sort of anomaly but, in practice, line by line costing with complete accuracy is more often than not impossible. Costs which cannot be allocated specifically then tend to be allocated proportionately and a brand making a significant contribution to total overheads becomes very important.

To sum up so far, the concept of the product life cycle is a useful way of describing the typical sales and profit pattern of either an industry or a product within an industry. Nothing about it is certain: the phases may vary in length, maximum profit may be reached during the early stages of decline, not all products require any introductory investment at all, and so on.

Examples of Life Cycles

Some industries enjoy very long lives, others barely start. The same is true of products, although a product may be short-lived in a long-life industry. Products may deliberately be made obsolete: fashion changes in clothes and cars are good examples. Changes in technology may make products or whole industries out of date. The pace of development in certain electronic components is so rapid that products often become obsolete midway through the growth phase and then the sales curve plunges almost vertically.

The confectionery industry is an interesting example of both short-life and long-life products within a total market determined by per capita consumption. At the one extreme there are products like Cadbury's Dairy Milk, which seems always to have been around, and products of the thirties like Rowntree's Kit Kat and Black Magic (one of the first great market-research projects).

At the other end there has been an ever-changing host of 'novelty' products which appeal for a relatively short time to a fickle public. These have mostly been count lines (sold by the unit) or filled bars of chocolate. Some have only accidentally fallen into this short-cycle pattern: others were always intended to do so. Many of the names would be unfamiliar to present readers but products like Rowntree's Nux bar and Mackintosh's Caramac spring to mind among those of the leading manufacturers.

The life of a product may be shortened by innovation by a competitor. Before instant coffee, coffee essence (Camp, Bon, Bev and Shieldhall) enjoyed a large market and was not really competitive with fresh ground coffee. The position of liquid coffee has been usurped by instant, and loose freshly roasted and ground coffee by packaged pure coffee. The latest situation is a more direct confrontation between premium grades of instant coffee and the packaged pure ground coffees. The latter have existed on a fairly static plateau for some years: if the counter-attack is successful, one might expect to see the decline phase set in.

It is worth recalling that coffee once occupied the position tea has today. Both total and per capita consumption of tea have shown a tendency to decline and there is every indication that saturation level has been reached and that a strong counter-attack is needed to create new growth. Otherwise a real decline seems inevitable.

Finally, in Figure 2, we see an interesting picture of how the life-cycle pattern appears for long-term usage (with forward projections) of fuels throughout the world.

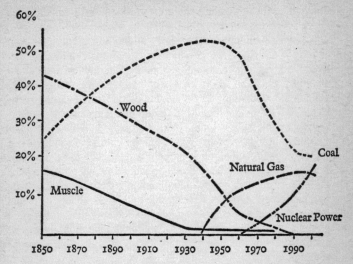

Figure 2. Life Cycle (Actual and Forecast) of Sources of Energy

Although incomplete in that the introductory phases are not always included and no profit figures are available, the validity of the general pattern is clearly demonstrated.

Taking Action on the Product Life Cycle

The classic reaction to reaching – or approaching – profit maturity is to revamp the brand to create a new cycle starting from a higher base, or launch a new product. In Figure 1 we saw an indication of the profit required from a new brand to remedy the fall in profit of an existing brand. In Figure 3 we can see how 'recycling' the brand would work in an ideal situation.

Earlier, we considered the case of Lyons Ready Brek. The successful repositioning of this brand was a classic example of recycling for increased sales and profit. However, such a successful turnround (which conformed to the pattern of

Figure 3) is rare and owes more to incorrect initial positioning than skilful remedial action. The more usual situation for a single brand is that shown in the next diagram.

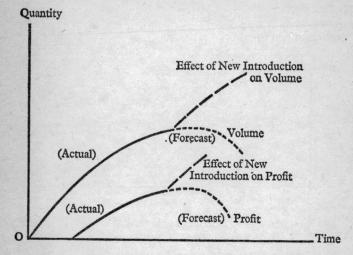

Figure 3. Effect of Successful Anticipation of 'Peaking'

In Figure 4, the primary cycle is the original product life cycle: the recycle has come in at a point where share of market, volume and profits were all falling. The aim in such cases is to restore the product to its former optimum levels. This secondary curve could arise fortuitously from some change in the competitive environment (a competitor's mistake, for example). Usually, the change is the result of planned effort (product, pack, price, advertising change, etc) and, more often than not, is in response to competitive action. Often the aim may simply be to slow down the rate of decline to acceptable levels.

Using the Product Life-Cycle Concept

The appropriate action required at any single stage of the life cycle will differ from that necessary during any other phase.

Everyday experience (backed up by a small amount of published evidence) shows that the primary use of this concept is in taking short-term tactical decisions relating to the present phase. Forecasts tend to be made from the existing shape of the curve with little regard for the possibility of what competitors might do.

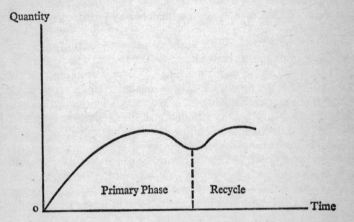

Figure 4. Primary Life Cycle and Normal Recycle

There is a tendency for the more experienced Marketing-orientated companies to attempt to forecast the duration of both the total cycle and individual phases and plan advertising, promotion and sales activity accordingly. In the introductory phase, rapid sampling and penetration is vital. Creatively, the advertising is designed for maximum attention. In the growth phase, regular promotional ratios will be established and steady frequency of message usually becomes more important than the sledgehammer opening-announcement weight of launch advertising. When the product reaches maturity and nears saturation, the problem of differentiation becomes more acute. Advertising may have the job of changing the whole image of the product or suggesting new uses to create a new, higher plateau. For example, Lea & Perrins Sauce – perhaps best known as an additive to tomato juice – turned to a recipe approach suggesting that almost any cooked dish would be improved by a dash of Lea & Perrins. Oxo had earlier successfully increased a very flat sales curve by the very successful Katie and Phillip campaign which taught a generation of young housewives how to make the best of the cheaper cuts of meat by using Oxo cubes. For a long period, no mention was made of Oxo as a drink, originally the basis of the brand's position.

Finally in the decline stage comes the decision either to allow promotional expenditure to fall in line with volume to afford acceptable profit margins or cease promotion entirely and 'milk' the brand, i.e. extract maximum profit recognizing that the period may be short. There comes a time, in any case, when the amount of promotional funds generated cannot support advertising, and effort swings to trade deals of various kinds until eventually nothing is worth doing.

A great deal more use can be made of the product life-cycle concept in planning future products and investment areas. This is especially true of multi-product companies. Unless product-life positions are carefully considered, there is the possibility of several products arriving at maturity simultaneously. This is the situation one very famous company found itself in a few years ago. A thorough Marketing and Financial investigation showed that four products accounted for around eighty per cent of total sales and that number five in the list sold only as much in a year as number four did in two months. All of the top four volume lines were in various stages of decline. Product variants worked in only one of the four cases. The company, a household name for many years, was sold at an absurdly low price (but a fair valuation in the circumstances) and the majority of its products have been taken off the market. We shall consider the importance of correct identification of stages in the life of a product when we examine (in Chapter 19) the timing of the introduction of new products to preserve corporate growth. For the moment, let us recognize that long-term growth demands products at every stage of the life cycle (and as few as possible in decline). There must be a planned programme of research and development aimed at producing products to defined turnover, investment and profit specifications at the appropriate times.

The Importance of External Factors

Marketing teaches us to look outside our business and consider the likely effects of all external factors. One of the more useful Marketing clichés is 'markets are people'. How many people there are in the market for our goods or services at any stage of the life cycle is crucial. Whilst for any given market segmentation by ability, desire and willingness to buy are of utmost importance, total population characteristics are important to all markets. The number of people in the population, their age, sex and marital status affect both the demand for goods and services and the labour force available to meet that demand. In our concern with the immediate problems of selling our particular product or service, we too frequently forget to look at things like population trends, levels of disposable income, sizes of families, ownership of appliances and so on.

In the last decade, we have recognized and capitalized upon the high discretionary income of the teenager. (By discretionary income, I mean the money left over from gross income to do whatever one wishes.) We are really only beginning to recognize the high proportion of working housewives: this can have a tremendous effect upon such things as convenience foods, refrigerators, automatic cookers and so on. We ought to recognize that our population is unbalanced with relatively too many teenagers and too many over-sixties. The latter proportion will increase. They will not all be pensioners and not all poor. They will mostly be living alone or with one other person. On the other hand, this could create pressures towards smaller portion packs ('dinners for one or two') whilst on the other, the work force will be depleted for a period. These are just a few simple examples of ways in which demographic characteristics can influence the life of existing products and create opportunities for new products.

We are all aware that the average wage has been increasing

steadily (although progress in real purchasing power has been less marked). In fact, the average weekly wage in Great Britain more than doubled in the fifteen years up to 1969. We have been able to see clearly what economists call the 'Veblen effect': as total income rises, the proportion spent on food and other necessities falls whilst wants, in total, seem to be 'indefinitely expansible'. The USA, the country with the highest disposable income in the world, spends more per head on food than any other country and yet spends a smaller proportion of total Gross Domestic Product on food.

Three factors combine to account for the 'Veblen effect'. Firstly, there is a limit to the amount one can eat and drink. One may spend more in buying better food but habits do not change with every rise in income and food expenditure rapidly gets left behind. Secondly, overall savings have been relatively stable. Share ownership – despite the rapid growth of Unit Trusts – is still not widespread, other forms of small saving schemes tend to grow only slowly (much of the saving being for a specific purpose, so that withdrawals run at a high rate) and we are notoriously under-insured as a nation (this can be a form of saving). In March 1970, the Prudential Assurance Company claimed to have one million policies still on their books where the premium was only 1d per week! Thirdly, and closely associated with the first two, what was regarded as a luxury yesterday becomes a necessity over time. Black-and-white television is now one of the first purchases of a newly married couple: colour television will inevitably move from the luxury class to a similar status as sets become relatively more affordable and services more extensive.

One of the prime skills of Marketing is analysing past events and situations and from them deriving future opportunities. Generalization is seldom valid. Predictions are hazardous but necessary. Projections of both existing and future markets are subject both to factors to do with the products and others due to population, environment, sociological and income trends.

Conclusion

It must be repeated that the product life cycle is no more than a useful representation of an inevitable situation. The security of business can be strengthened by continued attempts to identify the position of products on their life curve and by looking both inside and outside the business in order to anticipate future profitable opportunities. The methods used will include straightforward examination of sales and profit, measuring the cost of marginal sales, assessing market shares, sales forecasting and economic and sociological trends.

Although this section has talked in terms which suggest fast-moving consumer goods, the concept is applicable to all forms of industry. For example, the manufacturer of heavy machinery is supplying someone who acts as a converter (from raw material to finished article) and his customers are subject to all the influences we have considered. However long the chain, at the end there is a customer waiting to be satisfied. The life cycle of that final product will have repercussions upon the life cycles of all the industries and their individual products involved in the network.

Suggestions for Further Reading

The subject is considered in detail in Peter Kraushar's book *New Products and Diversification* published by Business Books. This highly readable book covers many topics raised in this book and does so in more detail.

Chapter 5

The Marketing Approach to Business Problems

The first problem a business has is that until it has customers it has only costs. We saw this clearly when we considered the development phase of the product life cycle. Even when it has customers, it needs a sufficient number before all its costs are covered and profits follow. In fact, the product life cycle highlights the fundamental problems of any business. Firstly one must run the business one has; secondly it must be optimized; thirdly one must judge the correct moment when the product – or the nature of the business – must change.

The Business We Have

The first duty of any Chief Executive is to run the business he already has. This often seems to be forgotten among all the injunctions to plan ahead for ever-increasing periods. The business you have pays the rent and if it is not looked after, you will lose the roof from over your head.

New products are exciting. Planning for new forms of organization can be intellectually stimulating and a welcome change from the everyday chore of a job you can do standing on your head. It is a more useful exercise to stand aside from your present business and try to look at it as an outsider. If you were starting from scratch, what would you do differently? If you were a competitor, where would you direct your attack?

Although no manager can afford to ignore the future or fail to spend some time actively planning for it, his first responsibility is to conduct the existing business as efficiently and profitably as possible. His first thoughts about the long term – assuming the present business is successful – should be towards the longest profitable life for the business as it now is. This is true of any business, whatever its state of development. The greatest dangers are with the developing small business and the very large company with a position of leadership with at least one of its products. For the small business, it is a full-time job just staying in business, and lack of time (a function of the small number of senior managers) can so easily lead to a concentration on problems rather than opportunities. The large brand leader is often so proud of leadership that it also becomes over-involved in problem solution as it tries to fight off competitive attack rather than look for opportunities to forestall activity by competitors. Leadership under these conditions can quickly become unprofitable.

Optimizing the Business

The definition of Marketing used in Chapter 1 very carefully used the word 'opportunities'. The shortest and surest road to success is through exploiting opportunities rather than solving problems. Of course, you have to face problems, but you don't have to go out of your way to find them. The best kind of problem to have is 'Which of these alternatives offers the best long-term opportunity for my company?' Solving troublesome problems leads to 'patchwork Marketing': it is rather like putting your finger in a hole in the dyke only to find water spurting out somewhere else, out of your reach.

Effort is habitually directed in the wrong proportions. The classic average is 80:20 – eighty per cent of the total resources of the company is devoted to areas producing only twenty per cent of total returns. This ratio (which not so long ago came as a great surprise to British businessmen) is now widely accepted. What few writers have commented upon is how difficult it is to get the proportions the right way round. It can frequently be open to question whether this is even desirable. It is seldom that any two situations are exactly alike in Marketing: perhaps the reason why a product or group of products contributes eighty per cent of total profits is that only twenty per cent of resources are allocated to them. Uncritical acceptance of this effort/return ratio often leads to the deliberate sacrifice of volume. Nothing is harder to replace. I have myself fallen into this trap in the past. By delisting four minor products I was sure (and my Regional Sales Managers agreed) that the extra sales force effort directed against our lead brand would more than compensate. Both volume and profits fell. I didn't save a single salesman so sales cost was now spread over a smaller volume. The lead brand (for reasons of competitive pressure, mainly) did not respond sufficiently to the extra effort with the result that its share of sales force costs (and all other general overheads) rose. The brand contributed a higher proportion than before to total profit but a lower profit!

Looking back, the correct tactic would have been to allow the four brands that were withdrawn to find their own level whilst ensuring (so far as one can with salesmen) that no undue effort was expended against them.

It must be right to attempt to achieve a high degree of balance between the allocation of total company resources and the expected returns. It is unlikely (except in companies with only a very small product range) that the two proportions will ever be the same; for example, that one can actually achieve a situation where eighty per cent of resources are devoted to eighty per cent of the returns. The product life-cycle situation enters into it: there are periods when one has to invest disproportionate amounts of time, money, machinery and effort in new and developing lines. In the long run, however, the classic 80:20 ratio suggests that most businesses do spend rather more time and money solving problems than in creating problems for their competitors.

'Proceed from strength' is a sound motto in business. Spend the bulk of your effort on the most promising opportunities, against the growth products, the strongest areas, the bigger customers. The small amount of business available to be gained in a weak area (probably at greater cost) can so easily be offset by loss of volume or a reduced rate of growth in a prime area.

Determination to make a success of a project is commendable

and an essential ingredient in the make-up of a successful entrepreneur. So, too, is the ability to give up when the going is too hard. Peter Drucker has said, 'If at first you don't succeed, try once more – then try something else.' One of the reasons for the spectacular success of the Tesco operation has been the way it has exploited opportunities in high-potential areas yet been ruthless about closing stores which do not come up to prescribed standards. Failure to do the latter and continuing to push water uphill by trying to solve the problems of low-turnover stores has caused the downfall of several of Tesco's once powerful competitors.

It is the ambition of practically every company to be the leader in its field. However, to be leader without being profitable is never worth while. Companies still exist (and often quite large ones) who expect to live on the laurels of reputation alone. Certainly, reputation is important – it may be your product plus – but it must be the customer's idea of reputation. And the best reputation in the world will not sell something people do not want. Wilkinsons make the very finest stainless-steel gardening tools but this will never give them a dominant share of the market for all garden tools because most gardeners are perfectly satisfied with technically inferior products. (This is no criticism of Wilkinsons' Marketing: they have chosen the segment of market which, having regard to their image, affords them the greatest opportunity. To attack the cheaper garden tools under the Wilkinson name would create a whole host of problems to tackle.)

As a generalization, leadership is partial and likely to be transitory. Here the word 'leadership' is used to mean the largest share of any market or segment of a market. Giants in one product field can be minnows in another. Brooke Bond have much the biggest share of the tea market: their share of the instant coffee market is negligible. Even within the tea market itself, there are sectors where the company is in a weak share position: the important thing is that they are strong in the largest segments.

Becoming a market leader can be tough enough but it is often tougher staying there. Many factors, of course, can influence the situation. How far ahead are you? What sort of start did you have? Is the market highly fragmented (like the fashion trade) or is it one where a few large companies have fairly similar shares (like the detergent market)? Frequently one comes across the confused situation where the company may have a range of broadly homogeneous products all competing in the same generic market yet operating with different products in the separate segments. Such a company may be market leader in total but occupy minor places with products in some of the constituent sectors. This situation obtains in fields as diverse as pet foods, detergents, cosmetics, computers, cars and heavy machinery. Such a situation can have a profound effect upon tactics and strategy. In a relatively static total market, for example, any new brand will eat into the leader's share. It may be sound Marketing sense to fragment the market yourself: as long as you steal more sales from competitors than you take from yourself, your total market share will go up. However, because so many of your competitors aspire to leadership, the position can be unprofitable. The cost of getting there alone may be uneconomic. The price of staying there may be too high. Unless they have a fairly long lead (for whatever reason) market leaders tend to reach profit maturity at a fairly early stage in their growth period.

Achieving leadership is a matter of securing the competitive advantage. The greatest advantage comes from real innovation. If you can get a long head start on competition you have the greatest advantage of all: the right to set your own pace. You can choose (as the pharmaceutical industry tends to do) to set your price high and reap the rewards of your enterprise – as well as recover your development costs – and drop your price later if you have to. You can choose to promote so heavily that the level of expenditure required to compete can itself be a powerful disincentive. Or you may choose to set a different pace by starting off at low prices. Given a long *solus* lead you may even become an arbiter of taste (in the way that Heinz Tomato Soup is the standard for all other tomato soups: when Campbell's (American) soups came to this country again after the war they had to break a long-standing company rule and produce a local recipe in order to meet the British desire for a tomato soup that tasted like Heinz Tomato Soup).

A head start gives you another tremendous asset: time to develop the next stage of your development. 'Me too' products (that is, blatant copies) have to have something else to make them succeed; lower price, better value, better trade terms, advertising attributes, better after-sales service. Competition will either have to spend time developing a better product in the consumer's eyes or devising ways of making a 'me too' appear different. During this period, you can be preparing new developments which make sure your competitor is always shooting at a moving target.

Thus, to summarize this chapter so far, the first task is to maximize the opportunities available to the present business and, ideally, to do so in the way that gives the best groundwork for preparing for the kind of business you will need in the changing circumstances of the future.

Preparing to Become a Different Business

No business can stand still for long: if it does not aim to go aggressively forward, it slips back. Products have life cycles and markets are people. Products are affected by technical progress, obsolescence and changes in taste and fashion. People change – in numbers, in the numbers in any group, in the amount of money they have to spend and how they choose to spend it. A cardinal factor in long-term success is the early identification of these changes. Even more successful is correct anticipation of likely changes and the most successful is the creation of new demand. Each is more risky than the one before. Demand *can* be created but it has to strike a sympathetic chord with the consumer. If you can do that, the greatest (and usually longest) benefits of leadership will accrue. Anticipating trends involves careful forecasting and, despite increasing sophistication in techniques, forecasts are still wrong more often than they are right.

Analysis of the external factors is essential both for anticipating trends and creating future demands. With the increase in the average working wage in the U K in the last fifteen years, coupled with the shorter working week, should we expect an increase in leisure spending? Or will the recent trend continue whereby, although the average working week per job has fallen, the average number of hours worked per employee shows no significant decline. There is more overtime being worked and more people doing two jobs. Does that mean more expenditure on leisure or more on consumer durables, housing, etc? These are the sort of decisions that have to be made from the available facts. We saw earlier how the proportion spent on food decreases as total incomes rise. This tendency was wildly overestimated in the USA (and to a lesser extent in the UK) because manufacturers did not anticipate that various external and sociological factors (more working housewives and the desire for fewer chores) would lead people to pay a higher price for convenience. Whilst the proportion of total income spent on food has fallen in both countries, in neither case has it been to anything like the original forecast level.

It may be necessary to become a completely different kind of business and early recognition of this can solve many problems which would otherwise arise later. One-product companies are always especially vulnerable and signs of decline – such as increasing age of users – must be watched for closely. Long-range planning, diversification and mergers are all subjects to be considered later in more detail. The business that exists is growing old: at some stage it must change in nature. If it does not consider the direction of these changes very carefully, it may change in ways which will be ruinous or it may find itself – as many major companies do – in continual cycles of diversification to build profit followed by rationalization to cut losses!

Conclusion

Whilst we have looked at three problems as though they were separate, they are in fact interlocking. They all relate to considerations of the product life cycle. What happens tomorrow is profoundly influenced by what we do today. The Chief Executive and the Marketing Director, in particular, are concerned with all three stages, often at the same time. Some companies attempt to ease the situation by creating long-term planning groups and new development specialists. The Chief Executive and Marketing Director who are not closely in touch with these developments and party to them run the risk of sacrificing the future to the present or failing to safeguard the present upon which the future has to be built.

Suggestions for Further Reading

One of the great books on Management through the Marketing approach is Peter Drucker's *Managing for Results* published as a paperback by Pan Books. Anyone who has not yet read this book should get a copy quickly.

Chapter 6

Marketing Self-Analysis

Marketing is very much a state of mind. This section deals with some very basic questions about the business you are in and its strengths and weaknesses. Its purpose is to show how adopting the Marketing attitude to half a dozen simple questions can suggest a new light on any Marketing situation.

There is nothing new about the technique. Some people give it the rather grandiose name of the 'Marketing Audit'; others call it the 'Thompson T-square' (after the J. Walter Thompson Company Ltd who pioneered the technique with their Plan and Data Questionnaire and once had a T-square with the basic questions painted on the edges). The number of headings can be as long as your arm or basically short and simple (as in this example). The headings are prompts, however, and in a complex situation with a company that has never carried out any Marketing analysis could lead to hundreds of specific questions. Most consultants and advertising agencies going to a new client adopt an approach of this kind. My own personal experience is that most hate you when they first see the questions, say they can't provide most of the information anyway and can't see what use it would be if they did. They usually answer most of it and thank you for making them do it but say they have solved many of the problems whilst finding out the answers!

This is why I suggest that any business that has not done this kind of deep thinking about itself should do so at once. Opportunities will be more clearly defined, problems put in clearer perspective and help can then be called for where it is needed. Once it is done, the answers should be collated into a Data Book and continually revised. You will then have not only an excellent diagnostic history of your business but a ready-made 'hand over' document for changes of staff, sudden emergencies and the guidance of outside consultants and advertising agencies.

When you look at the questions, they seem facile and may prompt quick answers. This would be fatal. The Marketing man is distinguished by his ability to see in the round and broad perspective what others see only in the straight and narrow. There is an old advertising adage: 'Sell the sizzle, not the steak.' You must approach this self-analysis exercise in the same way. Look behind the obvious for the hidden reasons: look for the sizzle. This must be regarded as a creative exercise. Although specialists will be required to contribute many of the answers, someone (the Chief Executive and/or the Marketing Director) must be prepared to challenge statements and assumptions.

The questions we are going to ask ourselves can be summed up under the broad headings:

> What are we selling?
> To whom are we selling?
> Why are we selling?
> How are we selling?
> When are we selling?
> Where are we selling?

In practice, some other pattern may have to be followed. In Appendix A is (in outline form) an example of a questionnaire produced for an unsophisticated company about to be absorbed by a very advanced Marketing organization. In this case, as frequently happens, the initial questions had to be asked of each department. However, the underlying questions are those set out above: all the information is designed to answer questions about the whys and hows of selling so that performance can be improved.

What Are We Selling?

If there is any one area where it is important to be unbiased and totally objective, this is it. The easy answer is a technical specification. Certainly technical details should be recorded in any Data Book, and weights, prices, number of packings can all lead to important conclusions when questions of range reduction or diversification have to be considered. Factory capacity is important too. But we are really after something else. What desire are you satisfying? For example, does a ready-made cake satisfy the same need as a cake mix? In terms of final eating the answer is probably 'yes'. In terms of selling convenience, they may be less competitive. What real satisfaction does this product offer the customer? (You may require research to find out. Better to admit you don't know than just guess.)

Again, I must refer to the vexed question of your own ideas about your own product. I have an actual example which reads: 'We are selling products coated with the finest couverture available in the United Kingdom (and the United States for that matter) today.' There proved to be two things wrong with that statement. Firstly, they were hardly selling anything in this category at all and, secondly, the consumer did not agree that technical standards of quality had anything to do with what they liked to eat! It is our function not to act as judge and jury on people's tastes but to accept them for what they are. People can be moved 'upwards', in taste terms, only very slowly and a reversal can easily set in. (There are many examples of people moving back down to cheaper products as the result of tax changes.)

Industrial companies must look hard at this question. The majority of industrial companies are producing an intermediate product: for example, a machine for making carpets. The demand that is satisfied is the ultimate consumer demand for carpets of the particular type and pattern your machine can produce. Failure to recognize this may lead you to badly miscalculate your position on the life-cycle curve for your products. If, for example, your machinery can produce only all-wool, plain carpets when the demand is swinging to synthetic fibres made up into patterned or textured carpets, you are running into troubled waters. However, perhaps the conclusion that you are in the business of satisfying the demand for carpets is itself too simple: should it be widened to cover all floor coverings? Your conclusion may well be: our end-market is that for any form of floor covering; however, our skill is in producing machinery which will produce woven carpets. Thus, you will deliberately, but only after careful thought, opt out of the market for linoleum, rubber floor tiles, vinyl and so on. You will have defined a segment of a market, but you will have defined it in terms of ultimate end-use.

Inevitably we have touched upon the question of competition: in this example, all floor coverings compete with each other to some extent. This is the first place to consider competition. Again we can start from the technical: what advantages and disadvantages does your product or service have compared with competition. Then ask the same question again from the consumer's point of view. A very famous manufacturer of boiled sweets (sugar confectionery) saw the market expand dramatically with the advent of a heavily advertised newcomer. Even worse, its own volume sales fell. Factory tests confirmed the inferiority of the newcomer; consumer research showed overwhelming preference for the newer product. The chief chemist was instructed to give top priority to matching the competitor. He came back with the answer within two days. The preferred sweets were all artificial fruit flavours. 'We can not only match them flavour for flavour by exchanging real fruit for artificial fruit essences but we can even sell the product more cheaply.' This incensed the (then) Chairman. 'We have never compromised our standard,' he said: 'They'll have fresh fruit flavours and like it.' They did and they didn't! The product was off the market within two years and, realistically, could have been taken off within six months. Moral: be objective; the customer is the arbiter of taste.

It isn't easy to define competition precisely in most businesses. You can define the area of competition much too narrowly: there is the oft-quoted classic of the American railroads who had to learn that their competition was not just other railroad companies but long-distance buses, trucking vehicles and the airlines. At the other extreme, is a Rolls-Royce really competitive with a Mini? There is a whole area of uncertainty of definition, and circumstances change through time. It could, for example, be argued that soup is competitive to ice-cream in that very few people have more than two courses at a main meal. A person who starts with soup is, therefore, less likely to finish with ice-cream. The consumption of bread has been affected by the tremendous increase in dieting as well as by the generally improving standard of living.

'What are we selling?' therefore, is a matter of identifying the final (or end-product) desire, of identifying the competitive products which may influence its life, and identifying the general economic and sociological trends which either present opportunities or will, if not tackled quickly, present problems. All Marketing planning starts with identifying the market you are in.

To Whom Are We Selling?

This is another question to which the easy reply can often be the wrong one. The most common mistake is to answer in terms of selling to 'all housewives' or 'the textile industry'. It is very rare (and very fortunate for you) if this is the correct answer. What we are looking for is not the sector you are selling to, not even the person who buys, but the person who makes the buying decision. This is important for it influences our product design, our sales approach, our advertising appeal and the media we use and possibly many other factors too.

The best way to approach this question is to proceed from the general to the particular. First identify the market (what are we selling?) then the segment you are most directly concerned with and then down to the question of the buying decision.

This is an area where research is most often called for. Those smaller manufacturers who are envious of the sums of money spent on consumer research by large food and detergent companies should console themselves with the fact that they probably haven't got the sort of problems that make such expenditure necessary. Since 'research' seems to imply spending money, perhaps we should substitute 'careful investigation'. In businesses where the number of potential buyers is small, careful research through sales contact can often identify the person who makes the buying decision.

We can identify three main problem areas in determining the ultimate decision-maker:

1. The buyer is not always the decision-maker.
2. There may be several levels of influence rather than any one single person.
3. Some businesses have many different kinds of customer or, possibly, no easily identifiable customer.

The buyer is not always the decision-maker. Many people shop for others but there are some categories where a very high proportion of the shopping is done on behalf of someone else. Who makes the buying decision? A high proportion of razor blades are bought by wives for their husbands. What happens? Does the husband instruct his wife what to buy, is his preference for a particular blade so well known that no instruction is necessary, or does he just ask for 'some razor blades', leaving the choice to his wife? If the last, the whole direction of the promotion of razor blades could be changed and outlets frequented by women (e.g. grocery stores) could become more important than, say, men's hairdressers. (In fact, the frequency of female buying of male items – like razor blades, after-shave, shirts and underclothes – is itself sufficient justification for a change in distribution policy.)

Breakfast cereals is a fascinating area. In this category you have brands chosen by the mother as being good for the child and brands whose choice is dominated by the child's desire for the particular gift in the pack or cut-out on the carton. With many of these products, both the mother and the child influence the buying decision and promotions are designed which appeal to both. There are many more examples under this heading, but let us lead in to consideration of the next problem by saying that in many product fields there is a person designated as 'the Buyer': research shows that he exercises the actual buying decision much less frequently than is commonly imagined.

There are many businesses where there are several levels of buying influence. This is true of most channels of distribution, for example, but in most trades it is recognized that the final purchaser is more important. That is why food companies advertise to the decision-making public although they actually sell through often long channels of distribution. Head Office permission to stock and order a product does not ensure that the local branch manager will actually do so: consumer demand is more effective.

However, in dealing with this problem, let us dwell on the situation where the final user is ignored. For example, having decided that there is going to be a continuing market for Axminster carpets you are interested only in selling your piece of machinery to carpet manufacturers. There is generally a lack of adequate research data about purchasing-decision-makers in specific industries and many are either too small to commission such research, fail to appreciate the value of such investment in research or are unwilling to get together on an industry basis to do this kind of research. This, surely, is one of the most beneficial things any trade association could do for its members. However, for a general survey of buying procedures in British industry, the interested reader is referred to the 'Suggested Reading' at the end of this chapter.

In short, one can say that the purchase of expensive capital items and/or highly technical processes is not a single decision arrived at by a single decision-maker. The process usually starts with a survey of the alternative types of machinery or process available. (There is probably no real consideration of make yet.) From this preliminary study, specifications will be prepared and, when agreed, tenders invited or shopping around begins. The tenders are assessed (or the results of looking around considered) before a supplier is decided upon. All this takes time and there are many areas of this investigation where speculative sales contact and trade advertising (in whatever form) exert little influence, as the people involved strive fiercely to preserve the unbiased attitude which is in the best interest of their company. (Although there are buyers in industrial markets who do not behave with complete objectivity and rationality, they are very much the exception.) Advertising and sales contact is probably most helpful at the very first stage of surveying alternative types and at the point of deciding upon type and becoming interested in makes.

Research has indicated five main groups of people involved in the buying decision in various degrees:

1. Departmental managers – the operational people.
2. Design and development engineers (or the Research and Development department).
3. Purchasing officers (or buyers).
4. Production engineers (if not in 1 or 2).
5. The Board, Chief Executive or General Management (possibly in combination).

(Another advertising problem here: many of these decision-makers are not equipped to understand technical jargon; others want a great deal.)

The same research showed that the operating managers had a continuing influence throughout the whole decision-making process and thus were usually the most important single group. At the other extreme, the Board seems to play a much less important part than is generally assumed. They were seldom involved in decisions to purchase materials or components (although where raw materials involve heavy capital investment there is normally a Buying Director), but had the final say in deciding suppliers for major plant items.

In short, industrial purchasing is often fragmented but is generally carried out by technically qualified people after careful assessment. The primary role of a buying or purchasing department is to invite tenders.

The pharmaceutical industry is another with various levels which combine to produce a buying decision. For items on sale to the general public, creating consumer demand is vital. For drugs prescribed by general practitioners, the doctor and the pharmacist have to be convinced. In hospitals, there may be more levels. The pharmacist orders, controls and issues drugs. Although he may make suggestions to the ward doctor, it is the latter who decides how his patient's illness will be treated. Often there is a third party, the bacteriologist, who may be asked both to identify an organism and select a drug capable of destroying it. In a case like this, one must sell to all three.

Finally, we have the business with several different customers or no single identifiable customer. In a sense, this situation is already caused by what has gone before, but so many people regard it as a different and unique problem that it is as well to treat it as a separate question. The food manufacturer recognizes a certain segment of housewives as being his buyers although he actually sells to wholesalers and retailers. He takes this attitude because the nature of his product does not change on its way through the distribution system. The manufacturer of machinery knows that he has no market unless what his machine produces enjoys a market, but he has no contact with that end-market so he tends to push it to one corner of his mind. The question arises when someone like I C I invents a new synthetic fibre. It does not market direct to the public. It sells to people who make shirts who in turn sell to people who retail shirts who sell to customers who are buying the shirts for themselves or someone else to wear. In this case there is no doubt that men must be assured of the comfort, value and general viability of shirts made of the new fibre, otherwise there is no point in anybody's making them. Thus I C I acknowledges that it has customers who make buying decisions at each of these levels. Although it does not sell direct to the public, it certainly advertises direct and is prepared to assist other people to advertise. (Motor manufacturers behave in the same way although they have only main dealers and agents between them and the public.)

There are some businesses producing a basic product capable of so many different uses that the number of buyers seems almost infinite: for example, glass, paper and steel. In such cases, end-uses provide markets and within each market (or possibly segment of a market) there are buyers. Broken down this way, buyers will be identifiable. So too will competition. There is no single market for glass or for steel. However, packaging can be identified as a market. Over part of the packaging market, glass and steel are competitive; in other areas they are not. For example, glass has the advantage of providing visibility for some products; with others, light is a hazard. Cans withstand greater pressure than jars where this is required, and so on.

Somewhere, in all markets, there is a buyer or buyers. They are often difficult to identify and companies frequently give up. At certain points of time, the person exercising the buying decision may not be the best person to do so. This happens frequently in the building trade. At a time when most building is on an estate basis by private developers, the scope for individual variation is very limited. Although the house buyer may choose his own fireplaces, specify the form of central heating and choose the bathroom fittings, he is seldom allowed any say in what sort of window frames he has or what kind of door. These may be decided on by the architect, the quantity surveyor or, often, the site foreman. In some cases, changes in these items cannot be accommodated within the design of the house. More often, the economics of the whole site plan depend upon standardization of all basic 'framework' items. Hardly the Marketing approach, but acceptable to people faced with a price limit. In this case, the end-user is not the person who makes the buying decision. Another instance of how important it is to identify this person and not just the buyer or end-user. They may be one and the same: sometimes they are three different people.

Many of these self-analysis questions shade into each other and overlap to various extents. This is especially true of the 'what?', 'to whom?' and 'why?' questions. An overlap with 'what are we selling?' occurs in cases where a product has more than one use: to whom are you selling it for what? Are the buyers of Andrews Liver Salts who use it as a laxative also those who buy it as a refreshing summer drink? (The latter will get the same benefit as the former in any case!) Dual is regarded by some people as a polish, by others as a cleanser and by a third group as both! What are we selling and to whom is appropriate to all three areas.

For the small business competing with the large it is particularly important to identify the buyers: what is it about them (if anything) that distinguishes them from the buyers of the products of large companies? Are they of a particular age or social class or are they merely local? Who they are may determine why you stay in business: why you stay in business against the odds, as it were, may determine who your buyers are.

Once we have decided who makes the buying decision, we want to know as much about them as possible in order to decide which particular Marketing mix will achieve the best result. How many are there, where are they, what are their socio-economic characteristics, their sex; how many are married, have families; what do they read, do they watch television and if so how often? The answers to questions like these – appropriate to your business – are essential to the formulation of effective business plans.

Why Are We Selling?

The obvious answer is 'to make a profit'! But that is too obvious and we take it for granted. What is it about the thing you are selling that makes people want to buy it? How does it compare with competition? Are these real values or psychological; do you rely on price or quality; higher trade margins or better service? Those are just a few pointers.

Ideally an outside view is required. If you really are conducting a piece of Marketing self-analysis, someone (preferably the Marketing Director or Chief Executive) should act as devil's advocate: keep asking 'why?' It is always extremely difficult for someone close to the business to be really objective about it. Business history has proved over and over again that what people inside the business 'feel' about their product is more often wrong than right. This is particularly true of the small business where everything is so much more personal that objectivity is that much harder. It is harder still in the smallish company still mainly concerned with the first-generation ideas of its original entrepreneur!

The 'overlap' comes into play again. Why you are selling may have a great deal to do with what the customer sees himself as buying: you and he may have different ideas about that – you should get together! Very early on, I made some disparaging remarks about life assurance. Unit Trust-linked life assurance has provided a very satisfactory answer to that part of the public that can afford it. There is a scheme whereby a man can buy into a Unit Trust with the expectation of capital gain and cover against what he likes to regard as the extremely unlikely event of his death before the scheme matures. He is investing, not insuring! We have already mentioned Johnson's Baby Lotion and Lyons Ready Brek as examples of products for which the consumer found uses which were not originally intended. The reason why you are selling may be that the consumer has thought of a better use than you did.

Many competitive advantages will not be obvious. Examples of those that are obvious include favourable price, trade terms and quality (in consumer terms). Among the less obvious advantages are extra service, favourable plant location and access to markets and supplies of raw materials. These are often taken for granted but can be very important. Very few companies – even very large ones – are not strongest in their home area. Small companies can often find favour – and extra sales – by greater attention to detail as a service to their customers. An example that springs to mind is rationalizing price lists, order forms, dispatch notes and invoices. There is always a risk of being patronizing about small companies. A study by the Industrial and Commercial Finance Corporation showed that ninety-seven per cent of all UK manufacturing establishments have less than 500 employees, account for fifty per cent of the total labour force and forty-five per cent of all industrial sales. Many of these are one-man firms, very small or competing in highly fragmented industries where their competitors are like themselves. If you are a small company competing with giants you need to be particularly objective about why you go on selling. The answer may be found in the questions already considered. There are, however, both people and companies who prefer dealing with small companies. Two of the largest UK retailing organizations are in this category. One does so because it likes personal contact with the owners and believes it gets better service from totally committed Management. The other aims to be such an important customer that the small firm is highly dependent on its custom and thus the buyer can exert pressure on both quality and price. One is a very healthy situation; the other is potentially dangerous.

One 'advantage' which is often overrated is 'know-how'. It has been demonstrated time and time again, here and especially in the United States, that 'know-how' can be bought. The pace of development, moreover, is so fast in most businesses that knowledge is rapidly outdated. Failure to acknowledge that technical expertise can be overrated, is easily outdated, and may have no relevance to the consumer, can easily lead to selling an outmoded product based upon false standards. The biscuit and chocolate confectionery markets have had many corpses labelled 'superior products'. Similarly, it is not much good saying 'British Banking is Best' to a man who wants to cash a cheque at 5 PM or on a Saturday morning.

In the balmy days of advertising, copywriters used to be told to ask themselves of everything they wrote 'What's in it for Joe?' If you look objectively for the answer you will answer the question 'Why are we selling?' in the right spirit.

How Are We Selling?

This section can be answered much more factually from existing sources of information within the company. How is your product distributed: door-to-door, through agents, wholesalers, retailers, some combination? On what basis do you locate your shops: do you, like Marks & Spencer or Nurdin & Peacock (leading cash-and-carry wholesalers) believe in expanding footage before outlets ? Do you, like Sainsbury's, make a careful study of area potential before opening a new branch ? What are your trading terms, discounts, over-riding payments ? What kind of retailers, in numbers and pro-portions, handle your product ? What kind of industry buys your service, what type of man insures with you ? And so on.

How is your sales force organized, what are the levels of contact, and how frequently are calls and deliveries made ? What are the after-sales arrangements ? A whole host of questions that can be answered reasonably easily, yet very seldom does anyone take the trouble to set them down. I can virtually guarantee you'll find some strange old Spanish customs when you do this exercise for the first time and you'll soon be asking a lot more questions – especially about costs and productivity. The actual tasks required of salesmen and the time allotted for them to perform them should be carefully examined. The company for which the questionnaire in Appendix A was designed came up with answers requiring forty men to make almost forty calls per day – which perhaps explained low distribution levels, high out-of-stock situations, infrequent calling and a large number of lapsed accounts!

To offset these revelations about yourself, try to provide objective answers to the same questions about your competitors. Real knowledge of the size, calling frequency and duties of competitors' sales forces is invariably very low. It isn't the easiest thing in the world to find out about, but competitive salesmen run across each other more frequently than they usually admit and one can always find friendly and helpful buyers to provide odd snippets and fill gaps.

Details of your own and competitive advertising and promo-tion belong here too. Over time, this becomes a valuable and indispensable record of themes, schemes, expenditures and effectiveness. Human memory is both fallible and selective and is no substitute for adequate historical records.

Since this is such a factual section, we can interpret it as

including the answer to the question 'How well are we selling?'
and examine sales and profit figures, trends, market shares and
so on. These should be carefully annotated with the reasons
for any particular peaks, troughs, variations, price changes,
effects of purchase tax or any other relevant detail. Correlation
of results by types of shop, branch and so on with the details
of the method of selling will provide a useful guide to the sales
effort/performance ratio. We shall be considering examination
of a range of products in the next chapter and trends of sales,
costs and profits will be vital to any decisions we take.

When Are We Selling?

There will be parts of this section which overlap with the
previous one, and obvious duplication (like calling frequency
and delivery cycle) can be ignored. However, we are not just
interested in seasonality here. The outcome of this particular
analysis should be an appreciation of when the opportunity for
selling is best. It could be that you will discover that there are
economies to be achieved by producing a more even spread of
production and sales effort throughout the year. Perhaps
carefully timed advertising, promotional and sales efforts could
do this. It can happen that the diseconomy of shutting down
plant and putting off labour are greater than the cost of
mounting a sales promotion scheme at apparently the wrong
season. Seasons are often traditional, like the old Services idea
of greatcoats and coke fires on 1 October irrespective of
temperature. Weetabix breakfast cereal is a wonderful example
of a product that achieved a substantial ironing out of its sales
curve by mounting summer campaigns.

For companies selling consumer durables and industrial
machinery, average replacement times and depreciation periods
will help to determine the timing of effort. The husband who
has paid £200 for a suite of furniture is not going to replace it
(if at all!) for many years; the company that has installed
£1,000,000 of plant will expect it to have earned an adequate
return and be fully depreciated, all other things being equal. I
have found very few industrial salesmen who could tell me

the average depreciation period of their clients.

'When?' and 'Why?' are often closely related. For example, a long-life product in a declining market now sells only on special trade deals when retailers stock up heavily. The answer to 'when?' is four times a year; the answer to 'why?' is because a very favourable buying price could be obtained by waiting for the deal. By this means, too, the amount of effort put behind the product is much closer to the return it yields than would have been the case by manufacturing and selling fifty-two weeks of the year.

Where Are We Selling?

This is a matter of analysing area or customer strengths and weaknesses. It could be both. You may be very strong in the North-east but not represented in the largest retailer there. Industrial companies normally find analysis by customer (or even industry) more important. From this examination should come a clear indication of both opportunity and problem areas. In the example quoted, there is a problem in that the largest retailer in the strongest area is not a stockist. The people of the North-east must like your product, so your problem is an opportunity. If the North-east had been a poor sales area your problem would be a difficult and costly one to tackle and probably not worth while unless all opportunities had been fully exploited elsewhere.

Another topic we will discuss later is financial control. However, it is worth pre-empting a point here by saying that rigid financial analysis of area or customer profitability will probably indicate other instances of bad effort/performance ratios. Unfortunately many accountants regard area or customer cost and profitability summaries as too difficult to do simply because they cannot allocate items specifically. Even quite arbitrary assumptions about such items as share of general overheads can provide quite revealing results, and it is seldom that being 100 per cent accurate would change the conclusion. With the growing use of computers, both area and customer-within-area analyses can be carried out extremely rapidly, and many of the more sophisticated companies are doing this.

Summary

Although facts are important to many parts of this kind of analysis, it is also important to look for the real reasons why people buy, who the decision-makers are, what they see in the goods or services you are offering, when they are most prepared to buy, and where. Three things need to be added:

1. Someone, if not from outside then a thoroughly objective insider, should act as devil's advocate and question every unproven assumption.
2. The answers should form the basis of a Data Book to be religiously kept up to date with new facts and figures.
3. Despite the Data Book, the whole exercise should be gone through anew from time to time to obviate the dangers of opinions being accepted as facts, internal values being accepted as customer values, and changes in the economic, sociological and technical environment passing unnoticed.

Suggestions for Further Reading

An entirely different approach to that detailed in my Appendix is to be found in the *Marketing Check List* published by the Institute of Practitioners in Advertising. Industrial buying is covered in *How British Industry Buys* by Hugh Buckner, published by Hutchinson in 1966. A section of Lawrence Fisher's book *Industrial Marketing* (mentioned at the end of Chapter 2) is also relevant. *British Cases in Marketing*, edited by J. S. Bingham and published by Business Books, gives a good example of pharmaceutical selling in Chapter 3.

Chapter 7

Analysing a Product Range

The great majority of companies market more than one item: many have very lengthy ranges. In the latter case, products are frequently grouped in more or less homogeneous divisions. These may be by raw material, process, distribution channel, physical distribution (e.g. perishable, refrigerated) or by sales force. Range analysis can therefore be carried out by products, by division (i.e. considering a division as a product) or by a combination of both. Any company, whether new to Marketing analysis or sophisticated in its use, should regularly consider the range it is selling to analyse opportunities, eliminate problem areas and allocate timings for new developments, acquisitions, diversification and, possibly, changes of business direction.

If you have carried out the Marketing audit suggested in the last chapter, product by product, it would be surprising if you had not begun to have serious doubts about some of the products in your range. The thing to do now, if it has not already been done, is to combine the Marketing self-analysis with a thorough financial review. Get as close as you can to individual product costings even though these can only be 100 per cent accurate in the minority of cases. It is far better to make the best assumptions possible than none at all.

There are many ways of looking at the results of such an analysis and one (partial) actual example is shown later. The methods can be entirely numerical, in terms of life-cycle position and expectancy, in entirely verbal terms, or some combination. Obviously this last is most likely, for a verbal assessment will have to have the back-up of profit performance and potential.

One useful way of looking at the problem is to use a set of groupings, a technique unashamedly borrowed from Peter Drucker. The terminology is not the same nor is the list quite as long. Like any list, it is elastic. However, we can all agree that all but the most fortunate companies will be left with two kinds of grouping: the 'straightforward' and the 'problem children'.

Briefly summarized, the straightforward group will contain:

1. Profitmakers now.
2. Profitmakers in the future.
3. Profitable, worthwhile 'specials'.
4. Priority development products.
5. Failures.

The problem children include:

1. Yesterday's profitmakers.
2. 'Patchwork products'.
3. Unnecessary, unprofitable 'specials'.
4. 'Investments in Management ego'.
5. Unidentified or ignored opportunities.

Profitmakers Now

There is no problem about the product making good profits now provided you know where it stands on the life cycle and there are no accounting 'fiddles' concealing the true situation. Care should be taken to ensure that the level of resources devoted to it is such that the product really can stand on its own two feet. For example, a cosmetic item was a significant profitmaker only so long as sales-force costs were allocated *pro rata* to volume and not to time spent selling the product. On the latter basis, it would have been considerably less profitable. Moreover, without this 'overdose' of sales effort it probably would not have attained its leadership position.

A product in this category is not a problem now but must be

watched carefully for the time when it does become one. More justification for continual review.

Profitmakers in the Future

There must always be a slight element of doubt about any item in this category simply because of the unforeseeable effects of competitive action, changes in taste, technical obsolescence and so on. However, *now* it does not look like a problem. It is a product breaking out of the investment phase of its development into what, other things being equal, can be expected to be a period of profitable growth to maturity.

There may be a problem here. If the economics of today's profitmakers are wrong or too many resources are being devoted to problem areas, the real potential of the developing profitmaker will not be reached. On the other hand, if it is over-endowed with resources, it may achieve an artificial situation with a disturbing effort/return ratio. It is a great temptation to put too much effort behind promising products.

Profitable, Worthwhile 'Specials'

Speciality products tend to occur more often in industrial and service markets than in consumer goods industries although they are far from unknown there. Examples might be: a rare and fine blend of coffee appealing to a discriminating few; screws, nuts and bolts of non-standard size; insurance of special classes of risk (like injury to a footballer's legs or a conjurer's hands). The ideal situation is that they should be an easily achieved, low-risk by-product of high-volume items. Thus, if no one at all buys the special blend of coffee, the write-off of total stocks will neither cripple the company nor seriously reduce its profits. It is not unreasonable to expect such products, appealing to limited and specialized or discriminating markets, to enjoy higher than average rates of profit. This must not, however, become a temptation to devote extra sales and management time to trying to sell more. They are more likely to be profitable if they enjoy leadership: indeed, if the market is highly specialized or particularly discriminating, they may well be leaders in their category or their particular geographical area.

Priority Development Products

We are now into the area where the 'straightforward' and the 'problem children' shade into each other and the dividing line is fine indeed.

A development product is no problem provided it has passed all its preliminary screening tests with flying colours and there are no foreseeable clouds on its horizon. The whole question of developing new products will be considered in rather more detail later. For the moment, a product will qualify for this category only if not miscast from the problem areas we shall consider shortly. The greatest dangers of miscasting arise from a reluctance to be objective and kill the work of many enthusiastic people – as well as write off the cash investment involved – and from misplaced Chief Executive enthusiasm.

Failures

A failure is a problem allowed to go too far. Now it is reasonably straightforward: you have to kill it. All businesses have failures. Most are only partial; fortunately, few are total. The safeguard against failure is to have products at every stage of the product life cycle, and new developments under investigation ready to join the queue for the allocation of resources and priorities. Businesses can take comfort from the fact that failures in just one area, however well publicized, seldom affect the overall long-term health of the company. Perhaps the area where failure hurts most is when a company makes an unsuccessful first attempt on a completely new market: a second attempt can be regarded as prejudiced, to say the least.

Yesterday's Profitmakers

This category includes some of the great household names and certainly many of the biggest problems in Marketing. They appear along the life-cycle curve anywhere from the point where profits have reached maturity, but sales saturation has not yet been reached, to a point well along the volume decline sector.

This situation was fairly well covered when we looked at the reasons for diminishing returns setting in on the life-cycle curve. In the attempt to reach saturation, promotion continues beyond the point where a pound spent yields a pound in return, sales calls are made on lower potential outlets and customers with a consequent increase in sales costs, and ultimately marginal revenue fails to equal marginal cost. Such products often remain on the market, as we have seen, because their rate of profit is satisfactory, they earn a satisfactory return on capital or – more frequently – because they pay a large contribution towards an overhead bill that cannot be reduced. The problems here are that the company did not have a product ready to fill the gap caused by the declining products and it appears that its other products will not sell without the support of resources they are unable to pay for themselves. A company in this extreme position is in a very difficult situation indeed. If the bulk of its products will not sell without the support of resources which cannot be recovered without the contribution of a large but declining brand, then it has to find a large and profitable brand quickly. And these are the hardest to find!

A very considerable amount of total Marketing effort, especially in terms of selling time and promotional money, is devoted to slowing down the rate of decline until the new breadwinner comes along.

'Patchwork Products'

These are the products which seem to be in need of continual remedial action; some department or other is constantly plugging holes. It is a characteristic of a patchwork product that the repair will only hold just so long: that does presuppose, however, that you have correctly identified the fault. Take a bicycle tyre inner tube which keeps going down. You test and test the tube but can find no reason, so you throw away the tube and buy a new one. The dustman takes it home, fits a new valve and uses it for another two years! With another tube you mend one puncture only to find the air escaping somewhere else; you mend that but the tyre gives way somewhere else. By the time you have realized that the tyre is perished and needs replacing, the shops are shut! The latter was a patchwork product: whilst you were wasting your time on a hopeless task, you could have been doing something more worthwhile. In the first case, you merely gave up before you had diagnosed the trouble correctly: this was *not* a patchwork product but you made it one by wasting time looking in unfruitful areas.

Peter Drucker calls these 'repair jobs' and sets a number of conditions which *must* be stringently observed if the product is to be worth your attention. The product must have substantial volume, considerable growth opportunities, a significant leadership position and high probability of exceptional results if the action taken is successful. However, to qualify, it must have *only one* major defect and that must be clearly definable, relatively easy to correct and one which is depriving the product of the full benefit of immediate profit or growth potential.

Notice particularly Peter Drucker's insistence on *only one* major defect. A 'repair job' can easily become a 'patchwork product'. The example of Lyons Ready Brek quoted earlier was a good example of a product with only one major defect – it was being sold to the wrong market. Although several changes were made to the Marketing mix simultaneously, they were all geared to one aim: appealing to a new market. Genuine patchwork products lead to resources being misapplied with the result that present opportunities are not optimized and new opportunities not identified.

Unnecessary, Unprofitable 'Specials'

In the very early days of a company it is Marketing orientated (albeit intuitively) by virtue of identifying and satisfying a consumer need. It then, traditionally, becomes obsessed with that item and becomes production orientated (a phrase just as applicable to a service as an industry, indeed to anyone who has as his primary philosophy 'we sell what we make' rather than what the market demands). As the business expands, the voice of the sales force is heard with increasing insistence and more noise. They can sell more, they say. Not only will this add to volume and profit but it will actually help to sell our lead line. After all, if we can supply everything (say) an office needs, why should they buy typewriters from anyone else? This is the classic way to unnecessary and unprofitable specials: lines either unrelated or only related through the most tenuous of links to the basic business.

A staggering number of businesses have been forced (by economic circumstances) to practise variety reduction and very, very few have ever found the sales of their main line to suffer. Indeed, one famous manufacturer of business equipment found that sales of his lead product actually improved when he ceased to supply ancillary equipment. The fact that the prices of this ancillary equipment had been uncompetitive had reflected badly upon his basic machinery which was also expensive but, unlike his other products, regarded as justifiably expensive. No doubt the concentration of Management and salesmen on their main task had a lot to do with the improvement too.

There are many speciality products which are just plain unnecessary, and where there is no demand there can be no supply. There can be a lot of wasteful effort used in trying to create a demand which would be better used in satisfying existing demands. There are, for example, a number of highly expensive cameras on the market at the moment which are designed to appeal to amateur photographers at professional prices. Some research has shown that these sell only to the very rich, unsophisticated camera user demanding complete automation. To the mass market and to the large enthusiast-amateur market these cameras are unnecessary and unwanted, for they lack certain essentials (like low-priced simplicity at one end of the scale and things like interchangeable lenses, back-wind, manual override, etc at the other). Perhaps these cameras are made deliberately to appeal to a very small market: perhaps they really belong under our next heading.

'Investments in Management Ego'

This is one of the lovelier phrases invented by Peter Drucker.[1]

They come in all shapes and sizes. The most difficult for the manager to deal with is the one whose originator is still in the business. The confectionery manufacturer who insisted on producing sweets with real fruit flavours when he knew the public preferred artificial flavours was letting his ego show. So was the man who was putting the best couverture on his biscuits. So is the paper-hanger who believes his work is worth two pounds per roll when the market rate is half that.

Unfortunately, a corollary of the phrase 'Management ego' is the word 'boss'. And since it is usually the boss – or someone senior enough to twist him round his little finger – the tendency is to throw resources behind the product or service believing that it is only a matter of time before success is achieved. Nothing is certain in Marketing and many a product has failed because it was launched too soon, only to succeed later. Many men have become millionaires by hanging on. The Xerox copier had been around for years before it was taken up and became a success. Nearer home, between the wars, there was such a social stigma about shopping at the cut-price grocer's that my grandmother used to send me. The man who ran that store is a multi-millionaire and has been knighted! That same man, however, has been noteworthy in closing down newly opened stores which do not reach their profit targets within a predetermined time.

We all have our favourites, especially salesmen, and we are not always as objective as we really should be. Since this section in particular owes so much to Peter Drucker, let me repeat his most apposite rephrasing of Robert Bruce's famous remark: 'If at first you don't succeed, try once more – and then try something else.'

Unidentified or Ignored Opportunities

In a sense, this is a problem you don't know you have: all the more important, therefore, to look out for it. We have briefly touched upon some of the ways of looking for opportunities and we shall consider more later. There is nothing more frustrating, however, than to be sitting on a real winner only to see someone else steal it either through recognizing its potential before you do or pushing it hard enough to make it a success.

Opportunities are often ignored because they are associated in some way with one of our other problem areas. For example, there have been many national daily newspapers in the history of both this country and the USA which can only be seen as 'investments in Management ego'. The great newspapers that survive profitably have done so by correctly identifying what their readers want and marrying that with the needs of advertisers to produce profitable entities. They have also both grouped together and diversified into allied businesses for added strength.

Often, of course, opportunities cannot be adequately developed because of lack of capital. Two of the tragedies of modern Britain are the difficulties of accumulating capital and the general unwillingness of the large financial institutions to invest in pure ideas. A tragedy associated with so many businesses is the number of companies with impressive lists of 'firsts' who are not in those particular markets or are not in significant positions because they lacked the acumen to identify the real possibilities of their product, or the courage to give it the backing required. In this country such a list would include such diverse items as commercial computers, comminuted orange drink, instant milk and aero-engines.

A Practical Example

Table 2 (pages 74–75) is an extract from an analysis completed by a smallish company in a very large market. The background to the situation was that sales volume had risen continually for many years but profit had been falling for about five years, to

Product	Contribution to Turnover £	Contribution to Net Profit £	Analysis of Position
A. (one flavour, one packing)	308,000	Dr 40,000	Brand leader in its sector with 44% share. Volume grew steadily until 1966 then fell back but appears to have reached a plateau. Share falling (49%–44% in 10 months) almost entirely to lower priced own-label brands. Distinct consumer preference for our product is apparently disturbed at a price differential of more than 3d per packet.
B. (one flavour, three packings)	96,000	Dr 10,000	Now a marginal brand nationally (2% share) but reaches 15% in home territory. Always considered a superior product but recent consumer research showed it to be least preferred of all branded products. Volume down by 50% in last 8 years. Not advertised, heavily price-cut but never as cheap as competitors.
C. (low-price line also sold in packs of six)	30,000	Dr 3,900	Marginal: share too small to register in rapidly expanding market. Sales rising with market but at much slower rate. This is one of our oldest products. Because of expensive ingredients it has always been more expensive than competition and price has recently increased.
D. (one flavour, three packings)	31,000	Dr 8,000	Original product of the company – still included in company name. Has been slowly losing sales for 12 years. Rate of profit loss accelerated by 'improved' packaging which does not yield required margin.
E. (one flavour, one pack)	6,000	Dr 8,000	Test-market product. All preliminary tests (taste, appearance, etc) carried out in factory. Due for national launch February next (7 months).

Note: The analysis covered 48 lines in 64 packings in all. Not all were as depressing as this and the profit figures are slightly misleading in that advertising was charged against brands featured although it could be claimed to be supporting all brands. The overall position of the company would have been unchanged, however.

Analysis. Company 'C-C'

Short-Term Prospects		Long-Term Prospects	
With Changes	Without Changes	With Changes	Without Changes
1. Introduction of easy-open carton, cheaper ingredients (research confirms no significant difference from present product). Volume: no change. Profit should achieve objective. 2. Investment in advertising – area test proposed.	Further loss of share. Probable loss of volume. Increased rate of net loss.	Assuming advertising test works plus ingredient changes plus two new flavours: new growth curve and profits in excess of objective after 2-year pay-off.	Probable life 15 years assuming gradual run-down of promotional support. More profitable to 'milk' brand in 5-8 years.
Changes required so drastic and would require such heavy advertising that profit would only be further depressed. Brand leaders too strongly entrenched. Further decline.	Further decline inevitable.	Accelerated rate of loss.	'Milk' brand and it will not have a long term. (May still be best thing to do.)
Research being conducted to reduce ingredient cost. With advertising support in prime areas (at first) – more rapid increase but initial loss of profit.	Price change has not yet had any effect on growth, therefore assume continued growth in volume and profit.	Very good – if not too late with changes.	Lower saturation level than market sector. With recent price change, this may be near.
No change in trend.	No change in trend.	Demand for this product now largely satisfied by a new market. May be possible to move product over into this market (would involve changes to shape and pack) and cash in on the name which still has high recognition. Good basis for revamped product.	None
None	None	None	None

the point where a real net loss was predicted for the year in which the examination took place. Only a selection of the comments (made by the Commercial Director of the firm concerned) is shown and they have only been altered where necessary to protect the identity of the company. (This is necessary because not all the planned developments have yet come to fruition.)

This quite simple table arises from a combination of objective Marketing self-analysis, an appreciation of the product life-cycle concept and identification of both the corporate and individual brand positions, rigid financial analysis and categorization in terms of this chapter. The answers quoted vary considerably from the verbal assessments made before these exercises were carried out, and were generally more pessimistic than published plans in existence before the analysis began.

You may care to amuse yourself by fitting these products into the categories used in this chapter: they have deliberately been left out. What happened to the company? Based on the consultancy analysis, it decided it could not continue as it was; it could not maintain volume without the existing high level of overheads and its product development programme would be too slow in producing results. However, it had valuable assets in a few well-known brands, a valuable and modern factory and a tax loss! It sold out at a very favourable price.

Reference

1. Peter Drucker, *Managing for Results*, Pan Books, 1967, Chapter 4 – from which this chapter has been unashamedly adapted.

Chapter 8

New Product Development

New products are the lifeblood of business. Both the word 'new' and the word 'product' are capable of numerous interpretations and it would take an entire book to study the subject thoroughly. A few examples will highlight the possibilities, however.

A product may be genuinely new but within the broad expertise of an existing company. Thus when Quaker introduced Sugar Puffs it was producing a completely new taste sensation but was using the company's knowledge of 'blowing up' a product (gained with Puffed Wheat), its expert knowledge of the breakfast cereal trade, how to position such products to the consumer and how to sell the maximum amount through the grocery trade. On the other hand, the introduction of Instant Quaker Oats could be seen as an extension of the old-established Quick Quaker Oats and a defensive measure against the inroads being made by Lyons Ready Brek into the already declining conventional porridge market. The introduction of a honey-flavoured Quaker Instant Porridge was a range extension and aggressive anticipation of what the longer-established opposition might do when the time came for their main product to be recycled. Thus, in this one example, we have considered a company staying within its basic expertise and producing a genuinely new product, a product improvement (although leaving the old product on the market to find its own viable level) and a range extension which could be regarded – in product life-cycle terms – as an early recycle. (In fact, in October 1969 both Lyons and Quaker came out with national launches of flavoured products. Each had two flavours: Ready Brek with chocolate and butter,

Quaker with strawberry, and apple and brown sugar.)

There is often a shadowy area between what appears to be an entry into a completely new area and existing expertise. An interesting example concerns Polycell-Prout Ltd. Polycell first became known as the do-it-yourself man's wallpaper paste. For generations, professionals had used cold-water paste (Rex and Tapwata being the best known) and the amateur had to do the same. These products still exist and have many advantages over the cellulose products like Polycell. However, great care is needed to avoid leaving nasty paste marks at the joins. Polycell leaves no marks and under most conditions is the answer to the amateur's problem. From here on development stayed within the do-it-yourself area: producing easy, effective ways of achieving professional results. Polyfilla replaced plaster and sand and cement for repairing ceiling cracks, wall cavities and nail holes; Polyfix provided an easy adhesive for wall and ceiling tiles. Polyclens came along to solve the problem of cleaning paint brushes of hardened paints. All perfectly logical and highly successful Marketing development.

Now let us jump to the present. Polycell-Prout sell a range of small boats. How did they get there? Here I must confess to behaving rather like a book reviewer who may impute motives to an author which he never thought of. I can only look on, as an outsider, at what would appear to be the Marketing logic for this apparent diversification. Firstly, one can see the identification of an opportunity. More productive use of leisure, growing interest in taking to the water, increased car ownership. Opportunity: small boats easily transported *on top* of the car. Secondly, established reputation with the do-it-yourselfer. At present there are three designs, two of which are available in kit form. The third is moulded polystyrene – which might be construed as a development of the production of ceiling tiles and moulded cornices of the same material. This is one example of a rather grey area of diversification; the links with the market and the production techniques are there but the end-products are pretty far removed from the early items sold by the company.

Many diversifications have no common links at all although

there may be hidden reasons which make entry into these fields more reasonable than appears at first sight. The link between Lyons Bread, Cakes, Tea and Ice-Cream with Hayes Laundry and Normand Garages seems strange until one appreciates the amount of laundry generated by the Hotels sector, and the purchasing and servicing of cars and lorries by such a large company. Similar examples of wholly owned 'service' subsidiaries are to be found in most large companies.

Companies frequently diversify into completely new areas when they are over-dependent upon a single product or a single area, or where they are in a declining market and either the existing expertise is not applicable to any other closely related product or the opportunities so presented are scarcely worth pursuing. Defence can be a prime motive for diversification into completely new fields and a classic example is the Imperial Tobacco Group which (by acquisition) has diversified into such fields as potato crisps, frozen foods, sauce and pickles. (There is, however, no suggestion that the opportunities for further profitable growth in tobacco have been exhausted.) On the whole, acquisition or merger is the most usual method of diversification into completely different fields, even though the acquired companies are often developed and diversified themselves. For example, when Unilever acquired T. Wall & Sons Ltd they purchased a high-class butcher. Now the Wall's name covers meats, sausages, packaged snack foods, ice-cream and other dairy products.

By now it should be obvious that behind all range extensions – whether of existing products or completely new ones, by internal development, acquisition or merger – there is some definite objective and more often than not some defined expertise. For example, Heinz have probably said, 'Our particular production expertise is in canning and our Marketing expertise is in selling primarily to the grocery trade.' Only comparatively recently have Heinz sold products in jars and packets and this could be construed as investment to protect their existing business (and capital employed) in a wide range of canned goods.

Just as the best way to develop present business is by

exploiting existing opportunities, so the best way into new product development is by utilizing existing strengths and skills. The first step in a new product development programme is a careful analysis of what skills, technical and marketing, the company has and what product or service fields those skills can be easily extended to.

The development of new products, from finding the idea to eventual launch, is a highly complex subject in which there are numerous techniques available. A great deal has been written about the subject and the reader is referred to the 'Suggested Reading' list at the end of this chapter. Here, we shall deal only with certain vital problem areas rather than attempt to give sketchy and inadequate coverage to the whole field. These main areas are:

1. Finding the idea.
2. Allocating priorities.
3. Organizing the effort.
4. The human problems associated with new-product development programmes.
5. The high failure rate and cost of new products.
6. Identifying reasons for high failure rates.

Finding the Idea

The fundamental requirement is that everybody involved in the management of the company should be actively encouraged to *think new products*. Most people have their own pet 'crazy ideas' but few express them. Most of the great money-spinners were crazy ideas once and people must believe that an atmosphere exists where their ideas will be given fair consideration and never, never ridiculed. Incidentally, the word 'management', in the sense that it was used above, may be too restricting if taken too literally. It is seldom feasible to go to the other extreme and get everyone down to office and shop-floor level thinking about new products, but there are many skilled non-Management staff (laboratory technicians, salesmen, agents, etc) who can provide a valuable source of ideas.

A good way of encouraging the right atmosphere is the use of 'brainstorming sessions' – a valid source of ideas in its own right. In one of these sessions, a group of people are brought together and told that they are going to be asked for ideas for new products in a defined area. If this area is too tightly defined it can stifle contributions; if it is defined too loosely the session may yield more than its fair share of wild and woolly ideas.

Ideally, there should be only one person acting in what in any sense might be termed an executive role. In fact, his role is more secretarial than executive. Having tossed the subject in the air, he should withdraw to the role of recorder. People attending the meeting must know that they are freed of other pressures, that they will not be called to the telephone and that there is no limit to the amount of time they have available.

No doubt different people have their own ideas about the conduct of these meetings. My own view of the ideal circumstances can be summed up under the headings of logistics and rules of conduct. Under the heading of logistics, the ideal would appear to be:

1. Away from the office.
2. The group should not need to break up. (If you can't eat in the room in which the meeting takes place, make sure you don't have to eat at separate tables. A meal break has killed many a promising session. Al fresco lunches work best: most people can still write with a sandwich in the other hand.)
3. No distractions. Telephone calls in or out are taboo. Notepads invite doodling. Whilst some people – especially artistic people – find this an aid to thought, the attention of most people begins to wander when they put pencil to paper.
4. A large easel with an unlimited supply of paper and plenty of thick felt pens. As each idea is called out, the recorder will write it on the board. The colours come in useful to connect (by underlining or the use of asterisks) related ideas.

5. Plenty of room to pin up fully used sheets of paper. All recorded ideas should be visible all the time. Hence the objection to blackboards: even if you had enough, you could hardly carry them away with you as a permanent record.
6. 'Home comforts': water, cigarettes, etc.

More important are the rules of conduct and the Chairman/Secretary must have the authority within the meeting to jump heavily on any violation.

1. Status must be ignored: all men are equal in these sessions.
2. There must be no criticism of any idea put up. (There is only one valid criticism under certain circumstances: 'That is outside the area we are examining.')
3. Ideas should be expressed as soon as they are thought of. They can be embroidered later, either by the person who first thought of the idea or some other participants. Ideas should come tumbling out.

As a source of ideas, a brainstorming session can be both rewarding and exciting. It is only a start, however, and later the ideas must be ranked and quantified.

A more scientific variant of this approach is the technique known as 'synectics'. Sometimes this takes the form of meetings of specially convened groups: some companies, principally in the United States, have permanent teams. The fundamental differences between the two approaches relate to the degree of free expression and preparation. In a synectic group people are deliberately chosen from different disciplines and required to approach the problem from their particular point of expertise. They are provided with all possible relevant data and encouraged to seek out new data. The computer frequently assumes a significant role. Thus the essence of this approach is a common commitment to reach an agreed goal with each member using his own particular approach to the problem based upon the nature of the problem and the information required. By the nature of things, a continuing group is best since original research (which takes time) is usually essential.

An exaggerated example of the fruits of this approach concerns an American paint company which decided to try to produce an everlasting form of house protection – probably, but not necessarily, a paint. The problem was solved by the botanist on the team who produced a fungus with the necessary clinging powers, providing protection against the elements but with an acceptable maximum growth (it didn't need clipping every year). There are no prizes for guessing the Marketing reasons for not putting this product on the market! Nevertheless, the example indicates how different disciplines can produce different answers to the same problem. Results are best when each discipline contributes to the solution in the same free-ranging way in which a 'brainstorming session' will approach a problem.

An intermediate stage is a form of controlled brainstorming in which people most closely concerned with the current areas of strength (such as technical know-how) are invited to think up all the possible ways of exploiting existing technology, plant, distribution and so on. If they need outside help to examine the practicality of these ideas, they may call on it.

In fact, this is the way most companies go about the problem of finding new products. As we have already noted, it makes as much sense to maximize the opportunities presented by the present business structure in the new product area as it does with existing products.

Apart from pure hunch, the two other main sources of ideas are search and research. For many years now, there has been a steady stream of businessmen (especially in the grocery field) scouring the United States for ideas which can be quickly copied. More recently, Europe (especially Scandinavia) has become a fruitful source of ideas. There is no doubt that trends in purchasing behaviour are becoming more international and the time lag between the appearance of these trends in different countries is becoming shorter and shorter. Experience in many fields shows that the real value of this kind of search is in identifying trends which might be expected to appear in this country and, by research and development, adapting the goods or services to fit local conditions. There are innumerable examples where the straight translation of a product successful in another country has been a drastic failure here.

Research leads us towards the technique section of this book and for the moment we shall consider only very briefly the main research methods used to find new ideas – not to vet them for final acceptance.

Normal research techniques of choosing an appropriate sample and asking questions from a predetermined questionnaire can be used. However, asking people what product not now on the market they would like to see available is fraught with so many dangers that it is utterly useless. It becomes more useful, though still dangerous, if people are asked questions about specific product or service areas. If you ask people what would be their ideal vacuum cleaner, you may well learn a great deal about desirable attributes and present defects. However, if you produce a vacuum cleaner based upon an amalgam of points suggested by the panel, you will probably end up with a product very few people want. (This was part – but only part – of the reason for the failure of the American Edsel motor car.) One is reminded of the oft-quoted remark that a camel is a horse designed by a committee. If that committee had used consumer research, the camel might well have had six legs for extra speed and another hump for extra mileage.

A well-used and quite successful technique for helping to generate product ideas is the use of group discussions controlled by trained psychologists. Again these only work when discussion is channelled into specified areas. The main value of these groups is that not only do they identify present deficiencies and desirable attributes but the pseudo-clinical psychological approach allows fairly intensive probing into reasons – something which cannot be done at all effectively with direct-response questionnaire techniques. The output of group discussions into specified areas is not a way of finding new products (except by accident): it is a way of guiding product development along the right lines and is often the follow-up to one of the other search methods.

The latest vogue in research techniques for discovering new product possibilities is the use of market segmentation (which will be discussed later). When applied to new product search, the technique is used to identify gaps in existing markets. For example, it might reveal that although there are a large number of soft drinks on the market, there is none which combines the advantages of the cordial (which is mixed with water) with the taste sensation and fizziness of carbonated soft drinks. There are three major problems with what is otherwise an exciting addition to the research armoury for those charged with the development of new products. Firstly, it is expensive; secondly, it takes a long time (two years is not infrequent in complex markets); thirdly, many of the gaps which are identified exist because the product that would fit is unwanted or, when quantified, produces such a small market as to be completely unviable.

Allocating Priorities

Between finding the idea and allocating priorities there is a great deal of work to be done. Most of this concerns the screening of likely ideas. They will be subjected to market analysis: how big is the market; what share could we get, at what cost; how strongly entrenched are competitors? All this and much more. There will be thorough financial analysis: what investment will be required; what returns can be expected, how quickly? Technical expertise must be assessed before a decision is taken that here is a product that is worth spending development time and money on. Although it doesn't matter where an idea comes from, it matters a great deal how it is vetted before it becomes a firm development project. Where clearly defined business objectives exist, the task is made easier. If, for example, the criteria for a new product are that turnover must exceed £500,000, that it must be within existing production expertise, capable of being sold by the existing sales force and of yielding a return on capital of fifteen per cent, the first screening is considerably simplified. Some-one, preferably a Marketing man, must establish that the product represents a viable business opportunity or that it should be killed immediately.

The various aspects of screening new products are worthy of deeper study and several techniques, many involving assigning weighting factors to various aspects, are included in the books suggested for further reading. Here we are concerned with practical problems, and more problems arise before and after initial screening than during that process. The only real problems associated with initial screening concern the availability of information and, since with real innovations this can be scarce, the sophistication of the techniques applied to the job. Often it can be a very simple matter indeed: for example, the soup market in this country is so dominated by Heinz, and the minor places so keenly contested, that very few companies would be prepared to challenge in the field.

There is a close link between the initial screening (including financial viability) and the allocation of priorities. A high-return, low-risk project fitting well into the existing business environment and expertise deserves to rank high in the priority list. A low-return, high-risk project will often find its way into the priority list and this is among the hardest to fit. Since it usually only gets through initial screening because there are no technical or distribution type problems it is almost certainly one that can be tackled easily but deserves low priority. The other reason for such a project getting through the net is defensive: it may be necessary to defend one's total position by developing to cover all flanks even though some are considerably less attractive than others.

What is a priority project? What does it mean to the Research and Development man actually handling the product, to the technician at the laboratory bench or the manager on the factory floor? This is where the everyday problems arise.

I have experienced many systems for allocating priorities but, whatever their degree of sophistication, they all end up with High Priority and Low Priority projects. Although the ideal High Priority project offers low risk with high returns, it more frequently turns out that it will yield a high return if only it is possible to find a way of making the right product. High potential returns tend also to be associated with high marketing (if not capital) risk.

Thus, in practice, one tends to set as High Priority projects those which are technically most difficult to achieve, and to assign lower priority to those easier to deal with. This situation frequently leads to frustration, misunderstanding and inter-departmental friction. This last must be avoided at all costs in a successful new product development programme.

'High Priority' can only mean that nothing will be allowed to interfere with development work on this project so long as there is work which can usefully be done. 'Low Priority' means that, where there are conflicting demands upon resources, this is the one that goes to the bottom of the list. There will often be opportunities to work on low-priority projects when no immediate progress can be made on a high-priority one and it is frequently the case that a fairly simple product assigned a low R & D priority comes out of the laboratory first. It then becomes a matter of Marketing decision as to whether it is subjected to consumer research, test-marketed or launched nationally.

There are two things the Chief Executive, the Marketing Director and the man responsible for new product development must watch. The first is that the simplicity of the development task does not become the main criterion for the allocation of priorities. In many cases it can be a significant determinant, but no single factor can ever be more important than the size of the potential market and the degree of urgency with which it is literally waiting for such a product. The second is the temptation to finish off almost completed low-priority products to the detriment of a high-priority one. The human temptation is obvious. However, the finishing touches do not always prove to be so simple and there may be several of these finishing-off jobs around at the same time. The definition of 'high priority' I have suggested must be rigidly adhered to.

It must also be reviewed. There comes a time with many development projects when your technical expert has to say: 'In the existing state of knowledge, this is the end of the road.' The validity of this statement must, of course, be challenged but if, as is most likely, it is a true statement then priorities have to be changed. Usually such a project is 'put on ice' whilst someone is given the task of studying scientific papers, visiting trade fairs, listening to machinery manufacturers' representatives – and so on – just watching and waiting for the time when this project can come alive again.

Budgetary considerations may affect priorities. New product development budgets are notorious for the ease with which they are overspent. With so many leaps into the unknown in such a programme, this is not surprising. The decision to increase the budget is a high-level one which must include careful assessment of why the budget has been exceeded, the likelihood of more money producing the desired result and revised financial estimates of the return to the company after the higher R & D costs.

Finally, both priorities and the sums of money put behind the projects may be profoundly influenced by competitive activity. The sudden appearance of a competitor on the market may lead you to rush ahead, to slow down whilst you measure his progress and success, or to give up altogether. There are no set rules. This is a situation in which the Marketing Director will advise and the Chief Executive decide. It is a situation almost bound to lead to a change in priorities.

One final point on this topic. For a company setting out for the first time to create an organized and orderly programme of new product development, there is a grave temptation to try to do too much at once and to give high-priority ratings to too many projects. This leads either to chronic overload – which will not produce the best results – or to over-staffing. The over-staffing is probably only apparent in the first place to the accountant who sees the R & D expense budget shoot up. It becomes clear in human terms as many of the projects die and there are more people with less to do. There is a very strong argument for building up staff slowly even if this means a queue of ideas waiting for attention.

Organizing the Effort

There has been a marked change in Marketing thinking about the organization for new product development in the last decade and it is only fair to say that there are still considerable differences of opinion expressed. These basically concern the problem of whether one man should have overall responsibility within the Marketing organization for new product development or whether – in a company with enough product managers to do this – development products should be assigned to men already handling existing products.

For many years, experienced Marketing men favoured giving new products to men handling existing brands. There were several reasons: it widened people's experience, it rejuvenated them by providing a break from existing routine, it brought them into contact with more people and, possibly, more departments. All these, however, were ancillary to the main reason: the avoidance of bias.

All good Marketing men are rightly keen to ensure that all developments, tests, promotions and campaigns should be as free from bias as possible. If one man handled all new product development he would feel that he would be judged on the number of products that actually reach the market rather than on the quality of his efforts. A man who already had a going brand would be more likely to maintain his objectivity and be less swayed by the enthusiasm of others.

Unfortunately, he also has less time to devote to new brands. His first job is to manage the product he is already responsible for and achieve the agreed objectives on that. The number of product managers available and the amount of time they could reasonably be expected to devote to monitoring new ventures could also put an artificial ceiling on the number of new ideas under active consideration.

Most leading companies and those consultancies and agencies

specializing in new product work now agree that there should be a separate new product development team under the control either of a trained Marketing man or a manager who thinks in the ways outlined earlier in this book. Although he will have line responsibility to his departmental manager, he must have direct access to his Chief Executive. The Product Development Manager will need the help of his Chief Executive in providing resources and integrating the efforts of various departments.

Often, there is a degree of compromise between the conflicting views of new product handling whereby a Product Development Manager is allowed to 'grow up' with a major development which becomes a national product. Then he moves out of the new product department with it. However, this is very much tied up with management development and the size of the company. A man well versed in all the Marketing, production and financial problems of new product development is a man with a good training in some of the most important aspects of general management. There is another problem, too, with this compromise situation: it does assume a stream of potential new product development managers coming along. The alternative is recruitment, with all the attendant dangers of the loss of momentum whilst the new man finds his way around. This must be considered as one of the human problems of developing new products.

We have, so far, assumed that it is always right for a Marketing man to head up new product development. There are businesses where this is a debatable assumption. Take, for example, the field of ethical pharmaceuticals. It does not take a trained Marketing man to discover that the world is waiting for an effective cure for cancer or, for that matter, the common cold. This is just one of several industries where fundamental research involving gigantic and costly leaps into the unknown should predominate. Since these are almost invariably fields where the investment in product development is high and the likelihood of reaching a satisfactory result quickly very low, the man in charge has to be the Chief Executive.

Many companies do make a distinction between fundamental research and what we might term 'directed research'. Where such distinctions exist, that part of research which has been allocated priorities and fits the immediate objectives of the company is under the control of the new products man. Fundamental research becomes a completely laboratory exercise, under the control of someone like the chief chemist, and will be aimed at the great discovery that will give the company an enormous comparative advantage over competition. Simultaneously, or alternatively, it may be concerned, say, with the basic chemical or molecular structure of a basic ingredient. This is work which does not necessarily lead to new products but may well lead to new processes, new ingredients or the discovery of new competitive claims which the Marketing man may seize upon to improve his product, increase the effectiveness of his competitive claims about the product, lower its price or improve its profitability.

Exactly which functions should be included in a new product development team cannot be stated with any assurance without knowing the nature of the business, its size, its ambitions and its ability to invest in achieving those ambitions. Perhaps there are only two generalizations one can make with any degree of assurance. Firstly, make sure that what you want isn't already available more cheaply – or even free – outside. Many suppliers of machinery, ingredients and packaging materials, for example, have elaborate research set-ups and provide these services to existing and potential customers. Where such expertise exists, it is foolish to attempt to buy your own know-how when it can only be on a smaller scale. Secondly, just as it seems to be best to have the head of the new product team specializing in this area, so it also makes sense for him to have a support team of the necessary technicians who can also devote all their time to new products. Priorities become meaningless where this is not the case.

Human Problems

This whole area is fraught with frustration and human problems loom large. Perhaps the biggest single problem is the difficulty the Marketing man has in accepting that he cannot have a product for that vast virgin market he has so clearly identified because no such product can be made. Too often he sees this as lack of cooperation or unwillingness on the part of his technical people to try new avenues. (Often he is right: a good Marketing man is naturally inquisitive and often comes up with approaches that more rigidly disciplined minds have not considered – out of the mouths of babes!) The converse is also very often true. Technical people cannot always see the market potential for what to them is a crazy idea or an inferior product ('inferior' measured against their high ethical and/or technical standards).

Friction frequently arises in the early days of establishing a new product development function in an old-established company. Initially, the department will probably be one product manager working full time on new products calling upon the resources of people who have an everyday job of vital importance to do and who have spent their whole time in the company operating on very straight and narrow tracks. Overnight, they are expected to change the habits of a working lifetime, learn some new tricks and jump to the ever more frequent crack of a new whip. Small wonder that tempers get frayed and cooperation often falls well below the perfect level. However, to be fair, many technical people (especially chemists and physicists) respond with great enthusiasm to this new opportunity to break out of the rigid confines of their previous existence, and this can be a most exhilarating experience for all concerned. Ironically, this situation may cause more problems for the Chief Executive than the first, for it can be difficult to force people back to continuing with the very necessary everyday tasks which they now regard as dull, routine and mundane.

Once a new product development function is established, the human problems mainly concern the overlapping of the new product specialists with those handling going concerns and the transition from development project into full production product.

It is a fortunate company that can invest in pilot plant or

create spare capacity for development trials. This means, for the majority of companies, using existing production capacity for experiments which can either disrupt normal production schedules or seriously interfere with product development priorities. It is not surprising if jealousy is aroused and cries of non-cooperation abound. Production managers become even more protective of their plant when the R & D manager not only wants to borrow it for a day but is going to put in a few change parts or introduce an alien product which means another day for machine cleaning. Where development has to be done under severe financial or practical limitations it is almost invariably better, more efficient and cheaper, to go outside the company to do the development work. There are many specialist companies who can produce sound evidence that the average time span from concept to marketing is usually measured in years when done internally but only in months when done externally. Time is money, and the cost of development externally can be very much cheaper as well as avoiding the human problems we have considered.

Friction can arise whenever one department crosses another's boundary and rather more of it is generated by new product development than occurs in the normal run of business. Perhaps the problem can be simplified into one of interlopers ducking in and out of the main stream of effort. They start by being outside, they gradually come in as the product comes to fruition, and eventually they drop out once the product is a going concern. The problem is to get rid of the idea that an R & D department (for example) is an interloper and to substitute the concept that it is a service available to all according to their needs.

Faced with precisely this problem, a colleague and I doodled on pieces of paper until we came up with this simplification which we called the New Products Wedge.

In this concept we have identified two of the fundamental business areas: the people who produce the goods and the people who market them. The two loosely defined functions, Marketing and Production, are each represented by a triangle. The base of each triangle represents 100 per cent effort by that

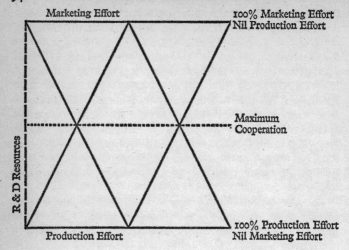

Figure 5. The New Products 'Wedge'

department, not involving the other at all. The apex of each triangle represents non-involvement. Thus the apex of one triangle touches the base of the other. In between they cross, and that represents the area of maximum joint involvement.

For example, the preliminary screening of an idea is done entirely in the Marketing department and Production is not involved. Ultimately, when the trials and tests are over and a full-scale production line has to be put in, that is 100 per cent Production's job. (Remember, we are talking about new products: once the problem is actually marketed, cooperation must be maximum.) In a very simple case, we would have a situation where the factory became increasingly involved in a project which had passed all the screening tests conducted by Marketing. Thus from a position of 100:0 (putting Marketing first) one gradually passes along the scale 90:10, 80:20 . . . and so on to 0:100.

However, such a progression is rare. A project may well jump from 100:0 to 0:100 and then 50:50. Where does Research and Development fit into this? In this example,

R & D is spread over the whole but is more closely associated, if and when required, with the more dominant role. To represent this situation diagrammatically requires a multi-dimensional model and is, therefore, better explained. Production may decide to share their 100 per cent effort with R & D. Marketing may choose to use R & D rather than Production. All three functions may be involved simultaneously, as at the moment of transition from pilot plant and test-market operation to full scale production and national launch. Similar 'wedge' diagrams can be constructed showing Production and R & D as the two prime movers and Marketing available on the sidelines as required and another putting Production in that role.

The two biggest human problems are lack of success and parting with success. In management terms, both create situations which require careful and objective measurement of performance.

Firstly, lack of success. Success tends to be measured by the profitable outcome of development efforts. In new product development 'success' can be having the wisdom to avoid further loss by knowing when to stop, or having the courage to keep going when a result seems distant or unlikely. The people working on these products may well be giving their best but simply, unwittingly, pursuing hopeless causes. The Chief Executive must be close enough to judge the people involved by the *quality* of their efforts and reward them accordingly: this helps to remove many of the frustrations. However, no company can afford continued failure to produce new products, however high the quality of the effort, and the people involved are likely to be rather more worried about their future than are people working on existing business.

Secondly, the problems of success. The plaudits may ring loud when a breakthrough is achieved, but they quickly fade and swing to the people associated with the success of the finished product or service in the wider market-place. It is only human to feel some resentment at not receiving the rewards of being in at the kill. This is where real management skill comes in and is a problem the Chief Executive and Marketing and

Production Directors must understand. A new products team needs every bit of encouragement if it is to keep a flood of new ideas coming forward. In its annual report every year, the American Research and Development Corporation repeats one paragraph which more than sums up the support that people engaged in new product development need:

> Creation of processes and products, of ideas and industries, depends on men more than money, on imagination as well as incentive. Seek out creative men with the vision of things to be done. Help breathe life into new ideas and processes and products with capital – and with more capital – with sensitive appreciation for creative drive; with support in management and manpower, with loyalty to the idea and to its initiator, the creative man.

High Failure Rate and Cost of New Product

Some of the most frightening figures quoted in business are those for the failure rate of new products. They seem to vary from 1 in 250 to 2 in 10. The truth is, no one knows. There is, too, a confusion between those ideas which never become final goods or services and those products or services which are exposed to the world at large and subsequently fail. There is also an inability to discriminate generally between those which failed without proper screening and consumer testing and those which went on to fail nationally after successfully surmounting those hurdles in representative tests. Finally, a product may fail not because it is a poor product but because it is presented to the public badly or because of unexpected competitive reaction or technological advance. What the businessman sees as a product or a service, the buyer sees as a mix of items. With consumer goods, many of these will be psychological: industrial goods are 'packages' of objective values (e.g. performance, reliability, price, etc). With so many possible items in the mix and so many permutations, the risks of failing to achieve desired goals *are* high.

I have had the opportunity to work with many companies

(mainly in the grocery field) and to talk to many people from other companies engaged in product development work, and it would not be at all unreasonable to say that most companies would expect to screen a hundred ideas to end up with two which will go to test market and one which will be launched nationally. We can represent this in diagram form.

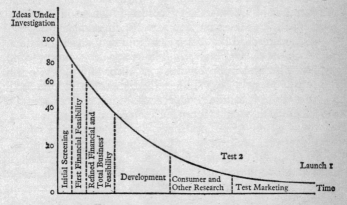

Figure 6. Typical Pattern: Screening to National Launch

The majority of the hundred ideas will be eliminated very quickly: more quickly if stringent criteria about turnover levels, return on investment, 'business fit' – and so on – exist. The next big sort-out comes under the heading of 'refined financial feasibility' and may well involve such techniques as discounted cash flow and decision-tree analysis to eliminate those likely to involve high capital risk and decide between contenders for a limited supply of capital. (One may have to reject a project this year in favour of a better-looking candidate although it may qualify next year when more resources are available or it is a better prospect than competitive propositions.) 'Total business feasibility' (or fit) will take the next largest toll as projects which satisfy purely financial criteria are seen to require a new sales force or put undue strains on distribution. Again, one must emphasize the importance of working to objectives: the criterion for rejection should be that the suggestions do not fit what the business *is* or *what it plans to be*. In the latter case, a company in newsprint (where the real selling tends to be at Chairman-to-Chairman level) would not reject the idea of making toilet and facial tissues simply because it had no retail sales force, if its avowed objective was to increase the sales of paper through whatever channel possible. It would have already tacitly accepted that such a policy inevitably meant investment in new distribution channels.

We have reached the first major 'go/no go' area: a product that has gone thus far is given a priority and development work begins. The proportion of products 'successfully' developed varies by industry. So, too, does the time taken. With a food product, once it can be produced the required shelf life will prolong total development time. Although accelerated tests can be done which represent longer periods of time, no wise company would market a product which had not performed under normal retail outlet conditions. Pharmaceutical products have their development time lengthened by the obligatory clinical trials. On the other hand, service industries develop ideas in the main and these can only be subjected to rigorous logical analysis before exposure to the public. Thus, the diagram cannot be to scale, but merely indicative of relative time spans. Time is money both in the sense of paying for assets and labour not producing a return, and in forgoing the return they might have earned by being employed on the going business.

Consumer testing is still regarded as an expensive luxury by many companies who fail to appreciate that even the most expensive consumer research techniques cost a good deal less than the loss resulting from failure in the market-place. Consumer testing and development cannot really be separated as we have done in our diagram. The normal pattern is for research to reveal total failure or partial rejection: very seldom does consumer research indicate an immediate success for the first attempt at the product. It usually goes back for some more development work: a flavour change, an alteration in texture, a modification to the design to make it equally acceptable to left- and right-handed people. Other tests will be running simultaneously. For example, can the quality obtainable in 10-lb lots in the laboratory be obtained in 100-ton lots in the factory? Machine trials, investigations into raw material supplies and so on will go on to make sure that the tested samples can be reproduced. Many a successfully tested product has failed to see the light of day because large-scale runs were impossible or could not reproduce the quality of test-batch production, or because supplies of a certain raw material were unobtainable in sufficient quantity. These are all cases which distort the admittedly high failure rate of products in development through inadequate screening or work carried out in the wrong sequence.

Finally we test-market our two or three remaining products (that is, try them out under actual market conditions in a limited area of the country) and hope to end up with one which will justify a full-scale national launch. We will consider test markets in a little more detail later but we should consider here the advisability of having a policy towards the number of test markets the company can afford – both in terms of cost and the disruption of present business (which may also be a cost) – and also the number of national launches. You may be lucky and get four winners in the same year and you need a policy to cover that eventuality. Nothing is more satisfying to a Marketing Director than a string of fully vetted new products waiting for the starter's gun.

Time is money and the more rapidly screening and development can be done, the better. There is no suggestion that these should be skimped. On the contrary, this is a strong argument for a complete new products development team – including accountants – able to knuckle down to problems as they arise. When directors are inclined to look at the cost of the new products unit they should attempt to mentally assess the cost to the business of using staff busy on existing business. The cost will be the disruption of their everyday work plus the cost of opportunity lost by delayed development times.

There can be no doubt that new product development can be a drain on current resources. This makes it all the more important that the timing and the scale of effort are related to the product life cycles of the business and its plans for the future. The two men who know most about those subjects are the Marketing Director and the Chief Executive.

Identifying Reasons for High Failure Rates

We have already identified the biggest single reason: insufficient (or no) screening and consumer testing. Analysis of inadequately researched products – including services – shows that they tend to fall down on one or more (usually more) critical points. One of the most frequent causes of failure is that the new idea just did not fit the existing business mix. Sometimes this failure expresses itself not so much in the failure of the new product as in the failure of the total business to achieve its goals because too much effort has to be diverted away from normal channels. An alarmingly frequent cause of failure is high capital investment without any attempt to measure the likely pay-out in terms of consumer demand. It can fairly easily be demonstrated that it is worth spending a proportionately high sum on research – and repeating it for reassurance if necessary – to ensure that the risk is justified (the subject of a later chapter).

Two kinds of product are often thought to defy research and this leads to their having high failure rates. The first is where there is a dramatic new product which creates a completely new category. Firstly, one should test the assumption that the product is so dramatic and does create a new category: the simple question 'What did you use the product instead of?' often produces surprising and disheartening answers, but prevents losses. The other category is for highly specialized items where volume is low. Unless the whole operation is geared to produce a satisfactory return at a low volume, results will be disappointing.

However, even products that have been well screened fail. Let us take as the first area of failure that of market assessment. Most mistakes are made about the probable market size, its estimated rate of growth and the profitable life both of the market as a whole and a new product within. Optimism is almost indelibly associated with the assessment of new markets, and where there is conflicting, inadequate or perhaps even no information available it is easy to be wide of the mark. Care must be exercised, in using published figures, to make sure you know what is included: including the catering market by mistake can make an error of £30 million in assessing the size of the tea market in the UK.

Particularly with new markets, there is a tendency to ignore competitive reaction and the possibility that their development may be in line with yours. You may see a market for £1 million which is just viable at that level. You expect to get it all and build it up. In fact, a competitor launches with you and neither of you will capture 100 per cent. Some allowance for the advent of competition must always be made. This is true even in those businesses which enjoy a period of patent protection: investment plans and Marketing action must take into account the effect of competition when it is allowed.

Multi-product companies often have as much to fear from themselves as from their competitors. If you have a range of products which shade into each other you may choose to further segment the market in some rather marginal way (the whole pet food market is a good example). The ideal situation is where all the sales of the new product come from the competitor or expand the market. Either will increase volume and share. The worst position is when existing customers merely substitute your new product for old ones. We call this 'brand steal' – taking share from yourself. This is another area where one is inclined to be rather over-optimistic. Often brand steal is encouraged by retailers who, reluctant to stock yet another product in the same range, cease to stock an older, less heavily promoted item in favour of the new one.

The second area which often slips through screening (but should not get by properly executed consumer research) is the lack of product difference which is real and meaningful to the customer and which they can prove for themselves. Often the difference is one which is clear only to the manufacturer. Sometimes it could be clear to the consumer if only the manufacturer did not assume so much. Two examples from a similar product field illustrate this latter remark. In the early 1960s, Revlon had a failure in the United States with a new addition to their range of hair sprays. They called it 'Super Natural'. The consumer didn't know what the name meant for, to her, the two words were contradictory in the common usage of the market: 'Super' meant more holding power, 'Natural' meant less. More recently, in the UK, Vitalis, a greaseless hairdressing for men which had earned a reasonable niche in the market and had a good proportion of regular devotees, came out with a spray. Unfortunately, the makers failed to make it really clear that this was a lacquer – not ordinary Vitalis in an aerosol form. Regular users of the normal product were dismayed; non-users didn't understand what the product was. When the consumer can discern a real product difference clearly, the advertising theme almost falls into place and the one strengthens and builds upon the other. Advertising cannot create a difference that does not exist, whilst some differences need explanation – and quickly – if the customer is not to be forced to retire in confusion.

The third area is the estimating of the cost of launching into the market and sustaining pressure against competitive attack. Obviously this will be all the worse if you have already neglected to allow for the possibility of competitors entering 'your' market. As we shall see later, deciding how much to spend on advertising is a chancy business with little science to guide one. It is a temptation, therefore, to follow the lead of competition or spend what the costings tell you seems to be affordable.

Finally, under the general heading of why new products fail, a few words on why they still fail even though they have been subjected to consumer research. New techniques are being developed all the time and accuracy is being increased. We have to admit, however, that standard consumer research techniques are generally much less effective with new products than with established ones. This is particularly critical when research in these circumstances is required to be predictive.

Many of the reasons for the failure of research successes can be found in the failure to test all the ingredients of the total

Marketing mix, the difficulty of accurately representing national behaviour in small areas, competitive reaction, the differences in customer behaviour in test and real-life situations and the persistent refusal of human beings to act in a consistently predictable way!

On the other side of the coin, research has often been wrongly interpreted to indicate failure when it in fact indicates success at a different level. Ready Brek, mentioned earlier, was a research failure as a porridge but the research indicated a (then) small but viable franchise for the brand as a hot oat cereal for young children. A market ostensibly more limited than that for real porridge but one which has not only been highly profitable to Lyons but has since been invaded by the conventional porridge companies. In the USA, the toothpaste Ultrabrite, like Ready Brek, lost on all the conventional measures but the tests revealed enough people who preferred its distinctive sharp taste to indicate a market worth having. There are two valuable lessons here: a small number of people preferring your product significantly can produce a viable market, and an isolated product attribute with strong appeal can produce a worthwhile market even though overall preference scores indicate the contrary.

Conclusion

This has been a long chapter touching on many topics which will be treated more fully later. It is worth a book in itself and the reading list is essential for those who wish to know more about this important subject. I have tried to concentrate on management aspects of the problem rather than mechanical ones. We have already seen (when discussing product life cycles) how vital it is to have a stream of new products coming forward to fill the inevitable and ever more rapidly increasing death rate of existing products. Company reports of successful businesses bear testimony to the number of products in existence today that did not exist five or ten years ago. Since 1968, America has dominated world markets in nuclear power, aircraft, electronics and medical products. Why? Because the

United States originated two-thirds of the successful inventions in these fields in the previous twenty years. Technical innovation is clearly even more vital to the British economy than the development of consumer goods.

Just as life cycles are shortening, so are development times. J. J. Servan-Schreiber, in *The American Challenge*, says it took:

122 years to develop photography (1727–1839)
 35 years to develop radio (1867–1902)
  6 years to develop the atomic bomb (1939–1945)
  3 years to develop integrated circuits (1958–1961).

The pace and speed of development is becoming frantic and the costs high. Companies which do not rapidly create the momentum for further growth will be unable to create it at all. They must acquire, merge, be acquired or go under.

Suggestions for Further Reading

Peter Kraushar's book (op cit) is especially applicable, more detailed but eminently readable. A good slim volume entitled *Synectics*, by William J. J. Gordon, is published by Harper and Row. Gordon Medcalfe deals with the Brand Manager's role in *Marketing and the Brand Manager*, published by Pergamon Press.

Chapter 9

Acquisitions and Mergers

In recent years, British industry has been going through what has been journalistically dubbed 'merger mania'. Acquisitions (obtaining total control or a controlling majority) and mergers (the coming together of companies without one having a significant majority) have been on the increase world-wide. In 1967 Richard Barber was saying (at the Harvard Business School) that some 300 companies would control seventy-five per cent of the free world's assets by the year 2000.

Types of Acquisition and Merger

It has become a common sort of shorthand to use the word 'merger' to describe both sorts of situation. However, it is a truism that only shareholders' interests can be merged: people get taken over. It is usually the case that most of those concerned find themselves directly or indirectly under new management or new regimes, if not both. In many senses, the characteristics of both acquisitions and mergers are similar and since assets are merged, it is a convenient term to cover all circumstances and we shall use it as such unless it is important to distinguish for some technical reason. However, before adopting the 'umbrella' term, let us look briefly at the wisdom of the two alternatives.

Generally speaking, where affordable, an outright purchase of a controlling interest is to be preferred. The human problems of any business get-together are such that one clearly dominant partner is to be preferred. A merger is usually advisable only where an outright acquisition – or gaining a substantial majority – is quite out of the question. An effective merger of equals or near equals puts the maximum strain on the people in the business and, although there have been very successful mergers, they are rare and their profit record tends to be less impressive than is the case with outright acquisition. The attempt to preserve separate identities in a merger situation usually creates an unsatisfactory level of overheads which becomes a drain on profits. Over time, the pattern within a merged company changes and either one side becomes dominant in the role of Chief Executive, or new professional management without prior loyalties approach their tasks in a neutral frame of mind and the company becomes indistinguishable from an acquired company. Even old names disappear. It will be interesting to see how long names like Brooke Bond, Oxo and Cadbury-Schweppes last.

We normally distinguish three types of merger:

1. Horizontal – where the goods or services of the combined companies are viewed by buyers or users as virtually identical. The Westminster and National Provincial Banks merger was of this type.
2. Vertical – where the combining companies have a buyer-seller relationship or could have had. Examples would be motor manufacturers buying accessory firms or a tea distributor buying plantations. Similarly, it could be a food company buying supermarkets. Many of the purchases by Associated British Foods (e.g. Twinings) fit this pattern.
3. Conglomerate – a situation which fits neither of the previous examples, where neither customers nor technology fit existing patterns. There may be diversifications into new fields, new products or purely financial in nature. Of late, they have been seen particularly in this latter light and prime examples often quoted are Ling-Temco-Vought (LTV) in the United States and Slater-Walker in this country. In fact, by the strict definition, companies like ICI, with their many different technologies and markets, and the Imperial Tobacco Company, with its wide food

interests, are conglomerates. So, too, are all 'holding companies'.

However, these simple definitions need some amplification to cover some of the fringe cases and it is appropriate that we should consider other typologies and phrases in common use before we discuss the pros and cons of merging. Here are three more terms:

1. Concentric Marketing Merger – applies to businesses with the same customer types but where the technology is different. The word 'technology' is used loosely; this definition could apply to several different industries where the term is not normally used. Schweppes, selling soft drinks, jams and jellies to the grocery trade, acquired Typhoo Tea. Same customers, different 'technology'. Banks sell Unit Trusts over the counter. Marketing capability is an asset which is often capable of greater use and can be applied to new business areas. It can also be heavily overrated: the problem of selling tea is quite different from that of selling jelly even if the customers are the same.
2. Concentric Technology Merger – businesses where the same basic technical know-how applies but to different customers. British Leyland/BMC combines once-individual manufacturers using the same basic technology but selling to widely different markets in quite different ways.
3. Verglomerate – this is a term coined by the famous American writer on Marketing, Theodore Levitt, and covers conglomerates like ICI and IMPS. Both are examples of companies which started from a basic technology and have broken out of it, encompassing both vertical and horizontal mergers on the way. Some horizontal acquisitions have been of companies already vertically integrated by merger, acquisition or natural development!

Finally, another set of three words which are in common parlance and will crop up again later:

1. Synergy – one of the most-used words in the vocabulary of acquisition and merger. Simply defined, it means a close fit between merging companies. That usually means a horizontal merger with roughly the same products, customers and supplies. There is a great deal of evidence, both from the UK and the USA, to show that synergy is an important ingredient in successful mergers, and companies with this sort of fit achieve the best post-merger results. This is particularly true of the synergy to management styles and growth objectives.

2. Symbiosis – describes the merging of seemingly unrelated products. However, there is usually some pre-defined Marketing core running through the company's objectives, which gives the merger a relevance not always apparent to outsiders. The most common of these are: concentric Marketing or technology; the perceived need for greater safety than existing markets offer; artificial limitations on growth in present areas; the high cost of further growth in existing areas. Such companies do not wish to become conglomerates in the sense of being involved in many unrelated businesses but, rather, choose to be in a severely limited number of areas, like tobacco and food.

3. Leverage – a Marketing Americanism for what economists have always called the economies of scale and the balance of countervailing power. These can be enormous – especially in areas like R & D, production and distribution. Size permits the use of modern techniques whether they be the most advanced pieces of machinery or the latest computer techniques for providing management information. Size is not, however, a guarantee of success. In the case of acquisitions, the main areas of effective application of 'leverage' are those described above. In merger situations, it has been shown that economies of scale were most easily achieved where financial resources were pooled. Pooling production, distribution or R & D facilities without pooling cash resources generally does not lead to real economies of scale. With this important proviso, opportunities for leverage should always be sought: the highest proportion of post-

merger failures has been shown to occur where the acquired companies' sales were less than two per cent of the pre-merger volume of the parent company.

Why Merge?

It has been said frequently that most mergers are accidental and opportunist. There is, however, an increasing tendency to consider buying or being bought as part of long-term strategic planning. The services of 'merger brokers' and merchant banks in putting prospective buyers in touch with possible sellers has hastened this desirable trend. However, much of the thought is shallow and a great deal of it is done by people without the necessary skills to carry a deal to its conclusion. The Marketing man can really be expected to do little more than assess growth prospects with and without the proposed victim and attempt to put a price on the task of achieving the same results by development of existing or new products. Acquisition is not always the golden road to success but let us look first at some good reasons for buying:

1. To safeguard interests in existing markets. One must beware of coming up against the Monopolies Commission here, but buying a competitor's market share is often cheaper and is certainly quicker than a competitive battle in the market-place.
2. To expand interests in existing markets. Much the same considerations apply as to the first reason for buying. However, this would encompass the concept of concentric marketing and those companies who have expressed their objectives in terms of broad market categories such as 'food', 'convenience food', 'household products', 'investment' and so on.
3. To obtain a freehold in a completely new market. I am not talking about property here, although it could well apply to a company who had always been in office premises and who wished to get into the field of shop premises rapidly. The best justifications for this approach are where the

right technology or expertise does not exist, where the cost of aggressive entry from scratch is too high, or where it would take too long to establish the right market share to be viable. To take the property analogy a little further, the skills required for locating shops are not necessarily the same as those for locating offices. Significant purchases of shops will push up prices but this is unlikely if another property company is acquired. Finally, it will take a long time to negotiate the purchase of a significant parcel of shop premises.

4. To obtain 'know-how'. The effort of starting from scratch to enter new areas of production, distribution, research and selling is often altogether too much – not only in cash terms but in terms of the effect on existing resources and the momentum of today's business (which must be maintained). A business which not only has the real experts but is totally imbued with an aura of specialist knowledge can often hold out against the most determined attacks of the richest competitors.

5. To acquire under-utilized assets. Let's start with physical assets. If you can find a company with machinery capable of greater use, buildings which can be sold (possibly to be leased back), vehicles which will be unnecessary when the companies are merged, then there is a golden opportunity to produce dramatic financial results in the merged company. Such opportunities are increasingly rare. Property is generally valued at correct market rates, capital is managed better, cash control is becoming better than it was and the chances of acquiring liquid assets correspondingly less. Under-utilized assets often mean an industry which has too much productive capacity for total demand (a situation true of the tufted-carpet manufacturers recently). More and more, one is forced to look for less tangible assets. For example, I have personal experience of an acquisition which added £400,000 to the profits of the new parent simply by disbanding the sales force and the distribution set-up of the acquired company. Moreover, by reducing the total capital employed in the two businesses

(now one) the return improved with favourable effects on share prices and the market valuation of the parent company. Maybe you can provide an asset – such as Marketing expertise – where none exists.

6. To spread overheads over a greater turnover. This pre-supposes that you have certain assets yourself which are under-utilized. Adding significant turnover to an existing force will reduce the overhead charge to each product it handles, thus improving profit margins.

7. To acquire under-capitalized companies and develop them. These companies will often come to you or be found on the books of one of the 'marriage brokers'. Obviously, you must satisfy yourself that this is a company worth putting money into and that it is a better proposition than starting from scratch in the same field. Many of the opportunist mergers arise in this way as one hears (by various means) of companies whose potential is limited only by the lack of an injection of capital. These are often private companies hampered by companies legislation and burdened by taxation.

8. To acquire under-valued companies. Everyone's aim – but increasingly unlikely. However, given the generally low level of financial reporting in this country and the uncertain psychology of the Stock Market, such buys are still possible if one can strike quickly and avoid a fight.

9. In the case of vertical integration, to guarantee supplies (and reduce their cost by eliminating profit margins at each stage) and/or distribution outlets.

10. To acquire liquid assets which might be better employed by developing the business. Cash control, as we have already noted, is getting steadily better and there are no longer many companies with large supplies of cash or near-cash available. In the past companies have literally been acquired with their own cash!

11. Where one can see profitable opportunities through modernization – of methods, production, selling and so on.

12. To obtain a market quotation (known as 'buying a shell'). One normally looks for a moribund company with a Stock

Exchange quotation and injects the assets of a private company into it. A company with a quotation may well fall below the criteria for inclusion yet retain its quote, whilst a private company performing better may be unable to obtain an official listing. The real value of 'buying a shell' is that one can acquire a company, thus obtaining a quotation, without diluting one's own equity to the same extent as with a public offer.

13. To re-capitalize an existing company. The purchasing of a new company can alter the debt/equity ratio (more of this later) and both allow it to grow faster and give shareholders a better return on their investments. This is the basis of operation of what might be termed the 'financial conglomerates'.

14. To increase (or keep on trend) annual earnings. The price/earnings ratio is vital to companies playing the conglomerate game. To maintain it, earnings must increase steadily. If one part of the business hits rough weather or is in a short-term investment situation, the necessary levels may not be reached. Buying earnings with borrowed money is a valid – if short-term – strategy, but the cost rises rapidly if one strays beyond the wooing of low-price/earnings companies. (There is a formula known to financiers to show how much one has to borrow per £1 million of reported earnings.)

15. To obtain a footing in overseas markets. Setting up overseas can be expensive and linking with existing turnover can be invaluable. There are many countries – the USA is one – where a company must own physical assets before it can obtain a public quotation. Buying a company with both a foothold and a quotation makes life much easier and makes international Marketing less of a drain.

Fifteen reasons, and all of them rationalizations for a course of action. They may act singly or several together. However, there is only one real reason for acquisition or merger: to maximize the returns to the owners of the business. This usually means increasing earnings per share. The acid test is how well they will do that compared with development from within. We can sum up the advantages of acquisition and merger not only under some of the headings already considered but also with a few simple statements. Buying an established company enables you to get into a market quickly, with a known share which can be added to your own if the expansion is into the same market, or which gives a more certain start than the launch of a completely new product if you are buying into a new market. Establishment costs and overheads can be reduced, for example, where the new total sales-force complement can be less than the sum of the two individual sales forces. There is also the possibility that some physical assets can be realized to either offset the purchase price or improve profits: perhaps both. Purchasing an established company buys goodwill that may be difficult to create. The greatest attractions of carefully planned acquisitions, however, concern investment time lags. Unlike most new product development, most acquisitions begin their pay-back from the day they are transferred: they start contributing to corporate profits from day one. There are none of the costly and aggravating time lags involved in building factories, installing plant, locating depots, recruiting sales forces and so on. These are particularly important factors leading to diversification by acquisition or merger rather than by internal investment and development.

Problems of Merging

Despite the many attractions and advantages, more mergers fail to achieve the objectives set for them than succeed. Lack of pre-planning is the biggest single factor, and a company with clearly defined strategies which chooses to merge with a company which fits its own objectives and which can reinforce existing strengths and assets (i.e. synergy) is most likely to succeed. Here is a list of some of the more important problems that can provide strong reasons against acquisition or merger. We shall consider the human problems later.

1. If the products are similar, can you maintain total sales of

the two products at the pre-merger level? (The answer is usually 'no', often due to economies in promotional expenditure on at least one product.)

2. Buying goodwill may be valuable, but can you maintain it? One company in the food trade lost the acquired goodwill very rapidly when it imposed its higher minimum quantity rates and inflexible delivery system on a business whose very existence depended heavily on its willingness to supply small quantities at short notice. The forecast economies never materialized as orders disappeared with the goodwill towards the acquired company.

3. The cost of acquiring goodwill can be very high when buying a successful company. (The goodwill element of the price Schweppes paid for Typhoo Tea was very high and reflected the latter's high rating in the profitability leagues.) The cost of acquiring goodwill – which is an important element in any good company's market valuation – may well be greater than that of investing in a new product.

4. Management and 'know-how' are frequently overrated commodities when associated with particular companies. Why not buy them without the attendant problems of acquiring a company?

5. The attitude of even the best Management often changes when they are acquired. This is especially true when the good managers are also the owners or where they have built up from scratch. The qualities required are seldom those needed in a large management team and the transition from one-man operator to even a fairly big cog in a bigger machine can be painful to both sides. Owners tend to cease to be good managers when they cease to be owners.

6. The two factors of goodwill and management may combine to assume great importance. How much of goodwill is due to the people in the company?

7. Many old-established companies have adopted traditional patterns of behaviour in their particular business. If they were starting afresh, would they behave differently? If the answer is 'yes', there is good reason why you should start

afresh rather than buy something which needs to be created anew.

8. How easily can the new company be amalgamated? Many things cannot be known in advance but every possible consideration should be taken into account and a decision made on the magnitude of the likely task and whether the means will justify the end. Even where there is a lack of sufficient prior information, a network of necessary events in any amalgamation can be worked out.

9. Are there any unknowns which could dramatically alter the situation if they were quantified? This involves a subjective judgement of the likely risk of what you might unearth. More of this later.

10. Despite the fact that a profitable concern starts paying back from the first day of the merger, the total pay-back period before the cost of acquisition is covered is usually longer than on an investment project. The reason is that when you buy a company you pay for its goodwill: for the value in a name, for the reputation of the business in the eyes of the public and, above all, for the Stock Market's anticipation of future earnings. All these have to be paid off by increased earnings: the company you acquire didn't *buy* goodwill, it *earned* it.

11. There is a further problem in that pay-back periods can never be calculated with absolute accuracy. At least with your own investment projects you have full access to internal information. Much of this vital detail is denied to you in a pre-bid situation where your calculations must be based upon market valuations, forecasts and anticipated future earnings.

12. A competitive bid situation will obviously push up the pay-back period. One's pre-planning should include calculations of ceiling bid levels.

13. A company may artificially inflate its performance prior to selling in order to get a higher price. There are many ways in which future profits can be sacrificed to today's expediency: if you are selling out you aren't all that concerned about tomorrow.

The biggest problems concern the many unknowns in a takeover situation, the notorious inaccuracy of forecasts and differences in accounting conventions. An example of an unknown concerns a large grocery company which took over a smaller company operating in just one field in which the acquiring company was already active. One of the most significant economies was to come from a major reduction in the size of the acquired company's sales force (of around thirty men). When the company was actually acquired, it was discovered that this smaller sales force had no relief salesmen, had only two weeks' holiday a year and that all took their holiday at the same time (when there was a factory shut-down). When all the planning was done and the journey re-routed, three weeks' holiday allowed at any time and management and relief salesmen ratios applied according to the parent company's rules, the number of actual selling personnel had to be increased! Over-optimistic forecasts and differences in accounting convention were both to be found in the Associated Electrical Industries (AEI) takeover by the General Electric Company (GEC). When trying to fight off the bid, AEI forecast – in November 1967 – a profit for the year of £10 million. When GEC were in control and did the accounts their way they found that AEI had produced a *loss* in 1967 of £4·5 million. £5 million was attributable to facts (lower sales than forecast, for example) but £9½ million was attributable to differences in the accounting conventions used in the audited forecasts on the one hand and the GEC reported results on the other. Even when there is cooperation between intending partners, there are many loopholes to trick the unwary. Where a bid is being fought off, there will obviously be little prior cooperation.

Again, any company considering acquisitions or mergers should first draw up a clear corporate plan and master network of activities involved in any merger. During the negotiation stage, it should attempt to quantify as many of these activities as possible and use subjective judgements of risk where no information is forthcoming or where there is reasonable doubt about the figures obtained. Considered with the other problems, this may lead you to the view that you can make better use of your resources by developing your existing business rather than face the difficulties of digesting other people's problems.

Human Problems

It has often been said that mergers are easy to make but that it is exceedingly difficult to make them work. Businesses are people, and motivating people to work is the key to making mergers work. In most cases, mergers are worse than acquisitions. Although it may not be seen as fair, it is seen as likely to be inevitable that an acquiring company will force the pace and that preference will be given to existing personnel. In a merger situation, there is great uncertainty. People expect the better people to stay but are fearful that one partner may prove to be dominant and give preference to his own staff. The situation is at its worst where the problems start in the Boardroom. This is especially likely with two equal partners. They have got together for greater financial security but they want to retain their old independence. This carries through to a paternal attitude towards staff. When Slater-Walker acquired the giant metal-window firm of Crittall-Hope it found a situation in which there were two head offices, two sets of sales forces with offices and administrative services, and two factories, each working below capacity. The two family businesses which formed the original merger had agreed from the start to rationalize but they had never managed to agree which bits should go. Within a year of Slater-Walker's takeover, the duplicated sales offices and depots had been rationalized, one factory had been closed completely and part of another one and several unproductive assets had been sold off. These moves are reported to have freed £2 million in cash, and changed £18 million of capital employed earning less than £950,000 into £16 million earning more than £2 million.

Should Crittall-Hope have faced up to the problem sooner? There are conflicting views on the problem which may be summed up as:

—Avoid problems for as long as you can.
—Do it now.
—Phase the merger out.

As with most management and Marketing decisions, there is no single answer which will be right for all circumstances. The theory behind delay is that bloody revolution will damage your trading position. The British Leyland Motor Corporation seems to have taken this view and in an industry where trade union action can be crippling they may well have chosen the best possible course of action for their particular circumstances. (Nevertheless, they endured a series of minor strikes plus one very big one at the Leyland Truck plant.) The fact that British Motor Holdings was rapidly approaching bankruptcy was probably a much more significant reason. There is often the feeling that more facts are needed to take a decision and that any action taken immediately may have to be changed as more detailed information becomes available. Under these circumstances, Management often feels that the cost of making a too-early decision may well be too high.

The do-it-now school believe – rightly – that it is going to be painful in any case and that it is better to do what has to be done quickly. It would be foolish to ignore the fact that many of the managers faced with the task of deciding between people and telling some that they are going to become redundant will also find the episode painful. (Since the Redundancy Payments Act many older employees actually find themselves in a very satisfactory financial position shortly before retirement and it then really becomes a case of 'This hurts me more than it hurts you'.)

Advocates of acting quickly believe that uncertainty – which assails almost everyone in a merger situation – is more likely to restrict the momentum of the business than making the odd wrong decision through acting hastily. Whilst the expectation of change is high, the climate is right: with the passage of time people may feel safe and suffer an even greater shock when they eventually face the fact that they are going to lose their jobs. If people in the merged businesses are kept in a state of uncertainty, some will look for new jobs. Those who find it easiest to move are the best and probably the ones you want to keep. This can be one of the costs of delay; others were instanced by the Crittall-Hope example.

The third school advocates a phased attack on the problem. A good example is the eventual merging of GEC, AEI and English Electric. This appears to be the ideal but it does depend heavily on knowing what you want to do, when, and on keeping everybody involved fully informed. (Even so, troubles can be experienced as GEC, AEI and EE found when they fell foul of the unions over the later stages of plant closure.) Experience indicates the vital importance of announcing major policy changes as early as possible, preferably coupled with the ending of speculation about senior and key appointments. Staff definitely required should be told early and all staff should know what will happen to them if the worst happens. Often, incentive payments are made for workers who stay with the company until their particular decision day. Obviously, careful planning and rigid adherence to timing is important. It is bad enough to hear in January that your particular fate will be decided in June, but when you leave on holiday at the end of July and you haven't heard from anyone, it is far, far worse.

Which approach is chosen will depend upon the degree of synergy, the complexity of the problem, the size of the market, the problems you inherit and so on. You must accept, however, that dismissal – even when softened by the word 'redundancy' and a generous cash payment – is seen by most people as a major personal tragedy. I have personal knowledge of chronic illness and even death directly attributable to these situations. Any man will first wonder why it should be him and not the other guy and then begin to wonder whether there isn't something lacking in himself or his own performance. They may simply be victims of 'rather the devil you know', and this will be all the worse when he sees his own boss go too and is probably confronted by some new face. 'To the victor the spoils', and this tends to be true of the human problems of acquisition (especially) and merger: the stronger swallows the weaker and when the Senior Management of the weaker go first, their subordinates have no voice, only their collective record – and that made them a takeover candidate in the first place. If there is any single thing that is more vital than any other in dealing with this situation it is telling people what you are going to do: tell them which method you are going to adopt and give dates where you can and incentives to stay where you intend to phase the effort or delay the integration. Try to make fact precede rumour. Fear of the unknown is the greatest of all human fears.

Selling

There comes a time in every company's life when there is a need for more resources. Frequently, this will lead to the conclusion that the time has come to consider selling out. There are, of course, other reasons such as avoidance of crippling death duties, breaking out of the confines of the close company (both apply to private firms) or making a capital gain.

Preparation of corporate objectives is just as important with a would-be seller as with a would-be buyer. What do you want to achieve and what company will best offer it? If the aim is capital gain on the sale of your holding, the tactics will be quite different from those of a company wishing to see the progress of its goods or services continue! The study should carefully consider what you stand to gain (as a company or an individual) and what you stand to lose. Then look for the company offering the best fit and likely to be in the bidding.

Prepare accurate and reasonable profit and growth forecasts and have a fair valuation made of both tangible and intangible assets. From this, prepare your own estimate of a fair market price. If your forecasts are reasonable and no bid is received at your bottom price (which, of course, you will not have revealed) then, all other things being equal, it is better not to sell. It is better to choose your own partner on your own terms and this will almost certainly ease many of the human problems we have considered.

There are two possible problems you may face. The first is

that your chosen partner is outbid by a less satisfactory one (from your point of view). The answer to this depends on where the majority of the shares are: if they are widely distributed the bidder may be able to acquire the necessary majority however forcibly the directors argue against it. Once you have argued that selling to A is better than going it alone you haven't much argument against a better bid from B. The other problem is that, although you may well find negotiations more harmonious when you take the initiative in selling, you must always be prepared to lose your identity – and your job – completely.

Finally, if after carefully considering the alternatives you decide selling out is not the answer, then start preparing anti-bid tactics. In the last resort there is only one effective answer – healthy profit growth reflected in dividends and price per share.

How Much to Pay?

From time to time, companies have used various formulae for calculating how much to pay. Because of changes in such things as taxation, share indices, the rate of inflation and so on these have little long-term validity – if, indeed, they are ever valid. From time to time, completely new considerations enter the market which change all previous factors. The Imperial Tobacco Company, for example, in their thirst for diversification paid considerably more for at least two of their more recently acquired companies than others with natural synergy felt worth paying. (They also promoted, very successfully, at very much higher rates than the norm in one of these cases.) Many very big mergers between large companies have been motivated by the threat of unwanted acquisition and some of these have apparently broken all the rules – not only of valuation but of reasons for merging. (The beginning of the series of acquisitions and mergers which led to Cadbury-Schweppes appears to have been motivated by fear of takeover of Schweppes.)

A company has four possible values:

1. Book Value – the audited and depreciated value of total net assets. At best this can be deceptive and at worst downright misleading. We have already noted how the permitted methods of valuing assets can vary between companies but even were this not so, what is the value of total net assets at any given time? The value may be £100,000 at the time of a merger if the assets will continue in use or are capable of conversion or realization. At liquidation, you may have a job to give them away! Book value is no more than a historical record which says nothing about performance. It may be an element in the framing of a purchase price but it provides no valid basis for framing a bid.

2. Market Value – represents the lower limit of the value of a company. If you bid below, the owners are better off selling their shares on the open market (assuming there is an active market). There is an old and very true saying: 'You can know the price of everything but the value of nothing.' Measuring a company's worth by the total number of shares issued, multiplied by current trading prices on the Stock Exchange gives total company market *price*, not *value*. However, it provides some framework for bidding: the buyer will want to stay as close as possible to market price, the seller will want to get as far above as possible. There is one major problem: all share prices represent to some degree the 'psychology of the market' and a low overall index for all shares may discount the value of earnings on a particular share below its real worth. The converse may also be true. A good example is a company for which I negotiated a bid of 250p per share. For reasons beyond the control of either company the deal could not go through. Four years later it was sold at 450p per share although earnings had not improved during the period. Two factors influenced the price of that share: the overall index of share prices (which had risen), and an inflated valuation based upon journalist-inspired rumours of a technological breakthrough.

3. Present Value of Future Earnings – this builds upon the method of valuing by market price. However strong the psychology of the market, a company performing badly will

be rated below average and vice versa. The value of a company depends upon its ability to generate profits in the future and the greater those prospects, the higher the company's value. Some guide is given by market price, subject to the strictures mentioned earlier. But care must be exercised in relying upon market reports as a source of information. We all tend to believe all the reports we read about market prospects until we read one on an industry we know intimately. Only then do the limitations become apparent. This method of valuation relies upon careful forecasts of growth prospects based upon past trends both in the company and its markets and upon future prospects. It is probably worth while spending a lot of money on market research to avoid the risk of a highly expensive bad buy. It is staggering that so little pre-bid research is commissioned when so much is at stake, but this largely reflects the frequently opportunist and unpremeditated nature of many acquisitions and mergers.

4. Value of Future Earnings to the Bidder – this is the crux. The value of future earnings may be calculated quite differently by competing bidders. The value of, say, Golden Wonder Crisps to Smith Crisps was probably far less – or so it may have appeared at the time – than its value to the Imperial Tobacco Company. The life cycle of corporate profitability will determine the necessary levels of future profit and how quickly it will be needed.

In short, book value tells you only what assets you will acquire valued according to some particular convention. Market price will put a minimum figure on the bid but the seller will expect something related to forecasts of future earnings. The final price will depend upon how badly you need those earnings (allied to all the other possible reasons for buying) and how much they are worth to your company. Once you have decided that, set a ceiling and be brave enough to drop out if the bidding goes too high: don't suddenly develop megalomania! The real reason for buying is to push earnings per share up: this will not happen if you pay too much.

How to Finance the Deal

There are basically two ways to pay for a company: with cash or with securities.

A cash purchase is reckoned to be an inefficient use of resources. It is an immediate drain on available working capital and will result in a loss of future earnings. The whole object of the deal was to increase earnings! Far from paying cash, the object is to get at cash and near-cash from the acquired business. (One must also bear in mind that present UK taxation penalizes the holders of shares acquired for cash.)

For these reasons, companies prefer to acquire with their own shares, issuing new ones if necessary (a deal may be part cash, part shares; it may even be by instalments). There is a danger that a straight share exchange will dilute the equity in the purchasing company. It frequently happens, where the acquired company has a major shareholder, that someone from the purchased company becomes the major shareholder in the new business, for his consideration is partly financed by the dilution of the proportion of the equity held by previous majority shareholders. If a high premium has to be paid, the dilution will be the greater and there could well be a short-term drop in market prices of the shares. This will not please existing shareholders. The question of dilution should be considered before bidding and every effort made to ensure that the increase in earnings will be an offsetting factor. Of course, in any kind of takeover, one does not have to acquire 100 per cent of the shares.

The whole or part of the exchange may be covered by an issue of convertible debentures. (A debenture is a loan acknowledged by the firm issuing it. Although normally unsecured – in the sense of having no specific charge against a company's assets – they nevertheless have prior charge against the assets of the firm if it goes into liquidation. A convertible debenture can be converted into ordinary shares under certain conditions.) Interest is payable on debentures and earnings must cover this extra burden. The market price of the shares must continue to rise in order to service the conversion of debentures to ordinary shares (a further dilution) as it takes place.

At the back of the question of how to pay for the deal are two important considerations: the price/earnings ratio and gearing.

The P/E Ratio

Companies playing the takeover game with their own 'paper' find a high P/E ratio absolutely necessary. As we have seen, the price a buyer is willing to pay for a share bears some relation to both past performance and anticipated earnings growth. If the price in relation to earnings is high this indicates a high market opinion. Holders of low P/E stocks will be willing to switch into your stock. The ideal takeover situation – from everybody's point of view (financially) – is when a high P/E firm acquires a low P/E company. A low P/E ratio always indicates a possible takeover situation, although one must be careful to discover why the ratio is so low.

Taken at its simplest, the P/E ratio indicates how many years it would take for earnings to equal total market value (both at current levels). It is calculated by dividing the earnings after tax into the number of issued shares times their current market price. Thus if 2,000,000 shares are issued at £1 each and earnings are £100,000, the P/E ratio would be:

$$\frac{£1 \times 2,000,000}{100,000} = 20.$$

If share prices then rise to 150p, the P/E ratio would rise to 25.

Both high and low P/E companies generally deserve the ratings they have. Whilst a low P/E company may be a good buy to another with higher rated shares, one must be able to see the opportunities to push up earnings rapidly and substantially or water down the P/E ratio of the better-rated company. It is by and large true that companies with the leading shares of their particular spheres of business earn the best returns and have the best P/E ratios. They are better off in the long run buying similar companies or companies where they can clearly see an opportunity of improving earnings to such an extent that the P/E ratio will at least be maintained. As is increasingly apparent, giants end up by buying giants: hence the trend towards 300 companies controlling seventy-five per cent of the free world's business.

Gearing

'Gearing' is the relationship of debt and the market value of ordinary shares. Its value is best illustrated by example. To take the simplest case first, if a company has £100 of issued shares and that is its sole capital, and it makes £10 profit, the return on capital employed is ten per cent. In such a simple example, that is also its P/E ratio. If, however, it had financed its operations by £50 of issued capital and £50 of borrowings, the return on capital would have been twenty per cent and the P/E ratio the same. (This, of course, assumes that all of the £100 is invested in capital items; the return on capital employed will almost always differ from the P/E ratio.)

Now let us take a more realistic example. Let us take the example from that used to illustrate the P/E ratio. This company had £2,000,000 of ordinary shares at market valuation. Its revenue was £100,000. Now, suppose that £200,000 of that capital is loan capital. The P/E ratio was previously twenty per cent (2,000,000 ÷ 100,000). It is now changed. First of all, the earnings figure must be reduced to pay the interest on loan capital. For simplicity's sake, let us assume a ten per cent rate of interest. The new P/E ratio will be:

$$\frac{£1,800,000}{80,000} = 22 \cdot 5.$$

The advantage of gearing becomes even clearer if we consider what happens when earnings improve. With the same relationship between loan capital and ordinary shares and assuming no change in market valuation, earnings improve to £120,000. After deducting interest charges of £20,000, net earnings are up by twenty-five per cent to £100,000. The increase in gross earnings (which would be net where there was no loan capital) is only twenty per cent. The new P/E ratio is:

$$\frac{1,800,000}{100,000} = 18.$$

However, this ignores an important fact: the market value of a share which has reported earnings twenty-five per cent above last year's will not stay at £1! The P/E ratio will be maintained at 22·5 if shares rise by 25p each. The value of gearing is in the higher returns which can be produced.

'Gearing', then, is the relationship between loan capital (of various kinds), preference capital and issued Ordinary capital. A highly-geared company is one in which the various forms of loans are large in relation to issued equity. A low-geared company has a much higher proportion of equity. Some businesses (Unit Trusts, for example) are not allowed the benefits of gearing, unlike Investment Trusts. It should be clear from the example that given two companies with equal reported net earnings and the same growth rate of gross earnings, the more highly geared will report higher percentage increases.

It would be wrong to imply that high gearing is riskless. Going downhill on a bicycle in top gear with the wind behind you is marvellous: going uphill against the wind, a lower gear is preferable. A company must consider what level of indebtedness it feels is a safe risk and this will relate to the forecast growth of earnings and their ability to service the debt and repay principal when due.

Conclusion

I have dealt at length with acquisition, for every Marketing man is likely at some time to consider the Marketing advantages of being merged, whether as the senior or junior partner. For the vast majority of companies, the odds will be against acquisition simply on cost, pay-out and future earnings prospects. To generalize wildly and to speak for the majority of companies rather than the giants or those seeking international expansion, the two best reasons for buying are to safeguard an existing market or enter a new one. In a sense, you are buying time in both cases. However, there is no substitute for setting clear corporate objectives and a set of desirable criteria for companies which one might acquire, merge with or sell to. And when the time comes, get the very best expert financial and legal help you can.

Suggestions for Further Reading

Mergers in Modern Business by Nicholas Stacey, published by Hutchinson, is the best known and most readable book on this whole subject. For those who want to get very deeply involved with the intricacies of takeovers, a difficult but excellent book is *Take-Overs and Amalgamations* by M. A. Weinberg, published by Sweet and Maxwell. The Index to each year's *Harvard Business Review* will provide a host of articles too long to quote here on specific aspects of merger philosophy. Beware, however, of devices which are only possible under American Law.

Chapter 10

The Chief Executive as Marketing Man

So far, we have looked at Marketing as it affects every kind of business and every manager within it. In subsequent chapters, we shall consider certain aspects of the various techniques available, look at elements of the total Marketing mix, consider how the Marketing effort can best be controlled and then look at the particular problems of managing the Marketing organization. Whilst the Chief Executive may often know little of what is actually going on in specific areas, he bears ultimate responsibility for the results. In particular, he shoulders responsibility for the failures. He will earn no praise from shareholders for a well-designed package but he will get some hefty kicks if the action of a brand manager results in a sharp fall in profits. And he will deserve them!

The words 'Chief Executive' are used to describe the most senior decision-taker in the organization. He may actually bear the title of Chief Executive (it is currently fashionable to do so). He may report to a Chairman yet still qualify as the senior decision-taker. He may be the Chairman. He can be a sole-trader, a divisional head or Chairman of a giant organization. He is the man who bears ultimate responsibility for the success or failure of the enterprise.

A Chief Executive (unless in a very small company) operates through other line managers. In the large organizations, he must lean heavily upon his own subordinates and hold them responsible for the actions of the people who work for them. He can no more be directly concerned with the execution of an advertising campaign than he can with the operation of a piece of machinery. Unfortunately, because we all regard ourselves as advertising experts, he will be only human if he is more tempted to do the former than the latter. The temptation is the greater if the Chief Executive is himself a trained Marketing man. He may be more skilled and more experienced than those he now entrusts with the Marketing department.

Whatever background the Chief Executive may possess, there is a real dilemma: does he perform the duty of Marketing Director (many Chief Executives do), does he theoretically delegate but continually interfere, does he abdicate responsibility for the Marketing department or does he evolve some system which acknowledges his ultimate responsibility but which involves the minimum of interference with his chosen Marketing Director? Clearly this last is the most desirable. Wearing too many hats is always dangerous: to choose to wear just one extra hat may unbalance the organization (for example, Production may feel that it isn't getting a fair crack of the whip). No Chief Executive who is to be held accountable for his results can afford to abdicate control over any single major area of his business. Thus, in all significant identifiable areas of the business, the Chief Executive must lay down clear guidelines, policy objectives, restraints and constraints upon individual and departmental action, and clear decision and reporting limits. In other words he must *manage*!

It is unfair to single out any one department as being more important than any other: this will vary from time to time. However 'Marketing', in its widest sense, is the single most important activity of any business: 'Marketing' – creating profitable, customer-satisfying goods or services – *is* the business, and it is the Chief Executive's job to stay in business and continuously improve results. In the philosophical sense, 'Marketing' will be his number-one priority. He should be continually asking, 'Will this satisfy our customers; how can we be sure; what is the most profitable way of doing it; which way gives us the biggest advantage, the best lead and the longest life?' Those questions alone will tax the resources of the most complex business; they are none the less appropriate for the one-man business.

What follows is a sort of guide to 'How to live with your Marketing Director'. For the last two words substitute whatever is appropriate to your business: Marketing Manager, Director responsible, Consultant, fellow Directors. The principles are the same through whatever channels the Chief Executive has to exercise his ultimate business responsibility: satisfying customers at a profit.

The first requirement is a clearly defined overall objective with quantifiable standards. Where there is a Marketing department, these may well be prepared there to a prescribed formula for the Chief Executive's approval. Otherwise, the objectives will give the Chief Executive's long-term direction for the business, the areas for priority (which may vary by department), and how the plan is to be achieved: by natural growth, investment, diversification, merger, acquisition, sale, etc.

The specific areas which allow the Chief Executive to exercise strict control without detailed involvement can be summed up by setting the following standards:

1. Long-term aims in terms of growth of profit and volume, earnings per share, share of market, etc, as appropriate.
2. The formula for measuring success: e.g., return on capital, profit/earnings ratio, etc.
3. Profit requirements (in cash) for the coming year.
4. Where appropriate, policy with regard to promotional investment and pay-back periods.
5. Any other identified and quantifiable area requiring correction and improvement: e.g., higher orders to call ratio for salesmen, improvement in brand image, reduction in withdrawal of outdated stock.

By sticking to quantifiable objectives, these can be translated to individual commitments and actual performance compared at regular intervals with budgeted or planned performance. Clearly, not all of these items can be reported on at regular intervals, but the majority can. Annual operating profit forecasts can be broken down into appropriate financial periods and action taken before it is too late. However, the temptation to try to look at too much must be avoided: pick on a few key areas of the business and examine performance in these areas critically. For example, although you may have set the Marketing Director the objective of improving the orders per call ratio, there is no point in calling for a weekly return. Set a time limit – say six months – and arrange to meet the Marketing Director with the figures (and the explanations) then. If, however, sales are bad, it would not be unreasonable to look for the reason in the orders to call ratio even though the time limit was not yet up.

A Chief Executive is a busy man and it is questionable how much detail it is reasonable to expect him to absorb on a continuous basis. The computerized company has the answer in the exception report: a procedure whereby the computer is instructed to print out all variances outside a prescribed level. Thus, it may print out sales figures wherever they fall five per cent below target, or shop distribution whenever it falls eight per cent, or cash withdrawals whenever they exceed deposits. For the large company without such sophistication it is usually best for the Chief Executive to look at divisional or grouped figures and identify the problem (or success) area and then go to the responsible manager for identification of the precise problem. In smaller companies it may be possible to look at each separate item.

The size of the company is clearly important but it does not change the nature of the Chief Executive's Marketing responsibility. The biggest problem he faces, with varying size, is what kind of Marketing organization – if any – he should have. This will largely depend on the complexity of the organization, the number of products or services it offers and how diverse are the fields in which it operates. At the one extreme is the Chief Executive who is his own Marketing Director. Next comes the Marketing Director reporting direct to the Chief Executive and who is either a one-man band or supported only by specialists (e.g. a Market Research Manager). Although there are various intermediate types of organization, the ones where the Chief Executive finds most difficulty in exercising control are those where there is a Marketing Director and many Brand or Product Managers or several Marketing Directors or

Managers, each with large brand organizations beneath them. The only solution is a carefully graduated set of management objectives, graduated by rank, and with each manager holding the appropriate information necessary to quantify the performance of his subordinates. The Chief Executive looks at the broad, overall picture knowing where to find the answers to points of detail. (This system also has the advantage that more subjective assessments of performance and development potential can be built into the objectives of those lower in the organization. We must always remember that there are circumstances beyond the control of the most efficient man and we must allow for this in any system.)

Many Chief Executives place heavy reliance on regular meetings to pore over the latest results and receive written or verbal reports. I can find only two good reasons for such regular meetings: firstly, to exchange information between departments (or Chief Executive and department) and secondly, to discuss longer-term interdepartmental problems. Larger, regular gatherings waste valuable executive time, cause people not directly involved in interdepartmental problems to take sides, and generally are more trouble than they are worth. Urgent problems should be tackled urgently when they arise. A more useful formula is for it to be known that all senior managers should be in the office (except for the most urgent business reasons) on the day when the figures are published. Regular meetings are increasingly being cut down to budget-fixing meetings, and in the best-ordered companies it does not take the Chief Executive to get responsible managers whose actions affect each other to talk together before submitting budgets.

There will be more to say about making and agreeing Marketing plans later and it is obvious that the Chief Executive has ultimate responsibility to approve or reject these plans. He has the right – indeed the duty – to receive reports on the effectiveness of these plans. Somewhere, he must draw a line and leave the rest to a trusted subordinate. If he has come up through the Marketing stream, the Chief Executive should forget it: he is an entrepreneur and a man-manager first and foremost now. If he has come up some other way, he should know what Marketing is all about even though he is not an experienced specialist. His prime Marketing duty, however, is to spread into every nook and cranny of the business the basic philosophy of Marketing and to instil in every employee a pride in satisfying the customers of their business, whether it is selling cat food or airline seats.

In the next section, we are going to consider certain aspects of some of the many specialist techniques available to the skilled Marketing man. We shall look at them only in so far as it is necessary to understand what we can and what we can't do, how reliable the techniques are and what use to make of certain kinds of expertise. In a sense, Part 2 forms a bridge between the understanding of the Marketing philosophy and the practical aspects of preparing, understanding and achieving a Marketing plan.

Part 2

Elements in the Marketing Mix

Introduction

In Part 1, we were concerned with the philosophy of Marketing and the ways in which we can ensure the profitable continuance of the business. Now it is time to turn from those aspects of Marketing which equate with 'business', in the widest sense, to some of the areas of specialization which are normally exercised by specialists and frequently employ scientific techniques.

Any product or service is regarded by its user or buyer not as a single entity but as a mixture of attitudes, prejudices and sensations. These may be highly subjective as with, say, cigarettes or highly objective as with the purchase of a piece of machinery. However, even aesthetic considerations may enter into the otherwise highly objective purchase of a highly expensive piece of capital equipment. Many of the 'omnibus' or 'catalogue' definitions of Marketing are no more than recitals of the elements in the total mix. They include items like: the product, product development, packaging, design, service, research, advertising, sales promotion, selling, profit margins, distributor's margins, brand identities, price, brand image, etc.

There is no general agreement among companies as to which of these should be in the domain of the Marketing Director. Some include selling, some do not; some put physical distribution under his control, the majority appear not to.

Practically every topic we shall consider in this section (and many topics can receive only passing reference) is worthy of a complete book. Indeed, some sections are covered by numerous books covering only one small facet of the subject (e.g. market-research techniques). It is the intention of this section not to provide exhaustive treatment of any of the subjects, but to outline their uses and values and use personal experience to illustrate the importance of understanding the limitations of techniques which are produced as supporting evidence for recommended courses of action. The busy Chief Executive, the Marketing Director and, to varying but usually lesser degrees, other directors and senior managers are bombarded with recommendations full of jargon: some is necessary, much of it is not. Under these conditions, even the most practised Marketing man may overlook the deficiencies of a technique or neglect an important item in the total mix. There are many pitfalls to trap the unwary or over-hasty.

Chapter 11

The Product

From all that has gone before, it should be unnecessary to labour the point that the product should be as close a fit to what your consumer or user wants as you can reasonably supply. There is a tendency with the sort of over-simplification adopted in my first chapter to over-emphasize the concept of consumer sovereignty. You start with the business you have and tailor its products to what the consumer wants, where, when, how and at what price he wants it. You can then develop into doing the same thing for the type of business you can easily become (e.g. the Polycell example quoted in Chapter 8). There may be a greater identified demand for a product in some totally new field but you are unable to supply it with your existing technology and the decision to change the basic nature of your business is a major one with enormous risk attached to it.

The first essential of success is that the product should perform as the customer requires in relation to the price he or she is prepared to pay for it. Obviously, one does not expect Rolls-Royce performance at Mini-Minor prices. However, the customer's expectations of performance will be conditioned by a host of things associated with the product such as its price, presentation, degree of personal service offered, prospects of after-sales service, attitudes created by advertising, and so on. Good advertising, good presentation and a price regarded as fair and justifiable expenditure will lead to trial. Only satisfactory performance will lead to repeat purchases. All this is apparent, but Marketing textbooks tend to ignore the importance of durability, frequency of purchase and availability of substitutes.

It is obvious that you will quickly discover people's reactions to a good product that is bought once a week. You will soon know whether people are going on buying or not. At the other extreme, will the man who has just bought a piece of machinery with a twenty-year life buy from you again when the life of that machine is up? Some of the more interesting examples occur in the service fields. There are both consumer and producer services with varying degrees of durability and differing frequency of purchase. Haircutting is a consumer service which most men use at regular and fairly frequent intervals. A good or bad haircut is immediately apparent. One may, however, be satisfied with a less than perfect haircut because the service is so good (the staff are courteous, there are no long waits) or the price is moderate. If a man comes to your house to repair your television set, you may discover immediately that he is a bad engineer, or this may take some time. Whether it is his fault or not, the likelihood is that you will regard him as bad if the set breaks down again fairly soon after his call. (Any service engineer will tell you that 'fairly soon' can be a long time: human memory is notoriously suspect when it comes to matters like this.) If, however, your television goes on working for another eighteen months without the need for further attention, then you will regard him as a good mechanic. The judgement is subjective but the important thing is that, at the time of your first 'purchase', neither the customer nor the supplier knows if they will ever enter into a buyer-seller relationship again. Some consumer services are so durable that they may never be used again by the same person – although he may recommend them to others. A man who has successfully passed his driving test will not need the services of the same company again, but he may send along his wife.

There are parallels with services provided to producers. Machinery repairs equate with both the haircut (it will be obvious if the machine won't start up again) and also with the television engineer. The equivalent to the driving lessons could well be a piece of consumer research which, having produced the required answer, will not need to be repeated. On the other hand, as we shall see later, consumer research can also be continuous and, in such cases, is usually on a medium- to long-term contractual basis. The great problem with the Marketing of services is the uncertainty of repeat demand: a good restaurant may pull in the same customers every day or once a week, a good garage repairman may never see that particular car again if he has done a good job.

Durability is also a factor in other industries than those engaged in the service field. A man who is highly dissatisfied with the car he has just bought is seldom able to afford to change it immediately. He may well decide never to buy that model or that make again. The same is true of most consumer appliances. On the other hand, a satisfactory durable product will have a long life: hence the pressure for 'built-in obsolescence'. Model changes, fashions, technological advances and so on can create both real and psychological motivations to change even though the performance of the present appliance remains satisfactory. As we have seen before, 'a product' is made up of many things.

We have considered frequency of purchase and durability as influences affecting usage and re-purchase. We now have to look at the availability of substitutes. There are many businesses, usually connected with consumer or industrial durables, where sole agencies or franchises are given either in total or by area. If you want a particular product you have to use that dealer, however poor his service may be. The more interesting case is where competition is more apparent than real. Banking is a prime example. With the exception of the Co-operative Bank CWS Ltd, all the leading joint stock banks open at the same time, close at some of the most convenient times, offer the same terms of business and provide a degree of service that varies only according to the personalities of the branch staff. (The Co-operative Bank is the only major bank with an extensive network of branches which allows interest on current accounts and opens on Saturdays.) One of the major banking groups recently produced a piece of research that showed that most of its customers did not object to Saturday closing. I regard this as a piece of spurious evidence. 'Most' of their customers represent a minority of potential bank customers and they have been conditioned to such limited hours of opening on Saturdays that the majority of them probably ignored the opportunity. A more interesting survey would have been to have tried to discover how many non-users might open accounts if banks opened all day Saturday and some evenings. However, that is only part of the problem of the banks: they still suffer from widespread fear and distrust and even many people with accounts regard a visit to withdraw cash as rather akin to a visit to the dentist!

Insurance is another field where competition is more apparent than real but this time it is largely the customer's fault. Any good insurance broker will tell you that there are wide variations in terms and benefits and the insurance companies must bear some responsibility for making comparison difficult for the public. However, insurance companies are dealers in death, doom and destruction – unpleasant things that people would rather not contemplate. People, by and large, do not buy insurance – they are sold it. Even when they do actively search out a supplier, they seldom consider the alternatives and having once bought they tend not to keep their levels of household, property and life covers in line with changes in their circumstances. (This is where brokers and service salesmen can perform a valuable consumer function.) The competition is there but the customer ignores it (although it can be argued that the insurance industry could do much to remedy the situation).

It is important to distinguish what the public regard as the complete product, for, in many industries, it is not entirely under the control of the supplier. The holidaymaker who buys a package tour does not see himself as dealing just with a man behind the counter at a travel agent's. He sees the end-product as a satisfactory, trouble-free holiday. He expects his mind to be made up, his travel to be arranged, his hotel to be booked, his rooms to be comfortable, the food to be good, and the weather fine. The agent may check all these (using probability analysis for the weather!) but any breakdown anywhere in the chain – even though beyond the agent's control – will probably mean that one holidaymaker will not go back to that agent. A person buying a television is buying programme entertainment.

If this were uniformly bad, the demand for sets would probably fall off sharply. The person who rents a television, however, goes a stage further and is paying for service: the promise of never being without a picture for an unreasonable length of time. To a lesser extent (particularly as TV sets have become more reliable) renters are gamblers: they are gambling on the average life of a set and its capital cost compared with rental terms over a period of time. (This analysis is becoming more and more hypothetical as the legal requirements regarding initial deposits and advance payments come closer to the purchase price of a television. At the time of writing, the initial deposit on a colour receiver would purchase a very good black-and-white set.) One could continue with these examples: buyers of cars, consumer durables and industrial machinery regard after-sales service and rapid availability of spares as part of the product mix. Buyers of cosmetics will pay a high price for the psychological assurance provided by expensive-looking packaging, and the outer carton and the inner container are part of the product. So too are the less tangible promises of youth and beauty.

I make no excuses for covering ground already touched upon in Part 1. It is important to understand that your product is usually seen by the consumer in quite a different way from the way you see it. To the customer the product is itself a mix made up of various kinds of satisfactions – many of them emotional – of a number of different qualities, some induced by the product, some by the presentation, some by the price, some by advertising, some even by the weight of public opinion. Not all of these aspects are covered in this book, for reasons already stated, but the reading suggestions will refer those anxious to know more about the missing items to appropriate books and articles. The obvious thing to examine next is price: demand occurs only at a price and the setting of the correct price is a crucial factor in both the initial and continued acceptance of products or services.

Chapter 12

Price

'Demand exists only at a price.' Thus price is an important determinant of how much of any product will be sold. But price alone is not the only determinant of value. 'Value for money' is a subjective judgement affected by promises of performance, expectations, actual performance, presentation and so on. Price does not occupy the simple place assigned to it by the classical economists as the meeting point of demand and supply in a situation where everybody in the market had complete knowledge of everything else in the market and all substitutes were perfect substitutes. Competition is imperfect and price is only an ingredient in the total Marketing mix, though a very important one. It is hard to separate the product from the price: we must always talk about the product at the price.

Given its importance both as an ingredient in the total mix and as a major determinant of profitability, it is staggering how haphazard so much pricing is and how many companies who profess complete acceptance of the Marketing philosophy ignore the customer in their price calculations. The most common method of price-fixing is based on cost-plus principles: raw material and manufacturing costs plus a figure to cover general overheads, promotion and profit. This approach implies that price is *not* an important determinant of demand and that potential customers are waiting like sponges to soak up products whatever their price. Alternatively, one might take the implication that the company is not interested in profit maximization. (We shall see later that there is some evidence to support this latter view.) From the number of known cases where sales have improved as a result of a price increase and

the amount of research findings which place potential customers' valuations above cost-plus pricing indications, it would
appear that most products and services are underpriced. You
quickly know if they are overpriced so the last statement
seems logical. However, underpricing – especially in times of
increasing costs – means pressure on profit margins. Careful
testing is necessary to discover how far the price can be
pushed up before sales will be adversely affected.

The extent to which any one manufacturer can determine
the price of his product will depend upon the extent of
competition, the closeness of that competition and the availability of effective substitutes, the strength of the desire for the
product, price-elasticity of demand, price/volume considerations and psychological factors. We shall consider all these, but
it is fair to say that the area that has received least attention in
the past has been the importance of psychological factors in
pricing policy. It is interesting that the people who have
recognized the importance of these values longest have been
those people closest to the final consumer, especially street
traders who have long recognized the importance of certain
price thresholds and have indulged in auction techniques to
obtain the highest price.

Before we consider ways of pricing and those areas that
cannot be separated from pricing, we must recognize that
'price' means different things to different people. For example,
the price of Heinz Baked Beans to a large grocer is not the list
price on the manufacturer's price list but includes all the
discounts, deals and offers that go with that basic price. The
grocer has a concept of total price – a best buying price – which
he will compare with other total prices of competitive products.
He will then estimate the profit he can make at those total
prices, times expected volume, to arrive at his buying decision.
Similarly, housewives are bombarded with special offers;
manufacturers with promises of service and so on. All these
come together in the concept of 'total price'.

Cost Approaches to Pricing

We have already noted that basic costs (of manufacturing or providing a service) provide the basis for most pricing decisions. Obviously, one cannot consider selling below cost; what is wrong with most cost approaches is that they make little attempt to reconcile what the customer is prepared to pay with what it costs the company to be in business and make a fair return. Such reconciliation most often occurs with the realization that the product or service is – or will be – overpriced.

The first costing method of pricing we shall examine is known variously as product-line pricing, absorption costing and on-costing. (Not all companies use these terms in precisely the same way.) The essential of this system is that all costs are reduced to unit costs, for example costs per ton, based upon expected volumes of business. Firstly, all costs directly associated with the product alone are collected together (e.g. raw materials, machinery, direct labour). This produces a total factory cost or manufacturing cost. To this is added a share of all general overheads (non-specific production expenses, clerical services, R & D, etc), sales and promotional expenses to give the final unit cost. In multi-product companies these costs are normally apportioned on a fairly arbitrary basis. Companies using this method should attempt to be as specific as possible in the allocation of these general expenses even if the end result still has arbitrary elements in it. For example, it is pointless to allocate a flat ten per cent advertising/sales ratio across all products when it is clear that some need to spend fifteen per cent and some only five per cent. This will conceal true product profitability. When all the allocations have been made, a percentage mark-up is applied as profit. All allocated costs plus mark-up equals price.

There is one important misleading element with this on-costing approach. Since it reduces both costs and profit to a unit basis, the method implies that a profit is made from the very first unit sold. This, of course, is patently untrue. A certain volume is necessary before even fixed costs are covered. (This will be seen when we consider break-even analysis.)

The other major cost approach is marginal costing. It is important to distinguish between prices arrived at as the result of marginal costing and the mistaken use of the term 'marginal pricing' adopted by many Marketing men. The marginal cost of a product is the cost of making just one more unit. The only costs charged to the product are those – such as cost of raw materials, direct labour and possibly plant cost – that can be directly identified with the cost of making the extra unit. The difference between marginal cost and price is a contribution to all other expenses plus profit.

This method overcomes the big objection to the product-line costing in that it makes it clear that no profit is earned before all costs have been covered. However, although many companies in industries as diverse as food and chemicals make use of the method, it is a difficult system to use. In the first case, the cost of making one more unit is hard to define in most businesses and, in the second case, the contribution area is almost inevitably greater than the marginal cost area; indeed, the indirect costs alone are usually greater.

Theoretically, marginal costing is a better basis for costing than the previous method examined because it enables one to see what happens to profitability as sales increase or decrease, and thus one can establish a relationship between profit objectives and volume estimates.

One other cost-based approach deserves passing mention and this is the concept of opportunity cost. This can only apply where any essential element has an alternative use. A notional value is put on the cost of using, say, a piece of machinery to produce A rather than B. One could almost call it 'lost-opportunity cost': if one decides to produce A rather than B, the price should produce a profit at least equal to that which would be earned by producing B. Normally it is obvious that one course is more profitable than another, but in business one frequently has to take tactical decisions and the opportunity-cost basis provides a way of either making sure you do not forgo profit unnecessarily or, alternatively, that you do it knowing what you are giving up. The opportunity-cost concept is usually of more importance in justifying the

existence of a product than in fixing its price. This is especially
true, where the sales force is concerned, where the addition of
an extra product may lead to lost opportunities of making
profits on existing brands.

Break-Even Analysis

All pricing situations are capable of break-even analysis, that
is, defining the point where all costs and expenses are covered
and net profits are made. However, in cost-based pricing
decisions, break-even analysis is often used to set the price at
which the product must be sold at an anticipated volume. The
simplest form is shown in Figure 7. Fixed costs are shown as
a straight line and all other costs are allocated on a cost-per-
unit basis to produce an ascending curve. Revenue is simply
set at, say, a rate per ton. At point A, revenue will cover only
fixed costs. At point BE all costs are now covered and all
future sales will produce net profits. A more sophisticated
model is shown in Figure 8. This shows the rate at which
various items in the mix are recovered. It starts with variable
costs at a unit rate and adds fixed sums for fixed costs, allocated
overheads and the required return on investment. At point A
fixed costs are covered, at C revenue covers both fixed costs
plus overheads and break-even is measured here (BE) by the
point at which the minimum profit target is achieved. Clearly,
not only are there two ways of looking at the same situation
but also two uses of the term 'break-even'. In the latter case
the argument goes that if one is in business to make a profit
one should not consider any combination of costs and prices
that does not ensure reaching minimum profit objectives.
Although, in both examples, only one price has been shown,
probability analysis can be applied to various combinations of
price and volume estimates.

The terms 'fixed' and 'variable', when applied to costs,
relate to periods of time. Plant costs, for example, are fixed
until maximum output is reached. Further output requires
more plant, and fixed costs rise to a new plateau. When
reduced to a unit basis, costs can only be fixed at a particular

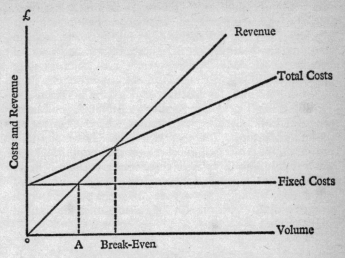

Figure 7. Simple Break-Even Analysis

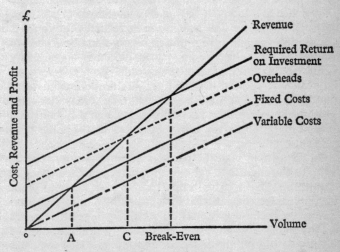

Figure 8. Sophisticated Break-Even Analysis

T—F

output: if output falls below the target on which unit costs were based, the share of fixed costs apportioned to each unit of production will rise. Variable costs, on the other hand, are often fixed for short periods. Sales-force costs (where they are allocated as costs rather than as expenses) are a good example: they tend not to respond rapidly to changes in volume since the size of a sales force is relatively static except in response to dramatic changes in trading conditions. Although you cannot dispose of half a machine when output falls, you can put off half the work force. You may well decide not to do this, especially if there is reason to believe you may need them back. Although theoretically variable, these costs are relatively fixed. The separation, although following fairly generally accepted conventions, is rather arbitrary, for there is a sense in which all fixed costs are variable and all variable costs are fixed at points of time!

Price in Relation to Objectives

Time and time again we keep returning to this theme of the importance of a company having clear objectives to which all its activities and possible actions can be related. Since price is an essential ingredient of profit, it clearly must be related to overall company objectives. Company objectives are generally expressed in terms of maximizing total profits, return on equity (plus accumulated reserves), return on total assets employed (including loan capital), return on turnover or some combination of the four. However, it is seldom that more than two of these objectives can be pursued at the same time without conflict.

In an existing market, the most common way of relating price to objectives is to use the cost-plus approach, arriving at a price yielding margins commensurate with declared profit objectives, and compare that with competitive prices. Alternatively, the exercise may start by accepting competitive prices as the ruling level and work backwards to producing at the right cost to give the required contribution. However, this approach assumes either that competitors are correctly priced (and in a well-established market this may well be decreed by habit) or that one has settled for the quiet life and wishes to avoid provocation by pricing low, or a restricted market by aiming above existing levels.

It may be the company's objective to undercut the market in the belief that this is the way to a higher share than could be gained by any other method. (Heinz, very significant brand leaders in tomato sauce and salad cream, have suffered such low-price competition from HP Sauce – among others – who clearly decided that the only alternative, and not a very satisfactory one, would have been to have marketed at the Heinz prices and fought an expensive promotional battle.) This kind of policy is frequently adopted by late entrants to markets with strongly entrenched brand leaders. In the case of a new market, one may well set out to pre-empt the market by setting a low price to keep competitors out. This can be a successful tactic where the volume yields sufficient return and competition does stay out. If, however, you do meet competition and you don't achieve the desired volume, you will have to increase prices (and hope your competitor does likewise) or suffer inadequate profit margins.

It is in trying to price low that companies often use what they term 'the marginal pricing approach'. Strictly speaking, 'marginal price' means the price of one more unit and would only be meaningful if, say, the 101st unit had a different price from the 100th. The approach is based upon a similar misconception of the meaning of marginal cost (already explained). In common usage, this approach assumes that producing extra volume will incur no more cost at all or only insignificant amounts of variable cost. It is assumed that no new plant is required, no extra salesmen, perhaps no extra labour and so on. All this reduces unit cost and allows a lower price to be charged. In effect, the product costed in this way is getting a free ride on the backs of other brands already paying for overheads which are assumed to be fixed in the short run (although variable by convention). There are two great dangers with this approach and they could coincide. One is that the product costed in this way is so successful that it *does* require extra plant, more salesmen and so on. This may turn the balance between profit and loss. The other is that the strong products which provide the supporting contributions may become weak and unable to bolster the 'marginally costed' brand. This may mean a necessary – and possibly sizeable – price increase for the low-priced brand with a consequent loss of sales or a total fall in corporate profitability or, probably, both. Used in this mistaken way, marginal costing or marginal pricing is dangerous. All new brands should be capable of paying their fair contribution to shared costs and if the introduction of another item does not lead to an increase in certain of these overhead charges, then the total can be spread over a larger expected volume, lowering the required contribution of each existing product and allowing the option of increasing profit per item or reducing price. The latter course should only be chosen if that will be the more profitable in the long run.

Price/volume considerations are clearly important in any low-pricing policy. Going below ruling prices as a deliberate strategy clearly aims at achieving a higher volume and assumes that high volume times low profit per item will be more rewarding than lower volume times higher profit per product. This is the basic philosophy of supermarket trading, but one should not run away with the idea that it is only supermarkets who have 'loss-leaders': products sold at or below cost to attract other purchases. Such products are found in the engineering field as an aid to selling a range of products. Often 'loss-leaders' and ultra-low prices are used to drive smaller competitive units off the field. Once successful, prices may well rise again.

The other end of the scale is to price high. Many companies have good reason to fear the damage that could be done to their overall image by being seen to supply low-priced goods. Even though it may not be true, a company with a tradition for selling high-priced quality items that offers a low-priced product will almost inevitably be assumed to be offering a low-class product at that price. Frequently, it is part of the objectives of a company when launching a new product to charge as much as the market can stand for as long as possible.

By so doing, it can cream off 'excess profits' (i.e. above-normal target requirements) to fund the possibility of having to reduce prices later as competition appears. Such a company will probably aim to reduce prices gradually and by as little as possible but by just enough to discourage new entrants. Frequently the extra contribution provided by high pricing will be used to give the new product heavy initial promotion, again with the intention of discouraging competition. However, it should not be thought that heavy launch promotion inevitably means high prices. Especially in the fast-moving consumer goods field, a technique often called 'penetration pricing' is used, where one combines low prices with heavy advertising to produce a mass market very rapidly. This usually involves a willingness to accept a long pay-back period on the initial investment.

From this brief examination it can be seen that pricing decisions must relate to overall company objectives and decisions about the ways in which the company is prepared to achieve these, coupled with policy decisions on the treatment of costs, the willingness to invest in markets and the length of time the company is prepared to wait before investment is recouped.

Examples of Pricing Situations

Obviously one cannot give an exhaustive list of examples but what has been said already may have greater meaning if exemplified by the situations prevailing in certain types and sizes of industry. An interesting place to start is the heavy industrial field. Products in this category are intermediary in the sense that a piece of machinery is used to convert raw materials into finished products for sale. Since R & D, engineering and tooling costs are high, price is normally set high in the first instance. The customer wants the machine and will buy it at the high price (in the absence of competition) unless the effect on his overall costs is to deny him a viable market. The concept of 'total price' (the inclusion of installation, start-up assistance and adequate servicing and spares) is important. Once bought, the price to that particular customer needs only to be reconsidered in the light of any subsequent competition either when he needs additional plant or when existing plant is fully depreciated and a decision has been taken to replace it.

In the case of raw materials, the cost-plus approach is normal although the plus element may be high if there is a high development cost behind the product and/or it represents a significant advance on other similar items. Manufacturing components rank with raw materials in this respect. Absorption costing is common with components and the lighter industrial goods. Price changes in either the costs of raw materials or component parts are normally reflected in the price of the end-product to the consumer only where they form a significant proportion of the final cost. (Switching from industrial products to grocery for a moment, the raw material cost of a packet of tea can be as much as eighty per cent of the final price: a change in tea prices obviously would affect retail prices if they were large enough to be translated to meaningful increases or reductions in the price of a quarter-pound packet.) Price changes by the whole market in the industrial field may well lead to the use of substitutes. The high price of lead has caused a swing to copper pipe in building. Plastic guttering is offered as a substitute for zinc. However, tradition dies hard in many industries (the building trade is a good example) and the switch to substitutes may take time.

Pharmaceuticals provide an interesting example of an area where enormous sums of money can be spent on years of fruitless research. When one comes up with a winner, one wants to recoup as much of that expenditure as possible and secure as much of the market as possible against future entrants. Prices are therefore set high on introduction but they may fall rapidly once a strong position is reached. Although it is easier to copy than to innovate, the costs in this particular industry are still high. There is an additional incentive to gain a quick return in that therapies are rapidly outdated both by the growth of bodily resistance against new drugs and by the development of newer and more effective treatments. The

Sainsbury Committee of Enquiry into the pharmaceutical industry found that overall production costs were forty per cent of sales revenue, with overheads and promotional costs accounting for another forty per cent. In the early days of a new product, the *gross* margin required could be between sixty-five per cent and eighty per cent of total ex-factory costs.

Any jobbing industry, producing a batch against a special order, is effectively barred from adopting a marginal costing approach to pricing. (Although if the job is an order for just one unit it is by definition a case of marginal costing.) In jobbing industries, one is never certain when the next order for a similar product will come in, and therefore some form of cost-plus pricing is bound to be used. Such industries do, however, have the advantage of knowing precisely how much they are going to make and are therefore able to be precise in their calculation of costs. Calculation of the break-even point is simple.

Jobbing industries frequently negotiate their prices or may even tender. They are not alone in this. Negotiated prices are common with industrial equipment and tendering is found in trades as varied as heavy industry, catering and the supply of private-label groceries. Negotiated prices and tenderings are really the same kind of situations. In the first case one has to assume there will be competition, whilst in the second one knows there will be. However, a negotiated price can include the concept of 'total price'; a sale may be gained by the combination of, say, price plus service. Companies or authorities inviting tenders for the supply of goods or services (usually over a period) tend to specify the standard of services required and the contract will go to the person able to meet the specification at the lowest price. There is an element of gambling in both but much more so in the case of tenders. Cost-plus is the normal basis of arriving at the eventual price but the gambling element does lead many firms to use the mistaken idea of marginal costing criticized earlier. Mention was made of negotiating prices for the contract to supply products to be sold under a store's own label. Usually, the product already exists as a branded item sold on the open market and thus cost information is there. The practice here is to eliminate those costs and expenses which do not apply to the own-label situation. For example, no sales expenses need be involved, there will be no advertising, if all goods are distributed to one central warehouse the distribution charge can be reduced. If an adequate return on capital is already being achieved, the company may be satisfied with a lower return on the extra business. The key is the word 'extra'. If you lose part of your own branded business by, in effect, competing with yourself, the overheads will have to be spread over a lower volume, reducing profit per unit.

In the service industries, the equivalent method of pricing to that used for a private-label brand can be found in such areas as air-charter flights and packaged holidays. If an aeroplane is only going to be half full, the airline cannot put on half a plane. Similarly, a hotel cannot dismantle half its bedrooms. Normal prices and expected margins in such businesses take account of average expected payloads and occupancy rates. Once an airline or a hotel is guaranteed its payload or occupancy, it can afford to accept lower prices in the *certainty* that its costs, expected overheads and a satisfactory rate of profit will be earned. This is how package-tour operators can fly their customers and put them into hotels at far lower rates than the customer could achieve by negotiating separately with the airline and the hotel. The whole field of hotels and travel also has problems of seasonality and adopts differential pricing according to season: one of the closest examples to the classical economists' law of supply and demand. Price is highest when there is a greater demand for, say, hotel accommodation than the amount available. Out of season, almost any contribution above that required to pay the costs of minimum service is better than having very few occupants.

Small companies tend to adopt the attitude that they must have a different price from that ruling in the market. In some cases, they aim for a 'prestige' sector and charge a high price; in the majority of cases, however, they tend to price lower. They rationalize this decision in two ways. In highly competitive fields, they tend to regard low price as the antidote to promotion. The more common rationalization is based on the fact that the small business has lower overheads and can achieve the same *net* margin as their bigger competitors from a lower *gross* profit. The twin dangers of this approach are, firstly, that as the company grows it will accumulate larger overhead expense items and may be forced to increase its prices and, secondly, that a lower price than that generally ruling in the product field may upset the psychology of the market. (More of that later.)

Fields like banking and insurance are complicated by the fact that profits do not come so much from the 'price of the product' as from the return earned on investing the customer's deposits or payments. In banking, there is a great deal of mystery so far as the customer is concerned in the way in which bank charges are arrived at. The basis is the cost per transaction modified by the amount of the customer's cash the bank holds (since the larger amount of money on deposit, the more opportunity it has to earn money by investing part of that deposit). In recent years, the joint stock banks have been effectively prevented by Government directive from earning money from one of their primary sources: interest on loans. As Walter Leafe put it, 'One of a Banker's chief duties is to make advances to its customers' (which rather puts banks in the same category as the Marketing man who accepts his job as being that of 'satisfying housewives' desires – at a profit!').

Insurance companies base their life assurance terms on actuarial principles and their non-life terms on probability assessment. Life expectation, occupation hazards, exposure to risk, value of chattels, power and speed of car – all these are taken into account. Unfortunately, very few insurance companies actually make any profit from their underwriting activities, which either means they are satisfied with the returns achieved by investing policy-holders' payments or they are in the wrong business! (They are certainly in a business which, structured as it is at the moment, suffers from competing objectives.)

The term 'conditional pricing' is sometimes encountered. This can cover a range of circumstances from something similar to the loss-leader situation at the one end to prices which really are available only if something else is purchased at the same time or subsequently on a contractual basis. (The latter frequently happens on a short-term promotional basis but we shall consider cases only where this method is used regularly.) The parallel with the loss-leader could be seen in the classic Gillette razor blade introduction where razors which would (then) only take the Gillette blade were sold at ridiculously cheap prices or even given away. Companies in the photographic field have also adopted the special combination idea (e.g. Kodak Instamatic films and cameras), whilst companies such as Dixons will give you a free film on the condition that it is processed by them: they ensure repeat business by sending another free film with the finished prints. (Some of these processing companies use film base which only they can develop.) Examples of a more contractual nature are common in the field of office equipment. A document copying machine, for example, will use a great deal of paper (and, to a decreasing extent now, chemicals) during its life. A low price may be charged for the copier on the condition that all supplies of paper come from the same manufacturer. (It is sometimes the case that a piece of office equipment can use only one make of paper, carbon or ribbon.)

Finally, it is worth mentioning the tendency in businesses where there are only a few competitors (or where a small number of competitors account for a very large share of the total market) for prices to be the same and for competition to be by advertising and short-term promotion in the main. The fight to gain or even maintain share is hard enough and one dare not price above competition if the market is well established. In a market with few competitors 'gentlemen's agreements' quickly spring up although they may not be explicit. It is understood that retaliation will be swift if one company reduces prices and a long-term price battle will only hurt everybody.

The Psychology of Price

There is an ever-increasing tendency for companies introducing new products (mostly in the fast-moving fields of food,
health and beauty aids and cigarettes) to do research on the
potential consumer's expectation of price. It is surprising how
often the perceived value as expressed by an indication of
willingness to pay a price exceeds that which would have been
reached by a cost-plus pricing policy. If, on the other hand,
one cannot produce an acceptable product at the price the
consumer is willing to pay, then the product is not marketed.

Such tests of anticipated price are now commonly incorporated into tests of the product itself and the two – as they
should be – are related. Consumers taking part in the test are
usually given a range of prices and asked to indicate, after
experience of the product, where they would place that
product in the range. Unfortunately, many companies leap
with joy when they discover that the product has an expected
price above that reached by cost-plus methods and then
market at the lower price in the belief that this must ensure
success. It does not. It can be as fatal to price below perceived
values as to charge too much.

Many years ago (under very different circumstances from
those existing in the market at the moment) I was responsible
for a range of pastry and pudding mixes. They weren't doing
too well. No consumer acceptance tests had ever been done so
we put some in hand. Tasting the products blind, i.e. not
knowing whose products they were, housewives rated them
very highly. Using them in their own homes, they rated them
even more highly. When we revealed the pack (which, to say
the least, was cheap and cheerful) and told them the price
(6p – which many of them, of course, knew), probing revealed
that housewives just could not expect the kind of quality they
wanted from such a cheaply packaged and cheaply priced
product. So we changed the pack to give a much better
impression of quality only to find that we had created new
doubts: something had to be wrong with such an expensive-
looking pack that cost only 6p. Doing the sort of research

mentioned earlier suggested that the price should be in the range 6½p to 7p. The new packs were put into two different areas at these two prices whilst the rest of the country kept the old packs and the old prices. Sales of the original pack at 6p continued to decline, sales of the new pack at 6½p showed a modest increase. Sales at 7p showed an immediate, dramatic and embarrassing increase (we didn't have enough packs). The product (unchanged) was introduced nationally in the new pack at 7p and sales increased steadily from then on. Part of the 'excess' profit was used for promotion which itself led to further sales increases.

The moral of this story – and there are many more like it – is that success was not achieved until the housewife regarded all the elements as being in equilibrium: the price had to reflect the value of the product to her.

People suspect high and low prices and, except for a minority of people who are suckers for 'bargains' or 'buy only the best' (by which they mean the most expensive), need a great deal of reassurance before they are prepared to pay prices above or below what they regard as a reasonable range. This was first identified clearly by the French psychologist Stoetzl who discovered that people have not a single price in mind but a range of prices which they regard as acceptable. He expressed this range as having an upper limit where price became too high and a lower limit beyond which they distrusted the product. His work has been developed by Gabor and Grainger who show how a 'buying response' function can be extracted from this range of possibilities by assigning probabilities of purchase. It follows from this work that the customer does not feel that he or she is taking a chance if the price asked falls within the expected range. No further reassurance is necessary because the price is in that area which equates with perceived value. Outside that area price alone does not say enough about the product. If it is a very low price, the reaction is, 'What is wrong with it that they can sell it so cheaply?' If a very high price, 'What is so special that the price has to be so high?' As we see in Figure 9, both price and the amount of information consumers require about the product can be represented by U-shaped curves. That for price is very much flatter than that for information. Within the acceptable range, price provides enough information and the information-conveyed-by-price curve is above that for information alone. Once the price is outside this area, the intending purchaser regards the situation as very chancy indeed and needs a great deal of reassurance.

For a single-product market, this analysis would appear to imply that advertising (in whatever form of communication that might take) is unnecessary if the price is right. In the great majority of markets where competition exists, price is of low importance in the Marketing mix when it is placed correctly within the anticipated range. Choice between competing products will now be influenced by other parts of the mix – such as the quantity and quality of promotion, packaging, special features built into the product or service, and so on.

Changing Prices

Changing prices is usually a matter of economic necessity and there is a natural desire to change them as little as possible (encouraged, of late, by Government action). However, this ignores completely the concept of psychological prices, some of which may be barriers to progress. One would like to test not only various prices for new products but also all possible price changes. Good pricing research can involve complex questionnaires and costs valuable time. The ideal – but it requires even longer time periods – is to run the product at different prices in different test markets. Some companies have done this when a price change has been imperative but there has been reason to believe that the necessary rise gave an unsatisfactory price to the consumer. The price is put up by the minimum amount but tested at higher prices in one or more areas. If the higher price seems better, prices everywhere are brought into line. If not, the price in the test area is dropped.

Companies are notoriously lax about examining past

records to see what has happened to volume when price has been changed and whether there are any significant price thresholds. Similarly, they should examine competitors' price changes and what happened to the sales of both their own and competitors' products. (The same records should be kept of short-term promotional price reductions.) Your ability to change price with the desired effects on sales depends upon the elasticity of demand for your product and your market position.

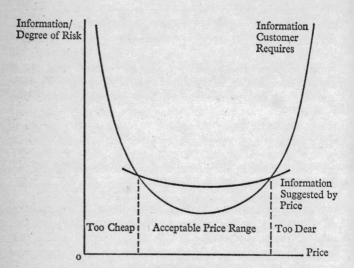

Figure 9. Information Conveyed by Price

'Elasticity of demand' measures the responsiveness of sales to price. Perfect elasticity occurs when a one per cent change in price leads to a one per cent change in sales. (Elasticity is perfect when the same figure appears on each side.) Some markets are highly elastic, which means that a drop in price will be followed by a more than commensurate increase in demand. This has been especially noticeable over a large range of domestic durables, for example washing machines and refrigerators. Other products, especially staples where consumption is regular and virtually at saturation point, are highly inelastic: price does not significantly affect buying patterns. However, it must be remembered that a product or a service is, in the eyes of the consumer or user, a mix of attributes. The demand for your product may be more or less elastic than that for your market as a whole. This is a measure of your competitiveness. Elasticity may occur at one remove. For example, it was discovered that a one per cent reduction in the price of whisky led to an increase of 0·75 per cent in consumption. However, an increase in total personal consumption of all goods and services of one per cent led to an increase in whisky consumption of 1·9 per cent! Consumption of whisky is clearly related to its price relative to all other prices rather than its price in isolation. This is indicative of a well-known post-Budget increase phenomenon and is applicable especially to cigarettes, beer and spirits but, more recently, few goods have escaped the sudden imposition of duty or a new rate of levy of an existing tax. Good intentions to reduce buying disappear as a function of time alone and partly because, in time, prices of all other goods creep up and so reduce the differential.

A dominant brand leader usually takes the initiative in price changes and the lesser brands usually follow, although they are frequently tempted to hold back on a price increase hoping to gain advantage. For example, in my days at J. Lyons and Company Limited, I would have regarded it as folly to either be first with a price change for Quick Brew Tea or fail to follow the lead of the number-one brand, Brooke Bond P G Tips. On the other hand, we were prepared not only to be first but to go it alone with Lyons Pure Ground Coffee where we held a market share more than double that of all our competitors. We had so much in hand that we had little real fear of being hurt by the failure of a competitor to match our price increase. The fact that our profits were of the correct order, whilst those of any competitor who didn't follow us weren't, meant that we could always exert pressure by short-term promotion to the customer or the trade. This is commonly done (although it was not appropriate to the ground coffee market) by a short-period price reduction to the consumer. Often, the price increase is disguised in this way.

The theme of this section of this chapter has been that people give products and services a range of prices which accords with their valuation of the item. One can imagine many readers believing that this may be fine for consumer products but has no place in, say, industrial marketing. Certainly, objective considerations rate higher with industrial products. However, the pattern shown in Figure 9 is different only to the extent that the high points of the 'information required' curve become more steep! The more objective and informed a buyer is, the narrower the range of price he expects to pay. This range can be extended by the addition of recognized attributes such as better servicing, durability, ease of maintenance and so on. However, because subjective considerations matter so little, much more information is required before an industrial buyer will consider products which are cheaper or dearer than his expected range. One more thing: industrial buyers are faced with almost as many new products or technological improvements as are housewives: they need information before they can frame their own price expectations.

Suggestions for Further Reading

Chapter 12 of Peter Kraushar (op cit) deals perhaps sketchily but none the less relevantly with pricing policy. Most modern work on the psychology of price is derived from 'Le Prix Comme Limite' by J. Stoetzl in *La Psychologie Economique*, edited by P. L. Reynaurd and published in Paris in 1954 by Marcel Rivière et Cie (pages 184–188 are the important ones). 'Price as an Indicator of Quality' by A. Gabor and C. W. J. Grainger in pages 43–70 of *Economica* in February 1966 is an important English development of this work, and any work by André Gabor draws together the work of the theoretical economist and the practising businessman in a most beneficial way.

Chapter 13

The Use of Market Research

If one of the tasks of Marketing is to take the guesswork out of hunches and eliminate as much of the risk as possible, then we spend far too little doing it. A great deal of what we do commission is bad and a great deal of false reliance is placed on work never intended to be interpreted in that particular way. There is, too, a widespread acceptance of, as gospel truth, research which can only be regarded as the best we have available at the present time. The purpose of this chapter is not to list research techniques (there are hundreds of books on various aspects of market research) but simply to consider some of the most used types and consider, from practical experience, the limits of their usefulness. Research is no guarantee of success: it is an insurance premium against the risk of *serious* failure.

Introductions to market research abound with clichés such as 'market research is only a prop, not a crutch' and 'the answers are only as good as the questions you ask'. They are no less true for the economy of their expression. A cripple may use a broom handle for temporary support but he would require something altogether stronger to get about on permanently. However, he is totally dependent upon his crutch: businessmen should not think that doing market research will answer all their problems. One of the better uses of market research is to reveal what your problems are, leaving you with a management decision (which you may test by further research) still to be taken. Research is offered in all sorts of guises. It can be bought ready-made like an 'off the peg' suit or it can be tailored to your particular needs. A bespoke suit is usually a better fit and gives greater satisfaction but it costs a lot more. If you are lucky, you can walk into a multiple tailor's and get just as good a fit at a considerably cheaper price. Market research is just the same. If you can buy 'off the peg' and it is going to fit the business need, then have no fear of doing it. Indeed, a good deal of research is done today by methods which are really unnecessary when perfectly good, quick, cheap methods exist. For example, if you have a problem that merely requires a quick quantification by age, sex and socio-economic class of how many people use your brand, there are several companies that make a feature of doing regular omnibus surveys incorporating several products, thus significantly reducing the costs per interview. The requirement is that your questions should be capable of simple yes/no answers or ones that can be pre-coded so that the interviewer has only to tick the appropriate figures, for example. On the other hand, if you want to know *why* people buy your brand you must go to other methods, be prepared to dig deep into your pocket and not feel too bitterly disappointed if you end up with an answer that makes no real sense at all. Every one of us buys something or other at some time without apparently conscious thought and we would find it very difficult to have to rationalize our actions afterwards, yet Marketing men are asking those questions all the time and expecting clear, logical answers (which generally means the answer they hoped for!).

Reasons why people behave as they do are rarely simple and straightforward. There are invariably so many factors at work (price, availability, social acceptability, product awareness, knowledge and so on) that identifying them all and assessing their relative importance to any purchasing situation is a skilled and expensive task. But expense is only relative: it may be minute compared with the benefit produced.

The Scientific Basis of Market Research

As we spread the net wider, into such realms as clinical psychology, in attempts to find answers to our questions, so we tend to borrow from more scientific disciplines. However, most market-research techniques are founded firmly upon the

twin bedrocks of probability and sampling. The two are
related: if you only interview a proportion of the total population (or inspect every tenth batch off the production line) you
want to know what degree of accuracy can be attached to the
findings. One can only be 100 per cent sure by asking the
right questions of every single person in the appropriate
population or examining every single product off the line.

Sampling theory demonstrates that it is unnecessary to
interview the whole population to achieve results with a
predetermined degree of probable accuracy. An adequate
degree of accuracy can often be obtained from quite small
samples, but, in general, you get what you pay for and the cost
of greater reliability rises disproportionately with the cost of
the sample.

I will make no attempt to discuss sampling theory but
merely suggest some practical considerations based upon a
formal statistical training and, above all, many years of practical
experience of devising samples, commissioning research and
interpreting it. Firstly, it is to all intents and purposes impossible to make use of a statistically ideal sample in mass markets.
Such a sample would be drawn from census returns or rating
lists on a basis designed to give every household in the country
an equal chance of being chosen for interview. If this were
done according to strict sampling theory, the cost per contact
(which is the major cost item in any piece of consumer
research) would be outrageous. Such an ideal sample would
send interviewers dashing out to all sorts of outlandish places
and travelling unreasonable distances. Thus, we normally
compromise with a 'two-stage' sample which means that one
lists all the districts (urban and rural) in the country and
chooses *districts* at random from that list. Households are then
chosen at random from the resultant list. This gives a less
scattered ('clustered') sample population without any serious
reduction in their representativeness.

The last word is important: any sample should adequately
reflect the population you are interested in. There should not
be significantly more, say, women with children than there
are in the population as a whole. If you are interested in

dog-owners, the right proportion of those should be in the population. We are beginning to introduce strictures which take us away from the scientific purity of the laws of sampling. We are talking about quota samples, where the interviewer is not given a list of individuals and/or addresses but a specified number of carefully defined contacts to be made. (In fact, the vast majority of samples are of selected groups such as car-owners, housewives, buyers of particular products.) A simple quota sample will define these contacts in terms of geographical location, age, sex and socio-economic group. This will become more elaborate when one adds requirements such as: x per cent must be car-owners; y per cent must use Shell petrol; z per cent Esso and so on. If there is a particular group that is of special interest, you may look for more of these people than the ideal sample warrants. You then weight each of the answers for the groups with correctly drawn quota samples by using an appropriate factor. To the purist, the very use of a quota sample is unsatisfactory because one can only measure the statistical accuracy of a random sample (although significance tests are commonly applied to quota samples). To achieve the same 'sampling error' as that produced by a random sample of 100 would require a quota sample of 600. An increasingly common compromise between random and quota sampling is the 'random route' technique. The interviewer begins at an address which has been pre-selected at random (a slight contradiction in terms!) and then calls on houses at prescribed intervals along a route chosen according to strict instructions (say, 'knock at every fourth door'). It is important to realize that progression through each of the stages outlined above increases the margin of error which can be placed upon the results. In such circumstances, I am inclined to generalize and say that such research is more to be trusted when it yields a negative result than when it gives a positive one: given the disposition of people to be kind to interviewers, if they say they don't like your product they really mean it! When they react favourably you have to examine the structure of the research very carefully indeed to see how reliable that finding is.

This leads us inevitably to the question of sample size. If

you want to double the statistical accuracy, the size of the sample must increase in a geometric ratio (i.e. not 2x but x^2 – where x is the sample). Thus, a sample of 4,000 people becomes not 8,000 but 16,000. An enormous increase in cost even with the less costly quota method. What, then, should be the ideal sample size? No two situations will be the same and one can only quote guidelines. The basic rule I have always adopted is very much a rule-of-thumb method: identify the smallest segments from which you require answers and devise a sample which ensures that there will be at least 100 respondents in the sub-section. Then scale up the sample so that the smallest section is represented in proportion to its presence in the population. It is unwise to attach much importance to the views of fewer than 100 people in any sub-group with conventional questionnaire techniques. A less expensive alternative may be to increase the number of interviews in the smallest population only and apply a weighting factor to the rest.

The devising of a sample should go hand in hand with the devising of the problem areas the research is designed to solve, for this will determine the ideal sample size. If the cost is too high, you must forgo some accuracy or some areas of examination or both. Again, I have a personal preference for questionnaire design and sample design to go hand in hand. Both should be done by experts but since clients expect (and are expected) to have the last word on the questions asked, the researcher must be strong enough to say, 'You won't get a meaningful answer without changing the question or the sample.' The choice is back with his client.

Wherever the word 'accuracy' has been used it has been in terms of the statistical measure of importance – 'significance'. As has been said already, it is strictly applicable only to a truly random sample but it can be – and is – used in all kinds of statistical contexts to give an indication of the value which can be placed upon results. Significance measures the possibility of a given result falling outside a predictable margin of error and occurring completely by chance. Thus 'five per cent significance' means that there is one chance in twenty that the result shown could have happened purely by chance. Do remember, however, that the other ninety-five per cent of cases are subject to a margin of error on either side of the figure quoted. This can significantly affect a conclusion: a result showing a 55:45 preference for your product subject to a margin of error of plus or minus five per cent could mean 60:40 for you or 50:50. Remember, too, that tests of significance can only measure what can happen by chance as a result of taking a sample. They can't tell you anything about errors due to not having an adequate basis for drawing the sample in the first place or interviewer error or bias or coding, tabulating and reporting errors. Some of these you can spot by careful reading: many stay hidden.

The two most commonly used levels are the five per cent and the one per cent level (normally represented as the 0·05 level and the 0·01 level, respectively). As one would expect, most research is conducted to give results which are significant at the five per cent level which is produced by taking two standard deviations either side of the mean (or average). Tests of significance are applied to examining the *difference* between two groups of data: for example, is the preference expressed for our product a significant one: are the services our customers require significantly different from those required by our competitors' customers?

Since the business manager can find so many other uses for the significance test, it is worth considering briefly, and as non-mathematically as possible, how to apply it to two sets of results. We can express the test for significance at the five per cent level as: the difference between the number of figures above the mean and the number below it must be greater than twice the square root of the total number of figures.

Let us take a simple example where the mean of one set of figures is already known, say 45, and we want to know if there has been any significant change since last year. We have taken 100 observations of which:

> 40 are more than 45
> 40 = 45
> 20 are less than 45.

The difference between those above and below 45 is 20 (40—20). Twice the square root of the sum of the observations is $2 \times 10 = 20$. Since the difference between the observations above and below the mean is the same as twice the square root of the observations, there has been no significant change since last year.

We can also take the basis of the test for significance to see if we are justified in taking action on the figures available to us. This we do by the calculation:

$$\frac{(\text{Twice the Sum of the Observations})^2}{\text{Difference}}.$$

We had 100 observations and the difference was 20 so our sum reads:

$$\left(\frac{2 \times 100}{20}\right)^2 = \left(\frac{200}{20}\right)^2 = 10^2 = 100.$$

Since this is exactly the number of observations we took, we would be quite justified in taking action on the data available. The more observations required to reach the desired level as given by this formula, the less reliable is the information and, of course, the converse is also true. (In practice, nearly all researchers use significance tables and an example is given as an appendix to this book.)

Although significance is a useful tool for managers to understand and use, in market research the best estimate is always the one you've got. Normally, researchers will apply significance tests only to key figures and take especial care to eliminate all the other sources of possible error.

Many more scientific principles are used in market research but they would be invalid without correctly drawn samples and ways of measuring the significance of the results. These techniques ('multivariate analysis'), such as correlation and factorial analysis, are used to analyse figures in new ways; to discover if different findings are associated in any meaningful way, which influences are strongest, and so on. Again one should be aware that many of these techniques, particularly those of association, can produce mathematically correct answers which are totally illogical. (For example, between 1924 and 1937 there was a strong positive correlation of 0·998 – 1·0 being perfect correlation – between the number of wireless licences taken out and the number of mental defectives. An extreme example of nonsensé correlation has been devised for pickles in the USA which shows that pickle-eating is associated with virtually all major diseases, breeds wars, leads to communism and to increases in crime: all because the vast majority of people involved in any of those groups or activities are pickle-eaters!) All market research starts with some hypothesis even where none apparently exists. One might claim that simply looking at hardened users of your main competitor is totally objective: there is, nevertheless, the underlying hypothesis that there is something different about these people and if you can only discover it you can take the advantage. However objective the survey itself may be, one is always involving subjectivity in research design and assessment. As one prominent practitioner, Tony Cowling, has expressed it, 'A test of a blue pack against a green one looks pretty objective, but it is really subjective about everything except the difference between blue and green.' Research is not merely only as good as the questions you ask but also only as good as the skill in devising the sample and questionnaire and the way the results are interpreted. We will now look at the kind of care necessary in interpreting some of the more common forms of research.

Continuous Research

Research may be *ad hoc* or continuous. There is little more to say about *ad hoc* research (within the scope of this limited examination of market-research areas) other than to point out that there is often a shadowy area between *ad hoc* consumer studies and continuous consumer studies. Often one is used where the other would be more appropriate. For example,

continuous consumer audit will give basic demographic
breakdowns four times a year but, if that is all you want, it is
a very expensive way of going about it. Moreover, in a market
where such things change slowly, if at all, it may be too
frequent.

Under this heading I want to consider continuous audits,
either of the consumer or the retailer. These are truly continuous in that one enters into a contractual arrangement to
receive information about a particular product field over a
period of time. Consumer audits are based upon some method
of identifying consumer purchases as customers bring things
into the home. Retail audit aims to provide the same end
result by measuring movement out of the shop. By looking at
the consumers one can examine their characteristics and their
buying patterns; by looking at the shop one can examine rate
of stockturn, distribution, prices and so on. A good deal of
information is common to both, such as consumer purchases
and price paid. Unfortunately, as any Marketing man who has
used both types of audit simultaneously will testify, the two
seldom agree about sales and brand shares. Apart from other
differences which will become apparent as we consider the
various techniques, sales and share discrepancies arise basically
because the brand share of *all* sales through, say, *grocers* is not
the same as brand share of purchases by *all housewives* from
all sources. These are differences which may well have actionable meaning.

There are two methods of continuous consumer audits. One
is based upon a diary panel whilst the other physically examines
purchases.

Obviously, a diary panel must be fully representative of the
population as a whole. Since normally only housewives record
purchases, care must be taken to ensure that their family
circumstances are such that the panel represents the correct
proportions of males and children as well as single women and
that the right age and class proportions are preserved. The
ability to identify actual buyers enables some particularly
interesting analyses to be carried out. We can obtain a buying
profile by class, age, sex, size of household, presence of

children, and geographical location. Comparisons can be made over time of changes in the brand profile and this can be compared with the characteristics of the market as a whole and with individual competitors. Many Marketing men prefer to regard consumer diary panels as continuous consumer profile analysis rather than as a method of measuring sales and market shares. This is certainly a very valuable feature of a panel operation, especially in a developing field or any other market where rapid changes occur or are likely to occur. However, if this were the only use for the panel, it would be a very expensive way of going about it.

The great benefits of consumer diary panels are to be found in the uses that can be made of the ability to identify individual consumers and their purchases. Thus one can examine the degree of loyalty they have to the brand, how frequently they buy it and whether they sometimes buy some other brand. (We talk glibly of 'brand loyalty' as though customers stuck to the same brand through thick and thin, refusing all substitutes. Examination of a large number of buying patterns in many product fields reveals that 'brand loyalty' means something like 'the brand people return to most frequently'. Housewives do accept substitutes, are influenced by price cuts and promotions, do try new products and are influenced by advertising. Conventional questionnaire research does not reveal this to the extent that a consumer panel can.)

Diary panels are not cheap (in terms of absolute cost) but they become so if the findings can be put to the best possible use. Frequency and loyalty findings can have a profound influence upon Marketing action. The question to be faced is: how do you define these terms and how often do you want to examine them? Many markets require frequency of purchase, loyalty and duplication of purchase analysis on a regular basis. Often, the best information comes from raw data. The Ready Brek success story mentioned in Part 1 was partly based on a hypothesis generated by study of diary panel raw data. This showed a pattern something like that in the following table.

Example of Breakfast Cereal Buying Pattern

Week	1	2	3	4	5	6	7
Housewife							
A	K	K	R	K	K	SP	K
B	Q	Q	RB	Q	Q	K	Q
C	K	K	RB	K	SP	K	RB
D	S	S	S	RB	S	S	S
E	SP	R	RB	K	RB	SP	RB
F	K	K	K	RB	K	K	RB
G	Q	Q	Q	RB	Q	RB	RB

CODE:

K	= Kellogg's Corn Flakes	RB	= Ready Brek
SP	= Sugar Puffs	Q	= Quaker Oats
R	= Ricicles	S	= Scott's Porage Oats

The pattern was clear: Ready Brek, promoted aggressively as an instant porridge, was not acceptable to the hardened porridge-eater (with the odd very rare exception). The advertising and product appeal invited trial: the product performance did not lead to a significant level of repeat purchase. However, two significant facts did emerge, one of which is apparent from the example. Ready Brek was ranked along with what are known as the 'variety cereals' as an occasional substitute for Kellogg's Corn Flakes. The other fact, which emerged from further examination of Ready Brek buyers, was that they were mothers of young children. From all this came a hypothesis which was subjected to test and eventually led to a reformulated, repositioned and highly successful brand. In time, the same pattern would have emerged from loyalty, duplication and frequency of purchase data taken over successive periods. However, it is doubtful if the facts would have been seen with such startling clarity as the examination of raw data revealed. The purchase of raw data is expensive and subject to certain conditions. It is also difficult to analyse because it has to be sorted by hand. Nevertheless, it can be of inestimable value to certain products in particular markets, especially new products.

Before we turn to disadvantages of consumer audit techniques we should consider one more advantage which becomes especially important when compared with retail audit methods and is partly responsible for the different sales results given by the two methods when used to cover the same field. The diary technique allows the recording of goods from any outlet. None is excluded because a retailer refuses to participate, and purchases can be recorded from any category of outlet. This is especially important with a product that may be purchased from the grocer, the chemist or a variety chain.

Now for the cautions. The sample may easily become biased. In the first case, people who are prepared to fill in a diary religiously (ideally, every day) may not be typical of the population as a whole if measured by psychological characteristics. (It is interesting to note that fifteen per cent of the UK population is illiterate: they obviously cannot be included!) In the second case, the presence in print of a list of product fields and brand names may gradually exert an influence on panellists. The diary contains only those product fields and those brands within the product field that clients have paid for. (There is room for 'all other' brands in each category to cover those not specified.) No attempt is made to disguise the information that is being asked for. The tendency for respondents to be kind to interviewers may also come into play. On the other hand, there is a danger of housewives becoming blasé, filling in the diary at less frequent intervals and relying more and more on memory.

Another major problem is that of fallout: people leaving the panel for some reason and needing replacement. It is simple to replace them with people of the same basic characteristics but their purchasing pattern may be quite different from that of the household being replaced. I know of one extreme case in the flour field where several changes were made in an area with low representation in the sample. The replacements were from another town. The town was close by the first but the company had no distribution at all in the new town. This showed up as a sharp fall in sales and share for the area although ex-factory sales to the area continued to increase.

The biggest problems still concern sample size. Although the sample is correctly drawn to represent the population as a whole, it cannot be correctly drawn to represent the proportions present in the market for every product represented in a piece of syndicated research. Moreover, there will be many brands which do not pick up enough responses to allow statistically valid conclusions to be drawn. Products with slightly offbeat markets may produce results which are patently false. Over many years, diary figures for Lyons French Coffee (coffee with chicory) in the London area were totally out of gear with the brand's movement and market position relative to other Lyons Coffee brands which showed movements in line with both ex-factory and retail audit figures.

Such quirks must be questioned intensively. There may be a genuine sampling error or bias which will quickly be put right. If the answer is that the pick-up on your brand is too small to yield either significant results or ones which exhibit the same trend as ex-factory sales, then the time has come to serve notice.

The other method of continuous consumer audit makes use of the pantry check and dustbin audit instead of a diary. A special bin is provided for all used cartons, etc. An opening count is taken by a physical check of the pantry (which often means under the sink, in the bathroom and even more unlikely places). When the interviewer calls for the bin, she marks each new purchase with the date of call to guard against double counting. What about purchases between calls? The used cartons go into the bin and any unused or incompletely used ones are stamped. Thus any purchases between calls will be in the bin but unstamped.

The consumer diary panel or audit – whichever one is used – may suffer from bias, frequently has inadequate samples for particular products and suffers from regional problems because the samples, though large, can only be structured on a common, not individual product basis. Nevertheless, the measures of loyalty, frequency of purchase and duplication of purchase between brands cannot be gathered effectively at comparable cost by any other method and this is invaluable information for any Marketing man.

In short, continuous consumer audit is an extremely valuable tool used wisely, but don't use it for the wrong purpose and don't use it if the sample cannot do justice to your product group, your brand, your particular levels of distribution and your regional problems. And if any startling change occurs or the trend line veers from that of ex-factory sales, immediately start asking questions about the sample.

Since we have dealt fairly exhaustively with continuous consumer research, we can afford to be rather more brief about continuous retail audit for, although this may seem surprising, many of the advantages and disadvantages are common.

The basis of retail audit is the simple formula:

$$\text{Sales} = \text{Opening Stock} + \text{Deliveries} - \text{Closing Stock}.$$

The system uses a regular panel of shops which are called upon and physically checked at every count. This involves counting stock wherever it may be (which, as with the dustbin audit, can be in some very strange places indeed) and examining invoices and delivery notes. It requires no questioning of the retailer, which precludes bias, but does require that he keeps accurate records. Many small shopkeepers, in particular, welcome the auditor as the man who tidies their accounts!

Retail audit covers two major deficiencies in manufacturers' own sales figures. Ex-factory sales measure the movement into the trade, not to the consumer. Stock could easily be piling up and, if this is not known, could result in a sudden dramatic reduction in demand on the factory with possibly drastic effects on costs. Additionally, ex-factory sales take no account of either the movement of the total market or sales of your major competitors. Retail audit is one very important way of tackling the problem we discussed in Part 1: the question of whether 'good' is good enough.

With the more sophisticated sales forces adopting stock-check procedures and using planned levels of replenishment, the danger of over-stocking is a great deal less than it used to be and, with increasing sophistication and the use of computer techniques, will become even less of a problem. However, no sales force attempts 100 per cent coverage of all outlets in its market and there is probably always going to be a large area of total possible distribution which will not be tackled directly. There are also many major multiples who do not permit branch calling and some who do but do not allow a full store-check by salesmen.

The main areas of information provided by retail audit are:

1. Proportion of all shops stocking the given product (measured as those stocking at the call and those who have stocked during the period but were out of stock at the time of audit).
2. Retailer purchases.
3. Consumer sales.
4. Physical stock-levels.

Without going into full detail, this base information can provide a great deal of vital analyses. Examples include measurements by volume and value, where the retailer obtained his stock, how many weeks' average sale the stock-holding will cover, sales per shop handling, and area strengths and weaknesses. All this information is provided nationally, by regions and by as many brands and pack sizes as you are willing to pay for.

Once again, the major deficiency is the sample. Ignoring sample size for the moment, there are two other major deficiencies. Firstly, no ready-made list of shops exists to provide the framework for an ideal random sample. Census of Distribution figures form the base for the sample but these figures are published infrequently and late. Secondly, the refusal rate is fairly high. When a multiple grocer refuses to cooperate, he usually prohibits access to all stores, not just a few.

As with consumer audit, the panel is representative of, say, the grocery trade as a whole and is therefore less accurate for products with a different pattern. A product with twice the normal rate of sales for all grocery products through multiple grocers will be using a sample which is not representative of his market; it will contain too many small shops. Information is most accurate for products in wide distribution enjoying a high and frequent rate of sale. It is poor for products in low distribution or those where distribution is heavily biased towards any particular sector. At all presentations of retail audit findings, the sales force should be well represented. Not merely is this a vital tool of Sales Management, but they can draw upon their closer knowledge of the market to suggest what special promotions by certain manufacturers and/or outlets may be causing quirks in the trend line and brand shares. Many companies cannot obtain distribution in certain outlets.

Retail audit is more reliable on turnover than it is on distribution. The method of sampling is primarily designed to measure sales movements and is geared to producing results from where the greatest volume of sales occur, not the greatest number of outlets. However, since this means that there are relatively more large outlets than their numbers justify, results tend to be more accurate for these outlets even though they are disturbed by non-participation of certain chains.

The great value of retail audit is not in the individual figures it gives but in the trends it reveals. One is interested in progress *vis-à-vis* the rest of the market. The movement of sales, distribution and brand share is of more importance than the significance of the individual results. Because the basis of *all* audit research is statistical we apply critical analysis to the various methods and find them all lacking in some respect. However, they are infinitely more reliable than subjective opinions of consumer behaviour and analysis of distribution, volume and share movements based upon stock checks of part of the section of the trade you call on and estimates from empirical evidence of competitors' movements. There is a tendency not to realize how lucky one is to have either kind of audit information until one moves to an industry that cannot use it or deals with clients who will not buy it. There are limitations and the techniques very definitely come under the heading of 'the best we've got' rather than the 'ideal'. If more businesses perceived the true value of these techniques they would be prepared to pay the sort of prices that would enable some of the deficiencies to be remedied.

Psychological Research

This is a wide and imprecise bracket which covers a host of techniques from extended interviews where opinions are probed, through group discussions which may or may not be structured, to the use of mechanical devices to measure various kinds of response. I have no intention of covering all these. Again, I want merely to indicate some areas where caution is necessary.

Not so long ago, any problem which was remotely psychological in nature was called 'motivation research' and, in its early days, some rather nasty smells clung to the term. Motivation research was concerned with pseudo-clinical psychological methods to probe *why* people behaved in certain ways and bought certain products, and an attempt to bring to the surface hidden feelings and motivations. I use the term 'pseudo-clinical' advisedly, for the basis of motivation research was the group discussion – an attempt to probe deeply into the inner self not individually and gradually over time but (for speed and economy) in groups and in single sessions. The nasty smells referred to arose from inexpert handling of this different situation which requires different skills of the person controlling the group, from the reliance upon hypothesis in structuring the sessions and from lack of subsequent quantification. The root problem is that so-called 'depth' interviews deal with the fundamentals of the psyche – love, hate, Oedipus and so on. Marketing, on the other hand, deals with what to the psychologist would be regarded as trivial – Nescafé or Maxwell House, red or blue, lemon or raspberry flavour. The fundamentals of the psyche – like mother-love, for example – are not much in use in a brand situation for, basically, a brand does not differ from its competitor at that level of abstraction. It may be helpful to be the first brand to identify a fundamental psychological attribute but you are then presented with the problem of pre-empting and maintaining that claim for your product when it is equally valid for other competing products.

It is not essential that group studies and extended interviews should be carried out by trained psychologists, although many companies make a great deal of the fact that they will be. What is important is that the group leaders and interviewers should be trained in the conduct of their particular operation. Extended interviews use open-ended questions; that is, they cannot be answered in one word or by ticking a box or figure. Open-ended questions have to be interpreted and grouped after the event and great care is necessary to ensure that the vocabulary used in summarizing a group of replies reflects the responses correctly. Extended interviews go further, for they begin to probe into reasons why. This forces the interviewee to think and, too often, to rationalize. The skilful conduct of extended interviews does not necessarily require trained psychologists but it does require the very best interviewers. There is a good reason for a representative of the company commissioning the research sitting in on the briefing session: no reputable research company can possibly object, for it will have nothing to hide. Another truism: if research is only as good as the questions you ask, the responses are only as good as the people who evaluate them.

Good group interview techniques start with pilot studies which ideally are unstructured and which lead to hypotheses which may be subjected to examination in further groups either by structuring them ('Today we are going to talk about corn flakes') or by gently guiding discussion if it does not take the right direction ('Today we are going to talk about breakfast', and introducing corn flakes later as a subject if it doesn't come up naturally). A good group leader will get people talking without unnecessary interruptions or feeding leading questions. He or she will bring the whole group into the discussions and will try to prevent dominant personalities hogging the discussion and influencing the meeting. However, just listen to the tapes of these sessions or read the verbatim reports and you will soon realize that a group of twelve (about the maximum) seldom yields the effective opinions of more than half. This must be borne in mind if you are building up groups to achieve a defined total number of responses. You may need to cover 150 people in groups to gain the same effect as 100 intensive individual interviews. In fact, most researchers will carry on interviewing groups until no new information is emerging.

Psychological studies are of most use in the fields of fast-moving goods and of little use, except in exceptional circumstances, in industrial markets. However, they have been used very successfully in service fields like rail and air travel, tourism and hotels, and also for a wide range of consumer durables. Cars – especially American ones – provide some of the more extreme and often apocryphal examples of psychological research (for example, the well-worn quotations on the sexual symbolism of cars which, among other things, equate a saloon with a wife and a sports car with a mistress).

Psychological research can unearth areas and creative Marketing ideas which cannot be discovered in any other way. However, by definition, samples are small and it becomes very expensive to build up a large enough sample to produce quantifiable results. Nevertheless, quantification is vital and group studies will provide hypotheses which can be subjected to other forms of research capable of significant quantification. Semi-structured or extended interviews are also useful ways of arriving at hypotheses in industrial markets.

The various kinds of research are not exclusive but complementary and additive. Psychological research is concerned with attitudes and motivations; other kinds of research are concerned with numbers. The two come together in another way when it is necessary to consider characteristics of customers other than age, sex and class, and location. For this, we use Market Segmentation.

Market Segmentation Research

Markets can be broken down in many ways. Because of the difficulty of asking pets their views on products, the pet food market tends to segment by product type (e.g. meat and gravy, meat and cereal, etc) and price. The motor car market has segmented by price in the past but currently relies more on engine rating. Of course, demographic breakdowns themselves are forms of segmentation and for some product groups may well be the most important for defining the size of the market. Baby foods and geriatric products would be good examples. However, although brand profiles might indicate significant differences between brands, the major influences on choice may still be found in some other form of segmentation. Most conventional methods of segmentation are only effective for producing some estimate of the likely size of a market; they seldom are of much value for predicting brand preference or indicating ways of increasing brand share.

There are two main methods of market segmentation research, one based on the consumer and the other on the product. The consumer-based approach requires extensive research to identify those variables that relate to consumer desires for satisfaction from the product or service. This is done for the market as a whole and individual brands can be compared both with each other and with the theoretical ideal (which may not be actually delivered by any product in the market). Product change or appeals can then shift your particular product in the identified desirable direction. Consumers with the same fundamental desires can be grouped together and then the basic market and brand usage data can be looked at by each of the defined segments to see to what extent the customers are being satisfied by the products available. From this may come product improvements, new ways of presentation, new product claims and possibly new products.

The product approach has the same objectives but approaches the problem from the other end. This is done by looking for gaps in the market which non-existent products might fill or which your existing product could be modified (in form or presentation) to meet. It requires the identification of real or perceived differences between products, describing possible products which would appear to offer the right satisfactions and evaluating the hypothetical product against existing ones. This technique is currently enjoying a vogue in new product development.

The problem with the 'hole-in-the-market' technique is that many (if not most) of the gaps revealed are just not worth plugging. One invariably discovers a number of small and often esoteric opportunities. Moreover, the identification of a gap does not constitute the discovery of a potential demand for the product that would fit. Further, conventional, new product research will be required before you know whether there is a viable product opportunity.

Whichever form of segmentation research you adopt, the absolute cost is high, the techniques are very complicated and consequently the results will be a long time a-coming. Inevitably, you will end up with premises that require other kinds of testing and viability assessment before taking action. However, there is no doubt that the segmentation approach sketched here will be used more and more as its predictive qualities are appreciated and the deficiencies of conventional breakdowns acknowledged. For this reason, even if you take no notice of any of the other reading suggestions at the end of this chapter, I most strongly urge study of this area.

Industrial Marketing Research

Managers involved in industrial markets must have been feeling out in the cold for much of this chapter. Continuous audit information is not available and comparison with Government statistics and figures published by trade associations becomes the only way of measuring brand share for most businesses in this category. Industrial marketing research, on the whole, tends to be more integrated with total business planning than in the consumer field. A basic reason for this is that the majority of industrial studies concern identifying present and possible future market sizes. Frequently such research is subsequently seen to have covered a good deal of interesting information but not all of it necessary to reach a decision. The broad-based study is increasingly being replaced by 'minimum-demand studies'. This approach looks at a segment of a market at a time in whatever depth seems necessary. The results of the various stages are additive so that a decision to stop a project or go ahead can be made at an appropriate time. This is obviously closely akin to the screening process used in all new product development. However, consumer products can usually draw upon a good deal of readily available information. In the industrial field, more reliance has to be placed upon market research as a means of gathering information as well as predicting outcomes of possible courses of action.

We have already noted the problem of identifying the person who makes the buying decision in industrial companies. Any piece of industrial research which does not seek to identify the real buying influences – the personalities, depreciation policy, reasons for replacing, importance of price on decision level, etc – is stopping well short of the ideal. An independent research company is much more likely to get the true answers to these questions than a company representative who is steered through 'normal channels'. It must be recognized that the market-research company may have the same difficulty ·in identifying the right men within a company to interview. A quite different level of skill is required to interview busy and usually quite senior people in their place of work from that required in interviewing a housewife in her own home – many of whom seem loath to let the interviewer go.

Thus, industrial market research should be left to experts and the credentials of any candidate company checked very carefully in an attempt to assess their success rate of achieving interviews at the sort of level that will be appropriate to your business and your problems. Nevertheless, virtually all the conventional consumer research techniques have been applied to industrial markets, often with the advantage that the universe to be studied is so small that the 'sample' is in fact a 'census'.

Ad Hoc Studies

By concentrating on certain techniques one may have inferred that these are the most used methods of market research. One definition of market research is: the systematic application of the techniques of social science in order to collect, analyse and assess data relevant to decisions taken in the Marketing of goods and services.

Most of the decisions that market research is called up to assist with are one-off situations and are concerned with usage of a particular product or service. Whilst it has been argued that segmentation research is likely to produce more positive actionable data, both cost and time (in particular) are against its widespread adoption. The bulk of research work in the foreseeable future will continue to concern itself with questions like what proportion of the population buy canned soup, how often do they serve it, to whom; are there significant differences between regions, age groups, in sex or in socio-economic class ?

Obviously, you will use an adequate sample, devise the questionnaire with care and ensure that the interviewers are well briefed. The main cautions to be considered are, firstly, that you design the research round the questions you want answered and, secondly, that the situation really is one best answered by *ad hoc* research. If you don't expect people to tell you why they buy your product then simple interviews will probably suffice. If you want to probe into any specific areas, then you will need semi-structured or perhaps even unstructured extended interviews. There really are few research situations that can truly be called once-only affairs. It may be two years before you want to repeat the research but the odds are that you will. You must therefore design the very first piece of research in such a way that it will become a valid base for comparison. Too often one hears the question, 'How does that compare with the last piece of research ?' and the answer, 'We didn't check that last time'. Obviously, there will be new factors you won't have taken account of, such as new competitors and product improvements. One should, however, be as far-seeing as possible when the initial piece of research is planned, for it may prove to be cheaper in the long run to produce more base-line information than is immediately necessary, in order to prepare the ground for future comparisons.

All that has been said about sampling, interviewing, questionnaire design and so on obviously applies to *ad hoc* surveys. This short section is merely put in to redress the balance and acknowledge the fact that not only are most pieces of research done on a non-continuous basis and concerned with usage but that this is one area we have considered which is available to all kinds and sizes of business.

Conclusion

Book-length bibliographies have been published about books and articles on aspects of market research: it is therefore a very difficult subject to do justice to in a single chapter. I have deliberately highlighted some of the pitfalls in some of the more frequently used types of research because one continually encounters incomplete understanding of the limitations of market research coupled with demands for answers from one piece of research which can only come from a different type or another piece of research. Even worse is the acceptance of findings based upon inadequate and insignificant data. The self-imposed standards of market-research companies are very high indeed but they cannot guard against Marketing men making fools of themselves. While writing this chapter I have been shown evidence of a product launched on what proved to be the favourable rating of seven people. If this chapter does no more than make every user of research realize that he must pay for accuracy but the cost is infinitesimal in comparison with the wrong decision, and that he should always seek the expert's advice on what degree of confidence can be put on the results, it will have served its purpose.

Suggestions for Further Reading

The two books by Vesselo and Moroney are both good on significance and sampling but this is a basic subject treated in practically every general book on statistics. Reference to Hugh Buckner's book is appropriate to the section on Industrial Research.

Chapter 14

Test Marketing

Test Marketing is an established part of the risk-reducing armoury of most of the leading companies selling the faster moving consumer goods. There is, however, a growing amount of critical comment reinforced by the obvious success of some brands which have gone national right from the word go, by the ultimate success of brands which failed to meet their test criteria and the well-publicized national failure of some that did. On the one hand there is an argument that speed is essential and testing is slow and declares your hand to competition. On the other side, the majority echo the dictum first phrased by Procter and Gamble in the USA: 'We'd rather be second than wrong.'

The recent spate of criticism condemns the cost of test Marketing, the delay factor and, above all, its failure as a predictive measure. There seems to be a high degree of only partial digestion of these criticisms and one of the purposes of this chapter is to consider these in relation to the alternatives. We shall also refer back to the question of 'Marketing and Risk' and see to what extent decision theory can guide us in the decision 'to test or not to test'.

Established Attitudes

What test Marketing is, what benefits it can produce and the disadvantages associated with it are well established. However, the cautions are ignored every day by even the most experienced practitioners. The Marketing Society Group on test Marketing came up with this definition: 'The testing *in the market-place* of one or more elements in the marketing mix of a product, in order to determine their effectiveness on a larger scale as aids to profitability. The test market, a scaling down of a larger market, is intended to scale down the loss if the test should prove a commercial failure.'

At one extreme, a test market can examine the effect of changing a single ingredient in the total mix and we have already referred to examples where a pack or a price has been changed. At the other end of the scale is the area test of a completely new product as a packaged deal of product, price, pack and promotion. Similarly, 'the market-place' can vary from a test in a single store to a different approach throughout virtually the whole country of a totally new approach (usually leaving a control area unchanged). The test-launch of a new product epitomizes the problems of test Marketing and involves all the essential ingredients and we shall use this type of test as our framework, deviating from it only for the purpose of example.

The biggest problem is choosing the area. It should be representative of the country as a whole, self-contained, well served by advertising media, small enough to contain risk but large enough to give the best possible indication of your eventual market. No one area possesses all these attributes and if it did it would soon become over-tested.

Firstly, representativeness. The area chosen should have the same age, class, sex and size of household breakdowns as are present in the population as a whole. The trade you are dealing with should be represented by the correct number of large and small shops. One element that is too often forgotten is that your own organization in the chosen area should also be representative: it shouldn't be an area where good or bad physical distribution may influence the results or one where an extra-efficient or an inefficient local sales organization may distort results. Those are the classic conditions. However, they should be varied according to the profile of the market segment you are appealing to. Pure ground coffee has more appeal to the higher socio-economic groups than to the lower, in general. If you choose to test in an area with too many ground-coffee drinkers you will overestimate the market. Similarly, an area may have the correct number of pet-owners but results will be distorted if their usage of canned dog food is well below average.

Secondly, a test area should be self-contained. It won't be! Therefore, one must attempt to identify the extent to which it is not self-contained and quantify the effect of the significant outside influences. The danger is greatest with a town test and is minimized as the area chosen gets bigger: it is the danger of people entering the area from outside. When you come to analyse sales results you will be doing so on a population higher than the apparent figure for the area. The hinterland problem is an extremely difficult one, for it requires extensive research to identify the purchases made by people outside the main area. The most effective answer is the establishment of a special consumer panel confined to the test area alone. Comparison with ex-factory sales and/or retail audit figures for the test area will give some indication of the extent of the discrepancy.

Trade problems are often impossible to overcome and these may either destroy the representativeness of your chosen area or render it liable to outside influence and interference. It is virtually impossible to tie up wholesalers' distribution areas with test areas, and accurate assessment of the results requires that an estimate be made of sales outside the test area. Retailers, especially as they become more sophisticated in stock control and handling, find it difficult to stock a product in one area only unless it coincides with one of their own administrative areas. If a major retail group stays out of your test, you can only estimate what the effect might have been if it had been included and how that might project nationally.

Thirdly, the test area should be well served by advertising media. By far the majority of tests in the UK are now run in television areas using that medium either alone or as the primary one. Although there are problems of overlap with other television areas, these are known and relatively insignificant. Initially, certain areas became well known as test areas but there is now a fairly even spread.

The problem is more acute with other media. Local Press

has different characteristics from National Press, particularly in the nature of the editorial and the standard of competitive advertising. Circulation areas are often difficult to tie up with test regions. Posters and cinema advertisements are seen by many people from the hinterland and, in terms of the objects of the test, are wasted on these people even though they may buy. Regional test facilities by colour magazines are still relatively recent and less used than other media although they close a gap which previously existed.

Fourthly, the size of the area. The object of the test is to minimize risk and this would normally indicate the smallest possible area. However, many other considerations come into the choice of the area. Media is one. If television is to be your prime medium if the product is launched nationally then it is futile to test unless you use television. Anticipated market size is another. Something like household detergents or tea would normally be tested in large areas in order to expose the product to all the problems it would have to face when it went national (problems like trade reaction, competitive response and so on). However, a product with a very small potential number of buyers might also be forced to use a large area in order to pick up enough trialists in a reasonable period.

Productive capacity will also determine the size of the area chosen and will involve risk decisions. The cost of plant may be so high that elementary caution dictates the size of the test. Sometimes, however, the margin of error from a small-scale test may be such that the risk outweighs the risk involved in extra plant. (This is an area where decision theory can help.)

These, then, are the traditional golden rules of test Marketing. Nothing has happened to change them. In circumstances where it is right to test, they are as valid as ever. However, it has long been acknowledged that test Marketing is, at best, a very blunt instrument giving often enormous margins of error. Before we consider the predictive qualities of test Marketing, let us consider the common errors which either invalidate many tests or substantially increase the error in scaling up.

Common Mistakes

Still the most common mistake is to make efforts which cannot be reproduced on a national scale. In a test market for a quick-cooking rice in the Midlands, retail audit showed a disappointing level of distribution. The local manager immediately drafted in an extra sales team and had them drive up and down streets identifying new outlets not already listed and opening new accounts. The cost of doing this nationally would have been prohibitive, quite apart from the fact that the test was designed to see what could be done with the normal resources. There is a tendency for salesmen, particularly, to feel either that they have been specially chosen or that they themselves are under test. Although it would be reasonable to expect that a national launch will put the new product to the top of the selling list for a period, the likelihood is that it will stay at or near the top of the list for much longer in a test area. This must be stopped. Too-frequent visits by Head Office personnel can also exert a subtle influence upon the sales force which may over-emphasize the amount of effort employed or act to the detriment of more important established brands. The effect of a test product upon sales of existing brands should always be measured.

Almost as common is the tendency to try to test too many variables simultaneously. (We have already seen how many alternatives even a small number of variables can produce.) When testing a new product one is testing the totality of the product mix: one should not expect to be able to separate out the answers to questions about advertising, packaging, price and so on. If there is reason to doubt any one of these, there is a case for testing that variable in isolation. For example, the rice test market already referred to revealed, in one piece of research, a low level of awareness of the brand. This prompted further investigation and led to a change in copy with quite significant results. It would be interesting to know how many multiple test markets are comparative tests of individual items like price, pack and advertising content. Provided the chosen areas match, this is a perfectly valid way of testing variables.

Too many variables tested at the same time in the same place make it impossible to say which caused what.

Another far too common error is to short-change yourself on research. No test should be mounted without first enumerating clearly the objectives to be attained. Then, ample research should be mounted at appropriate time intervals to check progress against these objectives. Research should be a major expenditure item in the test: it will be money well spent if it prevents a financial disaster. The sort of questions one will need answers to in the case of a new product will probably require pre-launch and post-launch checks to establish awareness, levels of trial, brands replaced, use made of the product and so on. Retail audit is necessary in most consumer product test markets as is consumer audit. Both will require specially constructed samples or augmented ones if an existing service is used. The alternative to retail audit is ex-factory sales and this is normally dangerous. However, with a perishable product delivered weekly a retail panel may be an unnecessary luxury. The alternative to consumer audit (apart from nothing at all!) is to do two or more pieces of *ad hoc* research following up on the same sample. Thus one may contact people who have tried the product and ask if they will go on buying and how often. After a reasonable interval, you can then check back on those who said they would continue buying and see who actually did so and why those who stopped buying changed their minds.

An example of such research in combination happened with the quick-cooking rice already mentioned. The aim was to achieve eleven per cent of the Leicester market for natural (as opposed to canned, creamed) rice. A retail panel was set up, reporting every four weeks, with the first readings being taken two months before launch. Six weeks after the launch we did a large-scale survey (we correctly anticipated that it might be difficult to find users) which showed that just over two-thirds of all housewives had bought rice but only eight per cent had bought our product. We found that this was closely related to awareness which, unprompted, was only seven per cent; after a little help, thirty-eight per cent of the housewives interviewed could recall our advertising (which was all in the Press). Of the eight per cent who had said they had bought the product less than half said they would buy again. Given the tendency to be kind to interviewers, the disheartening fact was that thirty-five per cent said quite firmly that they would never buy again.

All this might have caused us to shut up shop there and then but sales into the trade were very good indeed despite the fact that we were selling a six-ounce packet of rice at 5p, giving a twenty per cent gross margin to the retailer, whereas they were selling ordinary rice at 3p to 4p per lb with margins upwards of fifty per cent. Moreover, backed up by highly favourable product tests before the launch, we felt that things might brighten up if the advertising could achieve more impact. This was done and knowledge of the product rose dramatically.

Four months from the start of the test, with two more months to go, sales into the area were averaging some sixty per cent of the natural-rice market in Leicester and its hinterland. However, the retail audit showed an alarming stock-pile, for sales out gave us only a two per cent share of the market. In fact, our high sales reflected increased distribution, especially among larger shops. On the other side of the ledger were many shops with nil sales. The outlook was even more alarming when we did our second survey, calling back on those who had said they would go on buying the brand. About one-third had, but they had bought only two packets at the most and half of those had either stopped buying or said they would stop. As a result of this follow-up survey, it appeared that only two per cent of all housewives might become regular buyers. Converted into national volume this represented just over forty per cent of the viable level. The product was withdrawn.

Of course, we discovered the reasons. Basically, the product was acceptable and was regarded as being as good as ordinary rice. However, the appeal of quick-cooking rice was minimal, for the value placed on convenience was very, very low. As has been said, we discovered that housewives normally only baked rice pudding when the oven was already in use: speed was therefore no advantage!

The reason for spelling out this case history of failure is simply that with only ex-factory sales figures to guide us we would have believed that we had a very large share of the natural-rice market. We would have been involved in very heavy capital outlay which would have been almost totally wasted.

There was another way we could have found the same result without spending so much on research. We could have let the test run on. With stock piling up, our ex-factory sales would have reduced to a trickle and the lesson would have been clear to see. However, we were importing the product and had only a limited option. Nevertheless, this example does lead to the conclusion that sufficient time should be allowed to elapse for all the forces in the market-place to work themselves out. It is a great temptation when sales exceed their target very early in the test to begin the national expansion rather than wait to see whether you are going through the market or accumulating loyal users. The early heady days of Ready Brek were deceptive in this respect. Sales climbed as more people sampled the product but plummeted as no new buyers could be persuaded into the market and the majority of those who sampled dropped out. This is where consumer audit is so valuable: it gives you early indications of whether you are gaining loyal users or running through your potential market.

Time is money and time in test is seen by many companies in terms of opportunity cost. Procter and Gamble went into test market with Crest toothpaste with fluoride. Gibbs and Colgate jumped the gun without test Marketing, relying on the well-publicized success of Crest in the USA. (This success was enhanced by official recommendation from the dental profession: this was not forthcoming over here.) Many companies adopt the technique of monitoring a competitor's test market hoping to learn the lessons at least as quickly as the tester does and go national earlier if possible. Another tactic is to deliberately destroy a test market by heavyweight

promotions. This is not so effective as it may sound. A little
elementary calculation will reveal the chances of that rate of
expenditure being continued on a national scale. However, it
does mean going ahead on a calculated risk since there are very
high chances that the readings you expected to get from the
test will have been badly disturbed. You will find yourself
asking some question like: 'Our aim was fifteen per cent but
we only get ten per cent in face of four times our competitor's
normal rate of expenditure; what could we get if he only
spends at his normal rate?' Personal experience suggests that
you have a high likelihood of success in such cases if all your
pre-test market research was encouragingly conclusive.

Evaluating the Result

From the rice example quoted it can be seen how important it
is to have carefully established objectives. A volume objective
alone is not enough; a share of market aim is better. Coupled
with targets for regular and occasional users and heavy, light
and medium buyers the objectives become much more
meaningful. What are you trying to discover, what limits will
you regard as actionable, what will you do if you get no
clear-cut result, how long will you allow the test to run? All
this, and more, according to the nature of the test, must be
considered in framing the objective. Then suitable checks
must be put in to check results against objectives. Figure 10
shows the kind of results that might be discovered when
compared with objectives and targets, and the sort of action
that might be taken. Notice particularly that each conclusion
leads to decisions between alternatives. Complete failure may
lead you to start again: complete success may not necessarily
lead to immediate national launch. You may have production
problems, sales-force capacity limitations or just financial
considerations which lead you towards a phased launch until
you eventually cover the whole country.

The critical point in evaluating the results is the degree to
which results in an area can be scaled up into national figures
with any reasonable degree of accuracy. One of the classic

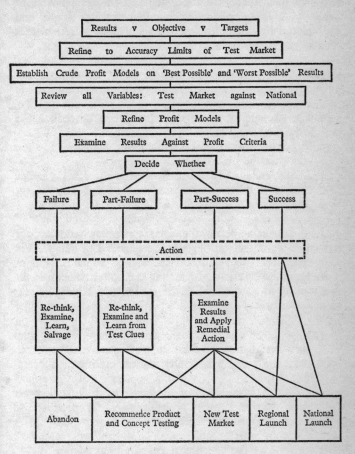

Figure 10. Analysis of a Test Market

pioneering pieces of research into this matter was done in the USA by Jack Gold. He concluded that the results were so meaningless that the test market might well lose favour and be replaced by consumer research simulations of test market conditions. His main findings were:

1. Employing a single test market is risky. Twenty per cent of cases gave projected results with measured errors of between +48% and −36%.
2. The probability of extreme error could be reduced by increasing the number of test markets.
3. Projecting from the share of market gained in the test area gave the highest degree of accuracy.
4. In any given case, one does not know which projection method and which area give a good facsimile of the country as a whole.

John Davis, at about the same time, was studying the results of 44 test-market patterns as recorded by retail audit. This provided two significant conclusions which should be borne in mind by those who tend to champ impatiently at the bit waiting to go national at the earliest opportunity. These conclusions were:

1. If, at any stage during the initial sales build-up, sales are more than twice the rate of the stable target level, there is a 3-to-1 probability that the product is successful.
2. *Unless* peak sales exceed the target by at least fifty per cent, there is a 3-to-1 probability that the product will fail to maintain its target.

Here we have the first useful early-warning system.

Staying with retail audit analyses, the A. C. Nielsen Company surveyed 141 tests both in this country and in the United States. Based upon this research, they reached the conclusion that the odds for correctly forecasting test results after various lengths of time in test were:

After 2 months: 1 in 9
    ,, 4   ,,   : 1 in 3
    ,, 6   ,,   : 1 in 2
    ,, 8   ,,   : 2 in 3
    ,, 10   ,,   : 5 in 6.

Success rates were generally higher for the shorter periods
in the USA. This was especially true of the 2- and 4-month
periods. From 6 to 12 months the patterns were similar. By
18 months, both registered 100 per cent success. This supports
the mythology of testing: never less than 6 months and better
12. Accuracy at 12 months was ninety-one per cent in the
UK and ninety-five per cent in the USA.

Of the tests examined by Nielsen, only 77 – just over half –
were not abandoned. A measure was then made of the accuracy
with which the test-market audit findings were borne out
nationally. The odds were:

1. About 50–50 that national performance will be within
$\pm 10\%$ of test results. (Gold's findings suggest that almost
half of the fifty per cent of cases outside this limit will be
wildly wrong.)
2. About 4 to 1 that the figure will be within $\pm 20\%$.
3. About 10 to 1 that the figure will be in the range $\pm 21\%$
to $\pm 31\%$. (Closer to Gold.)

Differences between the two countries were slight.

Nielsen concluded that going national without test Marketing involved a 50–50 risk but that, combining successful
detection of failures plus the 9 out of 10 hopeful cases subsequently confirmed, tests contributed to better management
decisions 19 times out of 20.

Turning our attention now to consumer panels, interesting
work has been done by Parfitt and Collins. Taking Gold's
point that the most accurate projections were based upon
brand shares, they examined diary panel raw data to extract
the cumulative growth in new buyers of a brand, the rate of
repeat purchasing, and comparisons between heavy, average

and light buyers. Their paper was presented in 1967 and drew
upon data going back to 1960. The first conclusion will not be
unexpected to any statistician: it is not necessary to wait until
cumulative penetration has been observed before prediction
can be made. A reasonable estimate is possible as soon as the
shape of the curve is determined and a declining rate of
increase observed. The second observation was that repeat
purchasing (if there is any) tends to be higher initially and
then declines. Prediction of the ultimate level is possible when
the repeat purchasing rate levels off. With brand penetration
predicted and the ultimate level of repeat purchasing estimated,
it is time to bring in the varying buying levels of consumers.
The predicted brand share is given by:

$$\text{Estimated Penetration} \times \text{Repeat Purchasing Rate} \times \text{Buying Rate Index.}$$

Taking the example used in the paper, we get:

$$34\% \times 25\% \times 1 \cdot 0 = 8 \cdot 5\%.$$

However, the varying buying rates give these figures:

Heavy Buyers	$34\% \times 25\% \times 1 \cdot 2 =$	$10 \cdot 2\%$
Average ,,	$34\% \times 25\% \times 1 \cdot 0 =$	$8 \cdot 5\%$
Light ,,	$34\% \times 25\% \times 0 \cdot 8 =$	$6 \cdot 8\%.$

Perhaps the most significant contribution emerged from
deep study of purchasing rate behaviour over a lengthy period.
This revealed that, on average, the earlier a buyer enters a
market the higher will be that buyer's repeat purchasing rate.
The first buyers will have a disproportionate importance in the
brand's final market share. Analysis of various promotional
devices showed what experienced Marketing men have always
suspected: that it is easier to increase brand penetration than
repeat purchasing rates.

We have looked at three pathfinding pieces of work in the field of evaluation of test-market results and their projection into national figures. Conflict between the findings is more apparent than real and they all three reinforce the plea for more research and ideally for a combination of *ad hoc* surveys, retail audit and consumer panels. Is all this becoming too costly: do we really need to test?

The Arguments Against Testing

The major arguments advanced are that test markets are not very successful as predictors of eventual success; they only become more effective given longer exposure to market conditions and this increases the security risk; they are relatively expensive to do properly and this is in direct conflict with the avowed objective of minimizing risk. All these statements are relative but, as we have already seen, have some validity. The evidence we have considered emphasizes the importance of thorough research and adequate time. The case against test Marketing is strongest where these rules are ignored and the predictions subject to considerable margins of error. The greater the error, the less point in testing since there seems to be a 50–50 chance of success without testing. Why not spin a coin?

Test Marketing comes very much under the heading of 'the best we've got' as a management tool. It should be seen as a part of the sequence of product development and not looked at too closely in isolation which has led to considerations of research simulation techniques which present all the promise of the product without actually exposing it for sale, mini-tests using single shops or a very small number of units, and mail-order testing techniques. No significant predictive results have been produced and conventional test Marketing, with all its defects, remains the most successful technique. The search for valid alternatives continues, however, basically because the cost of a properly executed test followed by subsequent national launch is greater than immediate national launch (assuming equal rates of success). Quite apart from research costs and other special analyses, diseconomies of small-scale operation come into play.

There has been a great deal of talk about mini-tests and I have encountered an alarming number of Marketing men prepared to accept this as the latest vogue and a cheap and adequate substitute for test Marketing. I am not aware of any leading advocate of mini-tests suggesting that they should be a substitute for a conventional larger-scale test. The point was well expressed by R. C. Davis in a paper delivered in 1968:

My own view is that there should be injected into that R & D-test-market continuum a greater number of primitive sales tests, far more mini-test-markets, and early on too. I want to see very limited sales tests of new products conducted very early on in their life, using hand made products if necessary, sold to and through (say) ten real shops – and *then* competently researched. At least such data will not be simulation data, it will be real post-sales data. And it will cut down the failure rate of subsequent more fully-fledged test markets. It will accomplish this quite simply by establishing beyond all reasonable doubt that the trade really did want it, the customer really did see it and like it and use it and came back for more. It will replace uncertainty based on research with probability based on facts.

This brings out the most valid criticism of test markets: the fact that they proceed on the evidence of research conducted in unreal situations which seldom produce more than declared intentions to buy. One more step in the sequence might show these intentions to be so flimsy that a test market becomes an unjustifiable expenditure. The argument is not against test markets; it is against a sudden transition from the unreality of the domestic interview to the harsh reality of the market-place.

Logic dictates that one should not automatically attempt to discover a facsimile of the total market for test purposes. Novelty products calculated to enjoy only short life cycles usually have such low risk factors built in that failure would not be a disaster. Fashion goods can only be tested on buyers. New magazines can only be tested on potential advertisers to see to what extent they would support a product designed to fit a segment of the market. The tooling-up costs prevent an area test of a new motor car. There is no point in testing a product, like an expensive gold watch, aimed at a minute section of the population. Similarly, many products will never appeal to a national market and an area is the market.

Current thinking is more inclined to sequential launching in which the whole span from product concept to final national launch is regarded as a series of stages, each with defined decision points. It is rather like those children's dice games. A throw may land you on spots where you miss a turn, advance several places or even go back to the beginning. In this game, sometimes the square you land on says, 'You've lost!'

Conclusion

Test markets are unlikely to disappear in the foreseeable future, if ever. More emphasis needs to be placed on the prior research and reality substituted for artificial situations wherever and whenever possible. Companies will calculate with greater care and precision the cost of testing relative to the likely benefits. However scientific we attempt to become, the basis of these calculations will remain subjective and therefore risky.

Suggestions for Further Reading

Two epoch-making papers were published in 1964: Jack Gold's 'Testing Test Market Predictions' in the *Journal of Market Research*, pages 8–16, August 1964, and John Davis's 'Test Marketing: an Examination of Sales Patterns found during 44 Recent Tests', at a conference of the Market Research Society in 1964 under the title 'Research in Marketing'. These jointly form the pattern for all further doubts and examination of test Marketing. Another significant contribution arising from a

Market Research Society conference was that by J. H. Parfitt and B. J. K. Collins on 'The Use of Consumer Panels for Brand Share Prediction', published both in the *Proceedings* of that conference and the *Journal of Marketing Research*, May 1968. An excellent book on the subject is *Experimental Marketing* by John Davis, published by Nelson, 1970.

Chapter 15

Selling

Selling has come a long way since the days when the textile salesman could have a three-word discourse with the buyer at t'mill: 'Owt?' 'Nowt!' 'Reet.' The modern grocery salesman from a sophisticated company dealing with efficient supermarkets will often walk straight into the stockroom, count the stock, check the goods in the shop, look at his computerized sales record and calculate how much stock that store will require to maintain an agreed stock-cover until his next call. Unless there is a special reason to negotiate a featured display, sell a new line, advise about new advertising or suggest reasons why the planned level is no longer correct, the salesman may have no more than common courtesy contact with the store manager. Mutual trust (checked by the store's own computer records) makes the formality of signing an order unnecessary. The salesman knows that he only has to deceive the manager once to be thrown out of that store, perhaps to get his company delisted in that chain.

These, of course, are extremes, yet the total spectrum of salesmen varies from non-selling order-takers who never do more than recite a long list (but more frequently ask: 'Need anything today, Joe?') to skilled negotiators cognizant of profitability figures and given a high degree of on-the-spot discretionary power. Unfortunately, the public image of the salesman is not much improved. (Although they enjoy a relatively higher status than their British counterparts, American salesmen also suffer a relatively low public image.) Non-selling managers, frequently encouraged by their Marketing people, are inclined to blame the poor salesman for all the ills of the company. The attention which has been devoted to other areas of management has been singularly lacking in the area of sales management. This must surely be one of the most fascinating areas of study, but no doubt the complexity of the task is discouraging and attention is focused upon management problems in less dynamic and very much more localized situations. One man who has done some practical research on some aspects of sales force problems, Derek A. Newton, has written: 'Sales management practice is like Topsy – it just grew. Each sales executive tends to work out his own style of managing from the assortment of principles he inherits from his predecessor, the customs of the industry in which he is operating, his own ideas, the expressed preferences of his corporate superiors, and so on. There has been a signal lack of method in this vital and challenging area of management.'[1]

With the growing tendency for sales forces to come under the ultimate control of people not versed in the problems of salesmanship and being a salesman, there is a need for much greater understanding of the basic difficulties of doing the job. Similarly, there is a need to encourage such managers to venture into new areas, new techniques, and new approaches and not use their ignorance and lack of personal experience as an excuse for continuing as in the past. The same objectivity that goes into the examination of brand plans and investment decisions can – and must – be applied but it must be tempered with humanity and understanding. A good salesman longs for the opportunity to give his loyalty, but loyalty, like respect, has to be earned.

The Psychology of Selling

The salesman's job is one of the loneliest and often the most frustrating in the world. He spends the bulk of his time travelling and waiting although he is probably (though not inevitably) gregarious and extrovert. Few salesmen operate from depots any more: unlike most of us, they don't have 'friends at work'. We can chat over our problems at lunch or pop into each other's offices, but the salesman probably sees his colleagues no more than once every four weeks, usually on a

Saturday morning or in the evening, and then only in a fairly contrived atmosphere. If you examined the habits of your salesmen carefully you might well find, as I once did, that they spend more time talking to their competitors (whom they meet in stores and cafés) than they do with their own colleagues.

The salesman dealing with trades like grocery, confectionery, tobacconists and chemists may find himself conducting high-level negotiations with a brilliant businessman at one call and being humbled at the very next call by a tycoon in a front-parlour shop who orders half a parcel of corn flakes! Empathy – total involvement with the customer's problems and understanding of his personal drives – is a highly necessary part of a salesman's make-up, but he is often sorely tried. Ideally, one would match salesmen with buyers, but in most businesses this is economically unjustified.

It is a lonely job because you are in front of the buyer on your own, bolstered only by supreme self-confidence, pride in your product, and some samples, literature and a set of key words and phrases you have learned from the last area meeting or Regional Managers' Bulletin. Frustrating, because your clearly argued case is often met with a totally illogical answer, unforeseen circumstances or sheer cussedness. One great argument in favour of the combined sales and distribution system (as with a van sales force who both take orders and deliver) was the fact that you all started out from and returned to the same depot. Ideas could be exchanged, grouses aired and settled quickly and like minds could discuss common topics. The salesman operating from home takes his problems home with him and there is a great deal of marital stress in the homes of salesmen up and down the country which is not exactly helped by three dozen dump-bins under the bed, six wire stands in the hall and the garage full of inflatable Donald Ducks!

Salesmen get to expect kicks and not to expect too many bouquets. Nevertheless, most salesmen would probably rather be kicked than forgotten. They'll take the kicks more willingly if they receive praise where it is due. The unfortunate tendency is to say 'He's only doing what he's paid for' when he does well, but 'He's not earning his corn' when he falls below target. Salesmen have a great deal to contend with. The older men are continually having to learn new tricks; parking, especially in busy High Streets, is becoming an ever-increasing source of frustration. Modern techniques require a great deal of homework in pre-planning tomorrow's calls and recording today's. In many trades, the salesman is expected to be part artist, part unpaid stockroom labourer, to keep abreast of the latest technical developments and read all the right journals.

A good salesman has a strong tendency to be naturally subjective. His whole instinct and training is to recognize the moment of human weakness his customer betrays: to recognize the moment when the glazed expression changes to a sparkle of interest at the seventh sales plus and then capitalize on that melting moment. Although he may put on a very good face of selling the whole range with absolute conviction, every salesman has his favourite. (In fact, as any experienced sales manager will tell you, the salesman who actively *sells* the whole of his product range probably doesn't exist.) There is no other explanation for side-by-side journeys with similar retail and population characteristics having wildly dissimilar patterns of sale for certain products. These are normally smaller, probably unpromoted products, where the enthusiasm of the salesman is passed on by the retailer. A large, heavily promoted product or one offering a substantial demonstrable benefit to the buyer is usually proof against apathy and hardly needs favouritism.

No mention of the psychology of selling could be complete without mention of 'sales force motivation'. It is a common belief that salesmen need to be 'motivated' to do things, persuaded to drive themselves in the direction chosen by the company. This is a complete misuse of the concept of motivation. People have certain inner drives but they differ considerably. 'Motivating' people means identifying that inner drive and capitalizing upon it in some way. One man may derive intense satisfaction from a sense of conquest: he may be best used for opening new accounts. Another man may have an intense desire for possessions: cash incentives or competitions may be best for him. It is obvious that no single motivating force will be equally successful with all salesmen, although money and pride of achievement are usually common. 'Motivating' a sales force requires one of two things: a group of people all with the same psychological driving forces or a management span of control which allows close individual supervision, encouragement and cajoling. Both are expensive but the latter is far cheaper in absolute terms and in terms of results. If a manager can spend one day a week with a man, he soon gets to know him very well and rapidly discovers who responds to the stick and who chases the carrot.

What are the qualities of a good salesman; is there such a thing as a typical selling type? In popular imagery, there certainly is. In reality, it is less likely. There may, however, be certain characteristics which are essential in particular kinds of salesmen, for we must recognize that the selling job is not the same for all types of business or for all tasks within the same business. A grocery salesman may be expected to be a highly sophisticated negotiator at one call, to chat about the shop-keeper's wife's ailment at the next and to hump heavy cases from the stockroom at the next. An insurance salesman is expected to service existing clients and be a friend to the family but change his tone every so often (usually when the inspector is with him) and try to sell new policies. Just two of many examples of quite different tasks calling for different qualities from the same man. The company must reconcile the cost of separate forces to handle different tasks against the lower effectiveness of asking the same man to perform several tasks.

The man who sells 'through' the trade rather than merely 'to' it needs to be capable of a high level of objectivity. High enough, indeed, to be able to see that it is in his best interests and those of his company to say: 'Your stock is getting too high, we'd better cut down the order to get the right stock-level'. That kind of man (who may be the stock-check and re-plenishment grocery salesman, a man selling to wholesalers, in the clothing trade or selling textiles) will find his motivation in the success of his customer and his ability to aid that success by careful control. High bonus payments and incentive schemes would run contrary to his objective, for they would encourage stock-piling. An ideal man for launching new products or giving personal selling assistance to his own direct customers would be younger, energetic and articulate. Salesmen selling complex technical equipment act like professional consultants in that they have to identify, analyse and solve their customer's problem. Again this speaks against the need for large bonuses or incentive schemes but for a high degree of objective analytical ability. They must be thorough in their preparation and willing to accept the necessity for frequent and often rigorous re-training as new techniques and processes are discovered. Cold canvassing for new business is a job generally best performed by older men. There is no reasonable way of targeting this job but incentives should not be ruled out, for new outlets of the right potential can be very valuable. This is one of the most soul-destroying jobs of the lot and one should not expect too many calls a day or too long a stint at this task without the opportunity of doing some selling where regular results can be achieved.

Just this brief examination of a few common sales tasks shows us that the conventional picture of the hale and hearty, beer-swilling, joke-telling salesman is totally false. Just as a matter of amusement, take a sheet of paper and write down all the qualities desirable in a salesman in your company. You can then fire them all, for it is a safe bet that no man will possess all those qualities! We commonly expect the impossible of salesmen: we have no right to complain at not getting it.

Organizational Problems

Any organization is both a function of the business you are in and the people available. The latter is important and usually ignored. Opportunity plays a great part in promotion; so too does the right chemistry between people. This is something to consider again later. However, these two facts are relevant here, for although most companies regard the sales force as the principal selling vehicle, it is rare for other people not to get into the act also. The Chairman or Chief Executive usually has a few very important buyers he deals with personally. This can often cause great problems on both sides when the seller offers or the buyer accepts something their subordinates are not empowered to do. All negotiation at whatever level should conform to predetermined rules which all other people dealing with the same organization should know about. They should also know when the rules have been broken, why and under what conditions. There are, of course, some businesses where the boss is the sales force and 'sales force' is a misnomer for servicing staff. The newsprint industry, which sells on long-term contracts at negotiated prices, is a case in point.

In most companies there will be a number of levels: Chairman, Chief Executive, Sales Director, Regional Manager, Area Manager, Salesmen. Each will deal with an equivalent level on the buying side. These relationships become formalized and often too much so. It is a good basic rule that every level of contact should have one superior level in reserve and, ideally, the Chairman be used only in the very last resort. The salesman can call on his area manager for support, area manager on regional manager, and so on. The more senior the manager, the more should his role be that of ultimate deterrent, peacemaker, and, if all else fails, persuader. However, once introduced, he loses his air of mystery and there is a strong possibility that he will become increasingly the man the buyer contacts.

Some companies organize by channel of distribution and may deal with all levels throughout that organization. In the grocery field, for example, the most common form of organization is a fairly conventional territorial one with salesmen calling upon all sorts of outlets in their area. However, Head Office contact is made by a small team of skilled negotiators who arrange for listings (permission for store managers to stock – seldom instructions to do so), arrange promotions, negotiate price cuts and so on. It is then up to the salesman calling upon the local store to convert that permission to stock into action by the store manager. Many sales managers in this country and the USA have experimented with the 'account manager' concept (myself among them). This places one man in one organization operating at all levels. The theory is that he is party to top decisions, gains an intimate knowledge of store policy and personalities and is seen by the retailer as going out of his way to help the stores, if necessary at the expense of his company. The concept has worked better in the States than in this country but everywhere the results have been well behind what the theory led one to believe. Practical experience shows that the salesman soon begins to wonder who he is working for and, therefore, cannot be left too long with one group. Frequent change, however, upsets the group, who have another new man to train. At store level, the account manager is frequently viewed with deep suspicion as a spy from Head Office. The more general pattern is for National Account or Head Office accounts managers to handle a small number of groups (on the personal chemistry basis) and leave the dealings with store inspectors and local managers to the appropriate local selling level.

In industrial selling (as in industrial market research) there is frequently a greater fusion of the pure selling function and the conventional Marketing analysis work. Frequently the total sales pitch involves major consultancy-type operations, as where selling something which constitutes a major technical advance may involve widespread restructuring of the buyer's operation. The 'sale' may be carried out by a project team. This often leads companies selling complex technical products, raw materials or components to say they have no sales force. Figures collected annually by *Advertiser's Weekly* on advertising, promotion and sales organization costs as ratios of turnover inevitably reveal companies who deny the existence of a sales organization. If they have no formally constituted sales force, they conceal its cost under other headings because they are usually employing a range of managerial, financial and technical skills on a project team basis and this is their sales force.

I suggest, too, that they are wrong not to employ specialist salesmen. They argue that such a high degree of technical skill is necessary that you would never find it in a salesman and you could never train him. The value of technical ability in a selling situation can be vastly overrated. A salesman sells benefits to the buyer and those can easily be learned. A technical man frequently does not adopt the Marketing approach of selling the benefit the customer wants but tries to sell the benefits he – the technician – has worked so hard to produce. A good salesman may find a way of reconciling the two or just selling the benefit the buyer wants, whereas the technical man may lose the sale by trying to sell what he wants to provide. Another organizational problem found with the project team approach is also common to any situation (for example, selling to hospitals) where several people in different departments influence the decision. In all these situations – and in the grocery field where many companies have buying committees – there are two golden rules:

1. Have one single person who is seen clearly by both sides as the funnel through which all final contact is made. It should go without saying that any conversations which do not involve him should be fully documented for him.
2. Unless it is absolutely impossible, do the final selling yourself, don't let your customer do it. However much you prepare for someone else to sell for you, he won't do it your way: he will interpret and interpolate, add his own opinions, make his own promises about your product and exhibit his own prejudices.

Advertising agencies present a good example of this kind of selling. The account executive is the salesman. The creative people, the media department and all the other services of the agency are the technicians. The executive may present the whole team, he may just present their work. All contact, in both directions, will pass through him.

Organization by territory is the most common in virtually every kind of business. Although this usually involves the psychological conflicts of calling on several different kinds of customer and doing often irreconcilable jobs, sheer economics usually swing the balance very heavily. Organization by class of customer comes second if only because the larger sales forces in the fields with large retailer universes do not find it so un-economic to have one grade of salesman calling, say, on a High Street supermarket and another grade calling on the small independent grocer next door. The benefits of specialization on similar tasks can easily outweigh the psychological conflicts mentioned above. Then comes specialization by type of product. It is not always advisable, practicable or economic to trot out both a salesman and a technical expert, and there are many fields where a fairly high level of product knowledge is necessary and where this is quite specialized. The man who sells typewriters may not sell his firm's duplicating machines; the man who sells life assurance may not sell non-life assurance. The channel and method of distribution may tie in with this kind of organization by product-type: one product may be sold direct to offices, another to retailers and another to wholesalers. Organization by function can be a method in itself but it is found most frequently as a layer superimposed upon some more basic reason for organizing the sales force. Thus, the basic reason may be the fact that territorial organization is more economic. However, a special pioneering team with the right qualities for this job may be drafted into an area at a time to open new accounts which then become part of the territorial organization. Most industries, as we have already considered, can find good psychological reasons why their sales force should be so organized that each man is asked to do only the job he is best at; few, however, can afford this ideal and stress and conflict remain part of the salesman's lot.

Call Policy

It is a rare business that finds it physically possible to call upon all possible customers for its products. It would be rarer still if they were all worth calling upon. The amount of sales produced depends upon:

1. The number of customers identified as being of the right potential.
2. The number of calls made.

3. How frequently each potential customer is called upon.
4. The order-to-call ratio.
5. The size of the order.
6. The cost of obtaining it.

You can juggle with all these items and changing any one may result in more or less profit and more or less orders: more profit, however, may not mean more orders – it could be the result of cutting out uneconomic calls. The leading companies selling to the grocery trade are continually pruning the number of direct calls they make, leaving wholesalers and retail buying groups to service the remainder.

The basis of all sales force activity by whatever kind of company is to concentrate its efforts where the bulk of the business is. Consumer goods should be in stock (and conspicuously so, especially when heavily promoted) where the greatest store traffic is; industrial goods should be in those units making the greatest use of the particular machine, raw material, component or whatever it is. This merely reiterates the principles emphasized in Part 1 of selling from strength and allocating the highest proportion of your costs to the areas giving the greatest reward.

The problems to consider under the heading of call policy are those of:

1. How many outlets?
2. How many calls per day?
3. How often do we call on the same shop/firm?
4. How flexible should we be to allow for changes in the future?

If you are starting from scratch, nothing is harder than defining the number of potential outlets (unless you are in a tight-knit industry where they are already defined for you). In this case you will probably start by doing only what you can afford, making cold calls but probably setting a minimum order level which won't give you an embarrassing number of uneconomic accounts later. An existing business should study its customer records carefully and decide which are likely to be uneconomic. I say 'likely'. Only careful work-study analysis can reveal the real cost of calling on outlets of various types. The size of store, the size of the order, the amount of waiting time, the complexity of the sales pitch, the number of people that have to be seen – all contribute to varying costs per call. Looking at the map will eliminate some calls even though they may apparently be economic by other standards. If you set the economic order at £1 but you spend that much in petrol and travelling time getting there, the order isn't worth having. There will be a recurring plea for more work-study techniques applied to sales forces throughout this section!

How many calls a salesman can make a day varies enormously. Van salesmen commonly do up to seventy per day and in the old days might often exceed 100. However, most van salesmen are order-takers and cash collectors – indeed with seventy calls a day they are hard-pushed to do that. The average grocery representative does twenty calls a day, whilst those concentrating on the top end of the trade seldom average more than eight. In many businesses you can only call when people will see you: I know one very well-paid salesman of extremely expensive capital goods (with an average twenty-year life) who is lucky if he actually makes two personal visits a week; he probably makes another dozen telephone calls.

The primary determinant of calls per day is the content of the call. A grocery salesman selling in a major promotion to a supermarket, pricing the stock and erecting a display, could well spend two to three hours at the job. (A supermarket on early-closing day is a hive of activity!) A sales pitch such as that made by Rolls-Royce for the sale of aero-engines in the USA in early 1969 took many months, a vast team of people and mountains of paper. The contact that kept those avenues open was far less time-consuming.

Call content is again something which can only be measured by work-study techniques. Most sales managers fear this. They have heard too many stories of factory strikes because men with stop-watches in their hands have stood over workers. Wherever possible, the sales force should have its own work-study manager. He should first carefully explain to the various levels of management what he is about and start by suggesting simple methods that local management can use to make the salesman's life easier. It goes without saying that the work-study man should not start work until he is thoroughly familiar with what the salesman's objectives are and until he has a thorough understanding of the many problems that will prevent perfection ever being achieved (things like early-closing days, interviews by appointment only, non-delivery days, one-way streets and so on). Then, and only then, he can begin his real analysis and he will do this as surreptitiously as possible. (You can usually tell a sales force work-study man: he is the guy standing behind the salesman with both hands in his pockets. He either has a stop-watch in each or a stop-watch in one and a pencil and notebook in the other!)

The normal method involves sampling and probability using a technique known as 'activity sampling'. You cannot, without upsetting the man you are selling to (if not your salesman also), openly record what is happening. You note as much as you can under each heading. The sort of headings of interest will be:

—Driving time
—Waiting time
—General conversation
—Selling
—Merchandising
—Stock checking
—Writing
—Meal breaks
—Parking

and so on. From these observations, the work-study manager will derive averages and will calculate the probability of any activity occurring by using the formula:

$$P = \frac{\text{Number of times Activity Observed} \times 100}{\text{Number of all Observations}}.$$

The adequacy of the sample and the standing error attaching to the results can then be calculated using the techniques mentioned in Chapter 13.

We will then know how much time a salesman should spend in various types of call, in performing various kinds of activity. Travelling time, parking time, meal time and other non-productive time will have been calculated and will probably be terrifying. From all this work, allied to customer analysis of business (both actual and potential), we can do five things:

1. Plan how many shops to call on.
2. Decide how frequently.
3. Calculate how long the salesman will spend at each call.
4. Plan the ideal journey.
5. Calculate how many men are needed.

Frequency and length of call will be decided by the volume of business in markets for fast-moving goods. Most large grocery sales forces work to a four-week cycle mixing weekly, fortnightly and monthly calls. Taking this pattern as an example, the theoretical result would be for a salesman to follow this pattern:

Week 1: All weekly calls, half fortnightly calls, one-quarter monthly calls.
Week 2: All weekly calls, one-quarter monthly calls.
Week 3: All weekly calls, half fortnightly calls, one-quarter monthly calls.
Week 4: All weekly calls, one-quarter monthly calls.

However, this would be unsatisfactory for a number of reasons. Weeks 2 and 4 will be less busy than 3 and 4 unless something is done to correct it. Moreover, the sales cycle coincides with the promotional cycle and it may be most desirable to see all the weekly and fortnightly calls – the more important buyers – in the same week before the promotion breaks. Weekly calls will be on supermarkets in the main. By the time you have eliminated non-delivery days, early-closing

day and Friday when they are too busy to see anyone, the
weekly calls get awfully crammed up. Thus there will be a
great deal of trial and error before the best fit is achieved.

Geography comes into it too. It will almost certainly be incredibly wasteful to visit all the weekly calls on the same day,
journeying from town to town. This is where journey planning
links with call frequency and content. Left to himself, the
average salesman gives a very passable impersonation of that
well-known creature of mythology, the Dingo bird. This
unique animal, as you will know, flies in ever-decreasing circles,

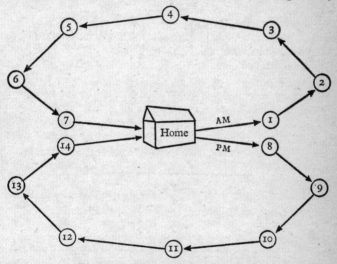

Figure 11. Typical Salesman's Route

eventually disappearing in the most remarkable way and
simultaneously performing an even more incredible feat! The
salesman has a natural, and wasteful, inclination to describe
large circuits, eventually disappearing into his own home at
lunch time and arriving back there at a time no later than that
at which he should finish his last call. Needless to say, his first
and last calls are close to home. Figure 11 gives a close approxi-
mation to this situation on any given day. It is immediately

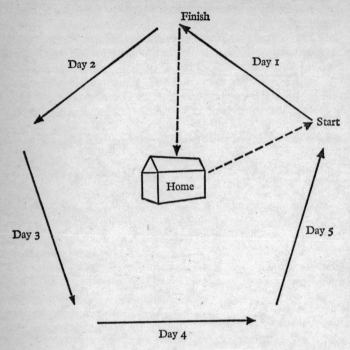

Figure 12. Effect of 'Linear' Journey Planning

obvious that calls 1 and 8 and calls 7 and 14 are close enough to be done in sequence. If a whole week is plotted in this way, stores will be seen to group in a way which enables a journey of much better fit to be produced. The work-study man's ideal would look something like Figure 12. Two points are of special interest. Firstly, the journeys are plotted as straight lines. In fact, they will not be absolutely straight, but the principle is clear: there is no retracing of steps, no travelling half way out, lunching, and then re-passing the same towns to finish the calls. Secondly, like the rest of us, the salesman now commutes to and from work; he no longer starts from home. (The dotted lines represent his journey to the first call and back home from the last.)

When all this work has been done, the necessary number of salesmen can be arrived at. To take a simple example:

Outlets = 40,000
Possible Average Calls per Day = 12
Sales Cycle = 4 Weeks
Selling Days per Cycle = 4 × 5 = 20
Therefore: Calls per Cycle = 20 × 12 = 240

$$\text{Men Required} = \frac{40,000}{240}$$

= approximately 167

To this will be added the chosen ratios of managers to salesmen and allowances for spares, reliefs, any pioneer salesmen and so on. (Normal management ratios vary from one manager to seven salesmen to one to twelve but seldom more than five managers to one more senior manager.) Work-study has enormous practical and financial advantages for the sales force but to be most effective it should be a continuing activity.

I recently conducted some not very scientific research by asking a random (but not truly representative) sample of sales directors what universe they called upon and how many men they employed in direct selling to that universe. I may say that I was staggered to find that most of my sample couldn't answer without reference to someone else. The results showed the largest sales force to be 902 and the smallest six – both dealing with the same trade and both enjoying roughly equal levels of distribution. Those were extremes, for one dealt only through wholesalers and direct orders from retailers whilst the other was a van sales force. More revealing was the difference in opinion between companies in the same business about how many shops they should call on to get the lion's share of the trade and the fact that where there was a reasonable level of agreement they used sales forces of wildly different sizes to deal with the universe. There is clearly room for a great deal of controlled experiment.

Training the Sales Force

We have already concluded that there is no one single salesman type, but there are types who seem particularly suited to certain kinds of sales task. The identification in recruitment of these types is thus critical. But can a man who can go out cold to an unknown non-stockist and sell toothpaste do the same with motor tyres: can a salesman sell anything?

The answer is a qualified 'yes'. A good salesman is an effective communicator (which means a good listener as well as a good speaker). He is adept at knowing when to close the deal and even when to close the interview without selling the deal. He is expert at interpreting the involuntary flicker of interest, at overcoming objections and identifying opportunities of presenting positive benefits. These attributes will stand him in good stead in any selling job. The first major qualification must be that selling skill can only be effectively transferred from one field to another if the salesman can really believe in his product: he will not successfully sell something he has a strong moral objection to. He will not be able to sell effectively something which he does not understand sufficiently to be able to relate its benefits to the customer's needs. The major training need is product knowledge.

The need for early product knowledge is most recognized in the fields of industrial, consumer durable and pharmaceutical selling. It is frequently skimped with products like food and toothpaste. A good salesman is a man who knows that his responsibility for the product doesn't cease until the consumer has used it in good condition. This means that he must understand the hazards to which his product can be exposed, how to recognize the date code and so on. Perhaps I know more about tea salesmen than any other kind so let me demonstrate the point by example. A good tea salesman has a 'feel', a 'nose' for tea. He instinctively picks up packets and looks at the code date. He uplifts outdated stock. Where long- and short-dated stock is on the same shelf he puts the older nearer the front so that it is sold whilst still in good condition. He can size up a stockroom at a glance and see if it is too damp for the storage of tea, if the parcels are off the ground (as they should be), if they will be subject to extremes of temperature. It is second nature to him to check that the tea isn't stored too close to sides of bacon or on the shelves next to jellies or any other highly flavoured product whose scent might permeate the tea packet. This is the kind of knowledge that puts a qualification before the word 'salesman' and makes him a typewriter salesman or a dairy-produce salesman or any other kind of specialized salesman.

After product knowledge comes trade knowledge. What conventions do they observe? Who buys what? What levels of authority exist? How do they calculate their profit mark-up or mark-down (as the percentage increase required to make wholesale price the retail price or buying price as a percentage of retail price)?

When the product and the trade are understood, it is time to introduce the new salesman to the techniques, conventions and reporting procedures of your organization. All training should be as practical as possible, but this aspect is best learned by observing and doing. Thus the initial training of a salesman will be both in the classroom (which may well be his own home with his local manager) and on the job with an experienced salesman chosen for his ability to explain clearly what he is doing and why. These men are frequently designated 'salesmen trainers'. Gradually, the newcomer will sell with his trainer alongside him until he is ready to be left alone. From then on, he should be trained continuously, by accompaniment, by refresher courses, by specialist courses in narrow areas of his job – perhaps to encourage him to become a specialist of some sort.

One area of in-class training that has become extremely important in the fast-moving consumer goods field is merchandising: building creative displays, calculating profits at various price levels, doing simple lettering and construction. There is a split in opinion as to whether a salesman should do his own merchandising or have specialist merchandisers following him around. Firstly, this depends on the nature of the task. Specialist merchandisers are very necessary for shops which do not normally receive a selling call: many voluntary group shops and some multiples served from central depots come into this category. Secondly, what do you mean by merchandising? If it is a matter of shelf-filling, pricing and perhaps getting several thousand display pieces around, not only may merchandisers be the best people to do it, but a contract merchandising force (where the cost is lower because it is shared with other manufacturers) may be an even better answer. Where a major feature is all part of the total negotiation with the store and involves the total business and creative complicity of salesman and customer, then (having tried both ways) I unhesitatingly plump for this kind of merchandising being part of the total role of the salesman and his calling time should recognize this.

One can only generalize about training, for the needs of every business differ and the funds available for training vary from firm to firm. Good sales training managers are like gold-dust: very hard to find. Many companies fear that by over-indulgence in training, they will become a sort of university from which competitors will continually cream off the talent. Of course it happens. However, take comfort from some of the findings of the research by Newton already referred to. He found that the turnover rate of a sales force, surprisingly, did *not* affect its performance index, although a turnover rate of ten per cent (which is low in my experience) is costly in the absolute terms of recruitment and training costs. A well-trained man expects better job satisfaction and opportunity. It is lack of these that primarily affects turnover and a good offer from outside tips the balance more easily where these things are lacking.

Finally, remember the training value of accompaniments (especially when the manager demonstrates by taking a call) and area meetings where experience can be pooled. But please, please keep it human. Don't reduce everything to slavish use of check-lists. I once accompanied a salesman who, his area manager told me, just could not close a sale. He took an order in every call we made. When I checked his records I discovered that he had exceeded his bonus target by a handsome amount in every quarter he had been with the company! He wasn't doing it by the book, but he was getting the orders. We changed the area manager! Managers need training too, something too often forgotten or regarded as a luxury.

Control of the Sales Force

Although cost control is a vital though frequently neglected area of overall sales force control, I want to deal broadly only with the 'creative' use of sales and call statistics for the moment: cost of control comes elsewhere.

The first thing to understand about all sales statistics is that they are just history. They don't tell you what is going to happen. This realization leads to two fundamental disciplines for anyone who calls for sales records:

1. What can you do with them?
2. Who can use them best?

A tremendous amount of information is generated which is produced in such a way that no remedial action is identifiable or indicated and too much goes to the wrong people. Too much paper gives you indigestion as surely as too much food. Eventually you ignore most of what you get across your desk, the valuable as well as the useless.

The person who is best able to take action is the man on the spot. The information collected for Head Office should be summary information in the main, provided the man on the spot has the sort of statistics that enable him to identify which men, which products and which customers are responsible for good or bad results. In summary, then, there are three main classes of sales report:

1. Sales and call information.
2. Identification of problems.
3. Special reports.

Sales and call information should be designed for the man on the spot, safe in the knowledge that the information can be summarized both nationally and regionally for senior management. This will record sales against targets, percentage achievement at various times (e.g. seventy-five per cent of target achieved at fifty per cent of time gone), comparisons with other relevant periods and details of calls achieved and the ratio of orders to calls.

This last is an important control item. There is a favourite American selling story about the lousiest typewriter salesman in the business. Everyone knew he would have to go but his sales manager decided to use him for one last experiment. He sent him to the top floor of the Woolworth building with the strict instruction to poke his head round every office door in the building, working his way down. All he had to do was say, 'You don't want a new typewriter, do you?' If they said 'no', he just went on to the next office. If they said they were interested, then he was to walk in, plonk his typewriter down on the desk and keep his mouth shut! If they asked any questions, he was to say, 'I'm very sorry, I'm a new salesman with this company. I don't know anything about this product. All they have given me is this typewriter and the price.'

He broke every sales record in the company and kept his job. That seems to prove something . . . like 'If you don't make the calls, you don't sell the goods'!

How often should these statistics be published? It depends a great deal on the business but in few businesses are reports received daily of much value. The next call on that outlet will be at least a week away and most managers leave home before the post arrives, which makes the daily report two days old at least by the time he gets it. If he then critically assesses each one for all his men, half his day has gone. My personal preference is for weekly records with daily performance incorporated and period-to-date totals against targets for, say, the sales cycle, the quarter and the year (or whatever other periods may be appropriate).

Now from these you can derive part of your identification figures: you will know which men are above or below par, but you won't know where or why unless you have customer records, channel of sales statistics and any other relevant breakdowns. For local management use, channel of sales statistics are usually enough. If Bill Bloggs is low on sales to multiple grocers, you can go back to his own sales records to discover that he failed to get an order from Tesco. For the region (and the country) it will probably be worth taking out a total for Tesco as a whole – knowing that you can identify which region is out of line, the region can identify the area and the area manager can identify the salesman. This is still historical information but it can be put to good purpose because you can identify the opportunity and problem areas precisely.

Finally, special reports may be required to measure, say, sales before, during and after a special promotion. It may easily be possible to do this from other existing records. It often becomes necessary to arrange some specially collated report because a promotion with one customer may cross reporting boundaries.

Later in this book we shall consider the role of the computer. Clearly it can be of enormous value here. However, the temptation to produce too much information becomes even greater. As Professor A. M. McDonough once said: 'The enormous capacity of the computer may lead us to build monuments of useless data that may be remembered long after the pyramids are forgotten.'

Information is data selected to fit a need. How little do you need and who needs it? You can answer that by asking two more questions: What will influence our actions and what detailed classifications do we need to take action? The information you collect must simplify the task of controlling the sales force.

Payment by Results

The phrase 'generous commission' features in most advertisements for salesmen. The majority of salesmen earn some proportion of their total earnings in the form of commission, the average appearing to be about fifteen per cent of total earnings. There are, however, still salesmen paid only commission and expenses and a growing number earning only a basic salary. The decision is obviously a company one, related to the business need and not necessarily once and for all. There are ways of paying incentive bonuses for particular achievements which do not have to become part of the scenery. Beware, however, of those that do. A salesman can't get a mortgage on the bonus element of his salary but he may take on other credit commitments. A bad period will put him into hot water and the bad period may be as much a result of poor sales targeting as of ineffective selling.

The simplest form of payment by results is some element of bonus on every sale made: so much per lb, per case, per ton, per machine, per £100. It is easy to calculate and the salesman knows precisely where he stands at any point of time. If he wants to earn £50, he knows what he has to do. However, this system does put sales achievement too much in the hands of the salesman who can literally determine his own target. Taxation levels being what they are, there may be a tendency to ease off at a certain level. Payment on a unit basis is, thus, usually made only for sales in excess of quota.

There are many more complex ways of paying for sales above target; how complicated the system is will depend very much upon the complexity of the company's business. A sales force selling, say, bread and cakes may have a two-part bonus scheme. Payment will be made for exceeding target on either cakes or bread but a higher rate will be paid for exceeding target on both – an encouragement to selling across the range. Most systems of this kind use defined payments for certain brackets of achievement, for example:

Target Level	Payment
100%	£5
100–105	£7
105–110	£10
110–120	£20
and so on.	

Many companies believe in making the first payment at a

level below 100 per cent to allow for possible errors and unforeseen events. Personally, I oppose any suggestion that a
salesman should be paid for not reaching the target upon which
the company bases its well-being. Adjustments can always be
made at the discretion of Senior Management in genuine circumstances (such as the transfer of direct calls credited to one
area to central delivery credited to another).

Within such systems, incredible degrees of complexity can be
introduced. Certain products can be assigned weights, payment can be withheld unless a minimum figure is achieved on
each product, distribution increases can be allied to volume
targets. However, it is generally true that the more complex the
scheme becomes, the less effectively does it spur the salesman
on.

Many companies use various kinds of points schemes, usually
tied to some special prize or a gift catalogue. This may be used
alone or on top of a conventional bonus scheme. They have the
great advantage of flexibility: you can telegraph all salesmen
with the news that, for the next two weeks, all new non-life
policies qualify for double points. They can be especially effective for new products, distribution drives and special promotions. They should be regarded as exciting, creative
promotions in themselves and presented in the most enter-
prising way to the sales force. One important caution: they lose
their effectiveness if they go on too long or if the points
awarded do not allow the salesman to collect something worthwhile in a reasonably short period.

Finally, as far as the salesman is concerned, should he be
targeted by volume, turnover or profit? Most are targeted by
volume, which overcomes problems of pack and case sizes. A
man selling a computer cannot be targeted this way and his
usual measure is turnover. Profit, however, is the ideal. Few
companies use this as a standard for setting the sales quota
although most would prefer their salesmen to sell the more
profitable item. A common compromise is the use of 'standard
units' as a measure. If product A yields £1 profit but product B
yields £2, A is rated as one standard unit and B as two. The
salesman gets twice the benefit from selling B as from selling

A. However, common sense must prevail. If A is a growing brand and B a declining one, there may be a good reason either to rate them the same or to look to total profit rather than unit profit and give A the higher rating.

The argument against bonus payments is twofold. Firstly, a salesman should earn a decent living wage which should not be subject to variations which are not always within his control. Secondly, the end of a bonus period in particular encourages selling to, not selling through, retailers and this is anathema to modern Marketing thought. However, the majority of salesmen welcome the chance to supplement their basic wage by their own efforts. I can quote only three cases from personal experience but I feel they must have been repeated many times. One company dropped bonus entirely and commuted it into a higher salary: sales progress slowed dramatically. A second changed from a bonus paid on area achievement to one paid on individual results, the third introduced individual bonus payments for the first time. In each of the last two cases, sales rose significantly from the date of the change to individual payments.

Who should be included? Some companies give individual payments by results to salesmen, payments on area results to area managers and so on up the scale. The argument goes that a manager earning bonus on the results of his team will push all his team hard. The other extreme is not to pay any manager a bonus for fear that this will lead him to stock-pile to achieve results which may not be to the longer-term benefits of the company. There are various intermediate solutions between these extremes. Again a personal view: it makes good sense to give bonus incentives only to managers where their span of control is small. Thus an area manager with eight men could well qualify. However, although the regional manager might have only five area managers to control, his bonus would be dependent upon the efforts of forty salesmen and five managers. This is too much.

What is a bonus – or an extra trade discount for volume above datum? In cases where bonus is paid above a defined quota it is a sharing of extra profit between the company and its salesmen. Extra profit arises because although no new men have been employed they are selling more than was budgeted; the costs per unit are lower. However, this concept can be badly disrupted if achievement is unevenly spread across the year.

Setting the Target

The sales force target is probably only one of many the company uses. The 100 per cent level, however, should ideally be the one the company is using for its financial budgeting. Far too many companies adopt a different and arbitrary figure like 'last year plus ten per cent'. Any target presented to a sales force should be attainable – albeit at a stretch – in the light of the support the salesmen will be given. Room for manoeuvre should be allowed and if the sales manager really can convince you that the first figure you thought of is really not on, then the other estimates – production, raw materials, distribution and financial – must be changed.

Most sales force targets are set by projecting a national figure, breaking it down according to the percentage each territory accounted for last year and adjusting by trends revealed by territories. For example, London may have accounted for twenty-five per cent last year but it was only twenty-three per cent the year before and twenty per cent before that. There is a clear upward trend here that, other things being equal, should be allowed for.

The more sophisticated targets (requiring the use of computers) are built up by projection of trends of individual units (shops, hospitals, factories) and then amalgamated into territories from which a final national total is produced. Thus one can break out both long- and short-term forecasts by product, size, price, customer, channel, time period and so on.

There are many mathematical techniques for sales forecasting but none does more than produce the sort of line that a good free-hand curve projected from an existing graph will produce. The advantage of mathematical techniques is that they enable one to determine the average slope of the curve – which is not always discernible to the human eye – and to give different weights to different periods of time. The simpler techniques of moving averages, seasonal trends and exponential smoothing can be quickly mastered from any good textbook and are especially valuable with products which fluctuate considerably.

From time to time, the need may arise to consider giving the sales force a psychological target rather than an exact one. For example, if your company has taken a pasting over the last three periods and very few men have earned any bonus at all, there *may* be a case for giving them something which is attainable. The opportunity to earn again may produce a lesser shortfall on the original target than the effect of knowing that they aren't going to earn again this period. One may wish to do it the other way round and stretch a too successful sales force a little more. These are valid techniques but they should be used with extreme caution, for they can easily blow back in your face.

Sales and Distribution

It is a rare company that has its sales organization and physical distribution in balance. Where the sales force dominates, delivery costs and the cost of holding packed stocks can be very high, affecting both capital and expenses. The tendency is for such sales forces to expect delivery within twenty-four hours against demand, however small. Retailers frequently make contact with distribution depots direct. Where the distribution department dominates, there is a danger that the effort to perform well as a cost centre may result in less than optimum service for the customer. The ideals of the sales force and the distribution department are irreconcilable. The one needs stock available for immediate delivery and standby drivers; the other requires the minimum of packed stock, no waiting drivers and all vans 100 per cent full – preferably going and coming back! Reconciliation must come in such terms as what level of risk are we going to take of not being able to supply a customer within so many days; how much are we prepared to invest in warehouses, packed stock, fork-lift trucks and vehicles? As with so many other areas of Marketing, it is a matter of achieving the best fit: the most profitable mix at the least risk. Science is creeping into distribution scheduling, and major changes and economies can be expected in those companies which employ the latest techniques. However, the distribution department should never forget its Marketing responsibility – to service its customers in the most effective and efficient way.

Retailers' Attitudes to Salesmen

I have commissioned two pieces of research on this subject at an interval of seven years. The results (dealing with the grocery trade) were surprising and remarkably similar although quite different techniques were used. Despite the frequent complaints about time spent (some claim wasted) on salesmen, research showed that the great majority of retailers looked forward to the thrust and parry of the sales pitch. They had profound respect for those who did the job well and these they regarded as salesmen who expressed the benefits of the product in terms of profit to the retailer, knew their product and their competitors and were loyal to their company. Disloyalty was seen as a cardinal sin. Retailers wanted information: facts and figures, details and diagrams.

Retailers liked salesmen who were customer-orientated without being disloyal to their firm or their superiors. The loneliness of the salesman showed transparently. The more cut off from his company he felt, the more likely he was to side with his customer – often against his company. On the other hand, certain companies produced salesmen who were aggressively company-centred and, on the whole, these were thrusting, showed little awareness of the customer's problems and were frequently intensely disliked. Perhaps we could sum it all up by saying that retailers like a friendly fight but on the business level: the more you talk about their business, the less they will fight and the more friendly they are.

The book *How British Industry Buys* reveals that industrial buyers like salesmen's calls, whatever they might say to the contrary. They rated salesmen's visits the prime source of information about new products and developments. However, they resent service calls which, they feel, could be done better and with less time wasted on both sides by telephone. This probably applies to many other fields, and telephone selling for replenishment supplies is common in frozen food, ice-cream and catering sales forces.

Managing the Sales Force

A sales force of any size is managed at various levels. I want to assume (and I argue the case elsewhere) that the Marketing Director is the ultimate figurehead for the sales force – even though control may be exercised through a general sales manager or field sales managers – and suggest ways in which he and the Chief Executive should influence the management of the sales force and how they should behave towards it. Firstly, remember the isolation of the salesman. He needs continual contact and encouragement from the centre. Many Chief Executives and Marketing Directors write to all salesmen only when they have cause to complain. Write with good news, tell them about the latest big order, the fact that you have moved up one place in the league table, prevent rumour by communicating facts about resignations, promotions, etc (if they are important enough). I always used a special italic type for my personal letters to salesmen if it was a letter of congratulation, promotion or other good news. It stood out on the mat amongst the pile of computer cards, daily report forms, bills and other unwanted circulars! Give salesmen every possible reason to feel proud of their company. It does help to know that your colleague at the other end of the country has just landed a big order.

Spend time with salesmen and their managers but don't expect a royal tour or special treatment. Many years ago, a certain district manager always arranged a splendid display of grocery products in the window of the shop at the corner of the street where his depot was and arranged it to correspond with the day when his general manager and his sales manager made their annual inspection. For the rest of the year, the shop was a

tobacconist's! The salesman has a job to do. Don't interfere
with it by dragging him miles off his journey to collect you or
upset his call time by long chats with the buyer. After all, you
wouldn't expect a machine operative to bring his plant to your
office and take it to bits to show you how it works.

House journals help the salesman feel that he belongs and,
with large sales forces, there may be a case of them having their
own magazine. Local bulletins serve a valuable purpose by
communicating product and promotional information, giving
performance figures and congratulating the successful and
encouraging the sluggards. (This is part of managing by
results.)

The Chief Executive and Marketing Director should be
vitally interested in management succession. At Lyons, my
two field sales managers and I used to play a game we called
the 'No 11 bus'. This uncontrollable vehicle was in constant
danger of decimating our sales force! Cards were written out
for all levels and the names of individuals printed on them. I
would then turn one over at random – the victim of the No 11
bus. We would then debate his replacement. Sometimes it
would be obvious. 'Joe Smith must be our next regional
manager, he could go anywhere.' Another time the answer
might be, 'Joe Smith will outpace Bill Jones who is already
in charge of Scunthorpe. Scunthorpe is more important to us
than Weston-super-Mare, let's move Bill to Weston-super-
Mare and put Joe into Scunthorpe.' On other occasions we
would find ourselves saying, 'Anywhere else Joe would be the
right man but the Scots will never take to him', or 'The personal chemistry is all wrong.' Try it. You'll find that the
'obvious' candidate may not be right for particular circumstances. There are horses for courses and there are complementary and opposite personalities. Obviously this exercise
can only be done if regular checks are made by accompaniment on all salesmen and managers recommended by their
superiors.

Another management trick. When you are interviewing, see
some of your own men whom you have already passed over.
We are often unfair to people we know well whereas we accept

an expert performance (which any salesman ought to be able to give) in a comparatively short interview. It then takes time to find out that his sins are worse than those of the man you passed over before looking outside. Your own people may look even better under interview conditions. You also have a well-tested standard against which you can judge the outside applicants.

All the techniques of man management can and should be applied to the control of a sales force. It is essential, therefore, that all levels of management receive training according to their station and are continuously trained along the path of management development. Selection is clearly critical. The first stage of promotion to management exposes a salesman to a new situation for which he has received no previous training. Yesterday he was a salesman; today he is a manager. This is a big step and he will need careful handling and guidance. But what about those who are passed over? One must recognize that those who are excellent salesmen do not necessarily possess the qualities necessary in a good manager. They should not be penalized for this. The more progressive companies adopt a salary structure which gives such men ample reward for the job they are good at. Whilst they may never earn as much as the manager above them can earn if he progresses well, they will earn more than junior managers in each grade. A typical example is given in Figure 13. The upper point of the salesman's salary bracket is above that of his area manager; the area manager's is above the lowest point of the regional manager. Of course, this theory is often disturbed by the level a man is on when he is transferred. Obviously, he will get an increase either when he is promoted or when he has served a satisfactory probation period. As one would expect, the higher one goes, the less the gap up to the point where it is unreasonable that the general sales manager should have to earn less than his regional managers. Total average earnings have to be taken into account, especially where some levels earn bonus whilst others do not. This whole theory works best at the lower levels but it has much to commend it.

Finally, remember that when a salesman joins your company his family joins too. They accept a way of life which means

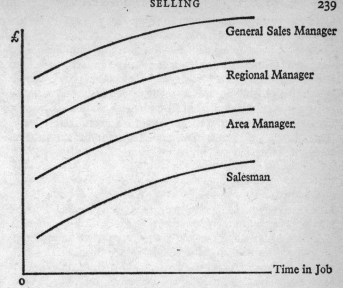

£

General Sales Manager

Regional Manager

Area Manager

Salesman

Time in Job

o

Figure 13. Graduated Sales Force Salary Brackets

moving home frequently, with all its associated trauma, children changing schools, making new friends and so on. Managing a sales force, directly or by delegation, requires recognition of these points and action policy for removal and disturbance allowances, travel allowances for the man whose family stays in the old home until the child has taken a vital school examination, and hundreds of other points which make running a sales force so excitingly and often exasperatingly different from any other kind of management.

Conclusion

In very few companies does any item in the total mix assume more importance for a going product than selling. Good selling has overcome bad advertising and presentation: it doesn't happen the other way round. In the small company money spent on one more salesman almost invariably produces a greater return than cash spent in any other area. A salesman is an expensive but valuable asset.

One last little experiment for you to try as an indication of the extent of empathy in a salesman. Meet him at the end of the day and ask him, 'How's business?' Unless there has been one outstanding highlight that has really made his day, he will play back the result of his last call and the opinions of his last customer! So when you accompany a salesman, try always to leave him on a high note of encouragement and congratulation where it is due.

Reference

1. Derek A. Newton, 'Get the Most Out of Your Sales Force', *Harvard Business Review*, September–October 1969.

Suggestions for Further Reading

J. O'Shaughnessy has published, through the British Institute of Management, an excellent practical approach to *Work Study Applied to a Sales Force*. Leslie Rodger (op cit) has some sound good sense in his Chapter 5 and Lawrence Fisher (op cit) does the same for industrial selling in Chapters 10 and 11 of his book. Douglas Smallbone's Chapters 5 and 7 of *The Practice of Marketing*, published by Staples Press, are also valuable. For a complete and thorough treatise, however, read Cyril Hudson's *Professional Salesmanship* from Staples Press, 1967.

Chapter 16

Advertising

So many people equate advertising with Marketing that I have deliberately relegated the subject both to a late stage in this book and a minor role. Indeed, many companies who really should know better fall into the trap of divorcing the two words. Try counting the number of advertising agencies who call themselves something like 'Bloggs and Co, Advertising and Marketing'. You will have identified a list of agencies who don't know what Marketing is and that should be valuable!

Why Advertise?

No one should think that a business has to advertise. In terms of sheer effectiveness, the pecking order of persuasion would probably be:

1. Personal recommendation. (Witness the remarkable early success of Wilkinson razor blades which, fostered by shortage, relied almost entirely on word-of-mouth personal recommendation.)
2. Blanket, door-to-door coverage by salesmen.
3. Advertising.

We use advertising because it is the most economic way of achieving the kind of coverage of potential buyers that makes for viable businesses. There are more effective methods but they are much slower and more costly in both absolute and relative terms.

However, there will be businesses whose market is easily contacted who will find one or both of the first two methods of persuasion both more effective and more economic. Most advertising media are wasted on someone who is not a potential buyer and the more localized and specialized your product the less reliance you are likely to place on conventional media advertising. Therefore, advertising should fall into place in the total Marketing mix as a sort of optional extra, to be used only if it is likely to be productive and affordable.

The first reason for advertising is to generate more profit than you would have done without advertising. Money spent on advertising should be seen as income-generating expenditure. This statement is just as appropriate on a downward sales trend as on an upward one. We can say, in a facile way, that advertising expenditure should always break even, that it should at least produce enough revenue to pay for itself and that ideally it should do much more than that. But we all know that situations have to be faced where we are forced to spend money in an attempt to hold a rate of decline to no more than the market rate, say. In such circumstances, there may well be an 'investment' element in the expenditure (in the sense that one is spending above a costed rate) but this is justifiable if, by advertising, the product makes a greater contribution to total company costs and expenses than it would have done if it were unsupported. The moment it can be demonstrated that your product is not doing better with advertising than without it, you either shouldn't be spending at all or you are spending too much.

The second purpose of advertising is to inform in a way which will result in demand. (There is, of course, a great deal of advertising whose purpose is purely to inform and which has no profit motive: examples vary from store names to public service – health, safety, etc – advertising in conventional media.) The simple model of the advertising process upon which generations of advertising men and businessmen have been brought up is based upon the mythical lady AIDA:

> Attention
> Interest
> Desire
> Action.

Arouse people's attention, interest them and create a desire. Desire and demand, as we have seen, are two quite different things and the circle is not complete until there is buying action.

A more sophisticated model is the DAGMAR communications spectrum (Figure 14) which shows the transition from unawareness through understanding and ultimate con-

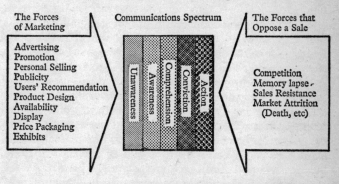

Figure 14. DAGMAR Communications Spectrum

viction to action as a wedge of situations between all the forces that attempt to create use (the Marketing mix) and those forces that oppose a sale. The point is made very clearly by this model that advertising is only one of the forces, and not invariably the best, that must pass through the communications spectrum and compete convincingly against the opposing forces before a sale is made. The time lag will vary considerably by product and by the time it takes for a potential buyer to move from stage to stage. It is quite common in, say, the grocery field for comprehension and even conviction to be high but for sales resistance (perhaps as brand loyalty) to prevent the final move to action.

We shall not be dealing with how to advertise or where to advertise but rather with financial and management problems, with a brief excursion into a fringe area and some consideration of the public's attitude to advertising, and questions of morality and advertising. However, having decided to advertise, one has to make an impact, do so with sufficient frequency to be memorable and achieve as complete a coverage of one's market as possible. As David Ogilvy has said, 'You can't save souls in an empty church!'

Setting the Budget

Advertising agencies commonly believe that there are only two methods used by the client in deciding how much to spend: by guess and by God! On the other hand, the commission system of agency remuneration has encouraged clients to believe that the agency is interested in recommending the highest figure they think they can get away with. Unfortunately, there are no guiding laws, not even guiding rules; only sets of signposts. They are most inadequate signposts too. They leave you feeling rather like the frustrated motorist diverted by the police only to find that once he is on the new route no one has thought to put up any more directions on how to get back on to the original road. The whole broad area of setting advertising appropriations, controlling the expenditure and assessing the results is full of hunch, guesswork, 'experience tells us' and – only very occasionally – a little research. Because there are no reliable rules and because we know so little about how advertising really works, most companies base their appropriations on some concept of 'what we can afford'. They prefer methods which are easy to calculate, can be readily compared with other years and other standard costs and – above all – guarantee that the expenditure is at least affordable if the sales targets they are based upon are achieved.

I have distinguished five methods of setting appropriations in current use. They are not mutually exclusive, they overlap and the discussion becomes almost circular, for what begins as one method frequently settles down to become another. Moreover, the part played by good old-fashioned compromise must never be minimized. A company with agreed yardsticks may change for just one year because of competing demands on resources, and sudden cuts are sometimes made to make year-end figures look good. Some companies even go to the other extreme if they have had an unusually successful year which they feel is unlikely to be repeated. The best solution to the question of setting the advertising appropriation may not necessarily be the best solution for the total business and any Marketing man and any agency executive will know that, however apparently rigid the system, figures get trimmed and altered to fit current circumstances. The value of these yardstick methods is in the ease with which they can be understood and rationalized both to superiors and subordinates. The dangers come from over-slavish adherence under changing circumstances.

1. *Historical:*

There are subtle variations of this method but the basis is the application of some factor to past sales (e.g. five per cent of last year's sales, £1 per case on last year's sales, etc). Its advantage, theoretically, is that you are spending money you've already earned. Theoretically! I don't know any company that carries over money from one year to another in any form other than reserves and I am not personally aware of any company that finances its advertising out of its reserves. In fact, one is really saying that this year's sales will at least equal last year's . . . or there is going to be a nasty shock!

The one time this method has real merit is when sales are going steadily upwards. Conversely, it has real disadvantage when sales are going down. In the latter case, one may run the danger of not spending enough to get out of trouble. Even in the case of rising sales, one may not spend at the optimum rate required to *maximize* sales opportunities. Not only does the danger arise of not spending enough on these specific occasions, but also there is the danger of spending too much because the formula allows it. This leads to the allied danger of still spending when the time has really come to stop.

But how was the factor set in the first place? Probably by reference to some other yardstick!

2. *Anticipation:*

This is nothing more than a refinement of the 'historical' method. Instead of looking back, you look forward. Budget anticipated sales, apply a factor of some sort – and there's your appropriation! This method does have the advantage that relationship to the future is usually more reasonable than relationship to the past. Anticipated success can be exploited and an expected downturn can also be allowed for.

However, applied uncritically, this method, too, has dangers. A simple percentage applied to an anticipated fall in sales is unlikely to do anything about reversing the trend. And, of course, estimates are notoriously inaccurate! This causes problems! Cancellation dates are long – especially for colour magazines and posters – and expenditure cannot always be adjusted rapidly enough to counter loss of expected revenue. It's usually rather easier to buy extra advertising time or space at short notice, although at certain times and in certain media that isn't always possible.

Some of the worst excesses in brand management have been committed in the name of this method. There is a grave temptation to decide how much money one would like to spend and produce that sales figure which justifies it. But you must have used some other method to decide how much to justify.

At this point, it is worth our while to consider the problem of the factor used in each of these first two methods. These can be grouped into case-rate methods and tonnage systems.

The case rate (£ per case, per pack, etc) is simple to calculate. A case is always a case and you can ignore changes in weight and price if you wish. However, there are dangers in ignoring such changes. When price goes up, a higher level of advertising may be called for. Conversely, a lower price may need less money spent on promotion.

Tonnage rates are easier to use where a product is available in different sizes and weights. This method is particularly favoured for joint industry campaigns (e.g. the Tea Council). Problems occur when weights are changed but prices aren't (e.g. the confectionery industry) and where the same number of packs continue to be sold although the weight per pack has changed. If you sell the same number of bars of chocolate as before but now there is less chocolate per bar, gross profit has increased. You could afford more advertising. However, because the actual weight has declined, you actually spend less! (The reverse is true when weight is increased without a commensurate rise in unit sales.)

One can never say with absolute certainty that a price rise needs a higher level of advertising. You may well, in fact, decide to spend heavily to make people aware that your price has been reduced. The message I want to get across is that whenever market circumstances change, the yardstick ratio must be reconsidered. This may be the time to compromise and say, 'I know the costing only allows ten per cent for advertising, but since our tonnage is going to fall because we are putting less chocolate in the bar, we must spend what we originally planned even if the ratio rises to twelve per cent.' There are no hard and fast rules which prevent your taking either offensive or defensive action.

3. *Competition:*
Very simply: how much is the other guy spending? Some regard to your competitor's activity must be built into any consideration of appropriation size. After all, you want to be seen and heard.

But who is your competitor and must you imitate him? The number of advertisements one is exposed to in an average day is horrifying. You can't set out to fight them all, but you must acknowledge that they all compete in some way for your prospect's attention. Again, one must never be uncritical. Are your direct competitors overspending or underspending? in the right media? using the right message? and so on. All in all, looking at your competitor's activity is likely to lead you to consider the *quality* rather than the quantity of your advertising.

One frequently hears Marketing men speak of the 'cost of

the club', meaning that a certain level of advertising expenditure represents the minimum entrance fee to any particular market. This is often true of the major section of the market but not of segments. Moreover, it has been demonstrated many times that high total advertising expenditure does not prevent the entry of competitors unless supported by clear product superiority (measured, of course, in consumer terms). The Wilkinson Sword Edge blade made such a breakthrough in the razor blade market against the might of Gillette; Xerox successfully invaded the copying machine market; Japanese motor-cycles have ousted many traditional British makes; before the swing to greaseless hairdressings, Brylcreem broke through in the strongly held field of men's hairdressings in the USA.

Following competitors' rates and ratios can be dangerous: how did he arrive at his figure? Perhaps he just plucked it out of the air. Someone else's guess can all too easily become the yardstick for the industry.

4. *The Task Approach:*
In its classic form, this method starts with a definition of the marketing objectives and then calculates how much will need to be spent to achieve them. If that sum is not affordable, something has to give; you must set your sights lower. As a method it is close to the ideal and it is certainly part of any really sophisticated approach to setting advertising budgets. By definition, it is a method which ensures the right relationship between objectives and cost. Nothing is going to be spent unless there is a fair chance of the money producing the desired result.

Unfortunately, however, there is no such thing as an 'ideal' advertising campaign. Rather than search for this mythical optimum, it is better to use the task approach as a means of setting the lowest or the highest rate of advertising necessary to achieve any given objective. Very few advertising agencies will agree on the coverage needed to reach all parts of the potential market: it's hard enough to agree on the potential market! Then there is the problem of what *weight* of advertising is required to make an effective impact – and what is an effective impact? As a method, the task approach has the great advantage of involving the total business rather than considering advertising in isolation. In practice, the method tends to be used in the following way.

It starts with a costing discipline. It assumes a ruling price and it assumes that that price is fixed in the short run. When the product is fully costed out, one is left with a certain percentage available for net profit and promotion.

Now, in this particular model, net profit is the key figure. The company has clearly defined profit goals and it will not succeed long-term unless it regularly achieves those objectives. Thus, in effect, the residual is advertising.

In the light of what has happened in the past, what is forecast to happen in the future, what our competitors are doing, and what turnover, brand share and profit goals we wish to achieve – we arrive at a cost for the job.

Is the advertising allowance in the costings enough to do the job? Supposing it isn't, what are the alternatives?

    (a) Aim to do rather less?

    (b) Forgo some net profit now (i.e. 'invest')?

    (c) Cut some other costs?

    (d) Put up the price?

This is not the place to examine the validity (or the ethics) of these alternatives. What must be seen clearly is that an advertising rate arrived at this way (rather than by the 'historical' or 'anticipation' methods) is not a *carte blanche* to spend but, rather, a *discipline on spending*. If you overspend your advertising rate without cost savings elsewhere, you cannot achieve your net profit objective. The decision is a total business one, not solely an advertising problem.

5. *Residual:*

Instead of costing to the point where the difference between selling price and total costs equals net profit, in this method there is no set advertising allowance and the residual is the 'sum available for profit and promotion'. Some decision then has to be reached on how much is going to be spent on advertising. And the minimum or maximum will probably be set by the 'cost of the job' method!

In a philosophical way, this method has a lot to commend it. All promotional expenditure must be income-generating expenditure, or it isn't worth doing. Conscious investment, on the other hand, is a deliberate reduction of net profit now to produce more later. Thus, in some respects advertising is complementary to net profit; in others, it is an alternative. Practically, however, it is an essentially short-period method. It isn't long before a certain level of advertising or net profit (usually the latter) becomes the norm. You are then likely to end up with a fairly rigid system in which there are standard ratios for every item of cost – including advertising. We have now turned the full cycle, back to a standard advertising/sales ratio!

Decision Theory and Appropriation Setting

The principles of subjective quantification are likely to play an increasing part in reconciling the task approach with the advertising budget on the one hand and the sales target on the other. Both are created under conditions of varying degrees of uncertainty and the assessment of reasoned probabilities can be of great value.

The first stage in such an operation is to take the actual state of affairs (turnover, cost per unit, appropriation and profit) and compare it with calculations for lesser and higher levels of turnover *but assuming no change* in advertising expenditure. One cautionary note. When doing this sort of calculation you must be particularly careful how you treat overhead expenses and you must take cognizance of the levels at which new capital expenditure may be necessary. Everything possible must be done to calculate true net profit at each turnover level.

All that is reasonably factual. You can go no further without being subjective. We are now going to postulate how much we ought to spend to achieve various turnovers. What are we trying to achieve? How important should advertising be in the total mix? What about the other ingredients: production capacity, sales force effectiveness, in-store distribution, likely response rates and so on as appropriate to your business ? Then decide whether this is to be an investment year or whether you plan to run your advertising at rates likely to be reasonable in the long run. Now use the task approach to calculate, for each of the turnover levels considered in stage one, how much you actually need to spend. It will probably be less than the current figure for smaller turnovers and more for higher ones. In all likelihood, one combination of turnover and advertising will stand out as appearing highly attractive. However, if there is only a low probability of achieving that combination it will not be worth while. Thus the third stage is to consider from all available evidence the odds of achieving any postulated turnover level at any recommended appropriation level. Turnover and appropriation probabilities can be assessed as single figures or as ranges. Whilst many companies prefer to quote a single appropriation and a range of turnover levels, the result is usually so confusing as to put you back into a coin-tossing situation: you probably end up with a five per cent chance that an appropriation of £250,000 will yield a turnover of £2,000,000, but a ninety-five per cent chance that turnover could be anywhere between £1,750,000 and £3,000,000.

The real cost of working out the sums correctly could be high and in many cases could exceed the likely benefits. However, an increasing number of companies can draw the necessary information very rapidly from their data retrieval systems. As we noted before, decision theory won't tell you how much you should spend: it merely helps you quantify the risk you are taking by forcing you to put numbers on what are little more than guesses. There is a great deal of benefit in this.

Measuring Advertising Effectiveness

Advertising is still a very 'hit or miss' affair. Appropriations are set in a fairly haphazard and unscientific way. From then on, almost the only form of checking by most companies is to make sure the appropriation isn't overspent!

The problem is: what shall we measure ?

There are some things which are relatively easy to measure, even if it is often expensive to do so. Our main concern is with profit and turnover and these will already be measured. We know our own sales figures. We can compare these with our competitors' progress by taking continuous consumer or retail audit information. The latter will also measure our in-store distribution, our stock levels and our rate of stockturn.

Although we can measure all these things, we cannot be sure that advertising *caused* them. We don't know if we spent too little or too much. It could be that the right amount was spent on the wrong message or the wrong medium. Competitive activity may have changed and negated our efforts. Perhaps we were unable to buy the space or time we wanted.

In the long run, our own sales and profit figures give the most vital information. One area where they are of no help is telling us what would happen if, say, we spent twice as much or half as much.

A favourite method is the 'pressure test'. A town, TV area, sales region, distribution area, or whatever else is a suitable unit, is given different treatment from the rest of the country. A national media expenditure schedule is worked out on the basis of, say, £500,000. In TV area 'A', spots are bought as if that area were getting a share of a £1,000,000 appropriation. Perhaps in TV area 'B', time is bought on the basis of a £250,000 appropriation. Perhaps again, TV area 'C' is left out completely.

The method has its uses, but it's a crude indicator at best. It is pretty good on such questions as half as much? twice as much? nothing? It isn't much help on questions like £25,000 or £30,000? And there are usually intensely practical difficulties. You can't always get the time you want – either the absolute amount or time of the right quality. It isn't much good buying the equivalent of £1,000,000 of off-peak mid-afternoon spots if the rest of your appropriation is being spent on £500,000 of Thursday/Friday peak-time fixed spots! All that has already been said about the factors that confuse the measurement of overall advertising effectiveness not only applies in a test area but may actually apply with much greater force in a smaller area. Your competitor can take action to disturb your test results at a level of spending which, perhaps, he could not consider spending nationally.

So far, I have dealt with the assessment of the amount of money spent. What about the medium and the message?

Who sees what advertising media is fairly well charted territory. The research suffers from limitations (for example, how many people seated in front of a TV set pay attention to the commercials?) but they can be accepted and used for what they are. The creative message is far more important. The production costs of any campaign usually account for only a small proportion of the total (in fact, the larger the campaign, the smaller the proportion). If one commercial performs twice as well as another, it is worth a great deal and may well be better than doubling the appropriation. Thus it is well worth while to make sure that any advertisement is communicating what you want it to. In this respect, pre-testing is better than post-testing. It is cheaper in research terms and immeasurably cheaper compared with the adverse effects of a 'wrong' commercial. It is a well-known and unfortunate fact of life in advertising that public memory of such 'wrong uns' is incredibly long and that they are played back faithfully as current advertising long after they have been replaced by new messages.

However, we are talking about sales effectiveness, and pretests of creative treatments can only measure communication – and we hope that effective communication of an acceptable message will be translated into sales. There have been two main schools of thought on measuring sales effectiveness of a transmitted campaign. The better known is the DAGMAR school. Basically, this school believes that advertising goals should be expressed in communication terms: sales goals require a combination of different Marketing forces. Nevertheless, the agreed communication goals should express realistic market possibilities and clearly must be expected to have an effect on sales appropriate to the role of advertising in the total mix (for example, it will be far greater for soap-flakes than is sales effort; the reverse will be true for heavy machinery). Clearly there must be benchmarks for measurement purposes.

The DAGMAR school attempts to isolate the factors causing change.

The other main school is based upon Moroney's Theory of Dynamic Difference. Unilever's dynamic difference model is the best known in this country. It tries not only to produce a measure of sales effectiveness but to be predictive too. The method is to measure changes in brand share against the competitive share of advertising expenditure. By plotting these on a graph (Figure 15) one can forecast what change in brand

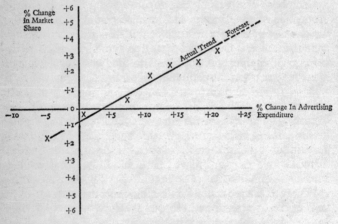

Figure 15. Dynamic Difference Theory

share will result from a change in advertising appropriation and, alternatively, what change in share of advertising expenditure will be required for any given change in brand share. A linear correlation would assume that all other items in the mix were either constant or relatively of little significance. Wild fluctuations would show that the theory had little relevance to the field under study.

It is most effective where there are a few very similar brands. However, the dynamic difference model cannot measure the effects of the creative appeal used: thus the essential difference between brands *has* to be in the amount of money spent. One final problem: since the prediction is in terms of advertising/ turnover ratios and is based upon shares of total market and total advertising, the model is heavily dependent upon a great deal of information gathered from other sources and it can only predict on the assumption that you know what total market advertising expenditure will be.

Other, more complex Operations Research type models have been built to take account of more and more variables. They are too complex to consider here but we can make a few generalizations. The first is that they need a huge input of information to be effective, and this costs money. In addition, they must rely heavily on a number of subjective elements and quantify them. The second is that any model capable of ignoring the computer is not handling enough variables to have the slightest chance of being any use!

Apart from the basic complication of our inability to isolate variables, we have not yet discovered how advertising works. Highly liked advertisements fail to persuade, whilst ones which people openly disdain result in very high sales. Experimental psychology has demonstrated that learning can take place without one's paying conscious attention and under quite uninteresting conditions. Absorbing information from advertising is clearly akin to learning theory, and the main ways in which information is transferred are:

1. By identification – when the prospective buyer can literally feel closely identified with the situation portrayed.
2. By involvement – a deeper level than identification where the situation is linked to some experience by the person receiving the message.
3. By cognitive dissonance. Simply stated, this state is produced when the message offends or cannot be reconciled with established feelings and beliefs about the product. The subject will either reject the message completely or somehow change his attitudes until the message is acceptable. This situation is commonly found with items like cars, where interest in advertising actually increases

after buying in an effort to provide reassurance that the choice was right.

Before leaving the subject of advertising effectiveness, there are, of course, a number of financial yardsticks that provide measures not only of national but also of local expenditure. These will be referred to in a later chapter.

Choosing and Using the Agency

If advertising expenditure is income-generating expenditure, the choice of the advertising agency is one of the most critical you can make. Many check-lists have been published and many readers will already have been solicited by agencies anxious to prove that if they are objective enough to produce a way for you to judge them there is no need to use the suggestions on them! Clients vary so much in their needs that, frankly, I do not believe in questionnaires or in eliciting testimonials from other clients (unless you know one well who is looking for the sort of qualities that you want). Agencies seldom have a strong corporate identity or hallmark: *your* agency is the group of people on your account. What happens on other accounts only provides reassurance (or perhaps the opposite) on the overall strength of the agency.

One of the most famous men in American advertising, James Webb Young, once said: 'Advertising is words and pictures: all the rest is just plumbing'. If an agency can't make good ads, all the plumbing in the world won't help. You must satisfy yourself as to the *real* creative ability of the people you hire. 'Real creative ability' means making ads that sell products, not just ads that win awards.

And when the ad is made, it has to be shown to people. The agency must have an efficient media department able to buy the best possible audience for the money available.

Great advertising and good media selection require correct interpretation of target audiences and effective 'trigger' appeals. Some agencies have specialist Marketing and/or research departments. Others do without but lead their account teams with men of good, solid Marketing experience. If there is any clear trend on the client side, it is to want a senior person capable of taking an immediate decision as the opposite number to a Marketing or Brand Manager.

So, simply expressed, the basics of choosing a good agency are:

1. Satisfy yourself as to their creative ability.
2. Make sure they have an efficient media department.
3. Be certain that the man who is going to run the account at the agency is thoroughly acceptable to you.

It is never very clever to go to an agency just to look at work they have done for others and then decide if they will suit you. Because speculative campaigns are (rightly) taboo, you will have to rely on examples of work done for others. But even these can be carefully selected to show how the agency has dealt with similar problems if you provide them with a detailed brief of your market situation and your problems and objectives. The agency can then tell you – in very broad detail – how they would go about tackling your problem and what success they have achieved with others like it. Don't be over-worried about security. Agencies are better guardians of secrets than people like packaging printers. Your best safeguard, in any case, is the certainty that any agency with a reputation for lax security will quickly lose business!

Now you have an agency, how do you treat them to get the best out of them? The fundamental premise to accept is that no agency can ever know more about your business than you do. But to your depth the agency can bring a breadth of knowledge and experience that no one company has. Experience of types of campaigns, similar media selection problems, distribution problems, redemption rates on coupon schemes, etc, etc, etc.

This leads to an important conclusion: no agency should have to waste its own time and money finding out something you have the answer to, and vice versa. Better to give the agency too much information than too little. Withholding any piece of information that could improve the efficacy of your advertising is like throwing pound notes down the drain. Profit information is absolutely vital. If advertising is to generate more profit, how can the agency really play its part if it has to prepare its plans in a vacuum, waiting for you to say if it is affordable or not?

Involve the agency in your forward plans. Another viewpoint and another set of experience could change things dramatically. All too often things that could have been changed before a launch happen months or even years later, accompanied by rousing choruses of 'Told you so' from the massed choir of the agency. A manufacturer's idea of a good selling proposition is not always the same as the copywriter's. In any case, it's the customer's view that matters.

Learn the time necessary to produce advertisements, to book and cancel space, and so on. If you really create hell, you *can* book space after closing date and cancel after cancellation date. In the long run, it doesn't do you much good, for media owners have a nasty habit of getting their own back! Rushed creative work can be extremely dangerous and ought never to be encouraged.

And you have every right to expect the same courtesy from your agency. When they have taken three months to produce a media plan it is absolutely immoral of them to blackmail you into an instant decision with threats of closing dates.

An agency/client relationship should be a perfect team relationship. The agency will accept reasonable criticism all the more readily if it is sometimes fairly praised too.

The Morality of Advertising

The small but vociferous minority who criticize advertising confuse economics and ethics. Before considering the ethical aspect it is perhaps worth noting some of the more significant findings of a distinguished panel of economists published in the book *The Economics of Advertising*. These conclusions provide formidable replies to some of the more frequently quoted arguments.

1. Advertising in total is quantitatively insignificant in relation to the size of the national economy. It tends to vary between 1·8 per cent and 2·0 per cent of total consumer expenditure and has barely kept pace with the growth of national income. (In fact, discounting rate increases, advertising expenditure has declined in real terms.) The actual proportion devoted to selling goods and services (as distinct from, say, classified advertising) is nearer to one per cent of total consumer spending on those items.

2. Advertising expenditure is only a small part of total Marketing and distribution costs (using the word 'distribution' in the economist's sense).

3. There is no proven systematic relation between advertising and the concentration of business into large-scale units.

4. Advertising is shown to be at least as much a weapon of competition as of restriction.

5. Thus there is no evidence that advertising acts as a barrier (other than a psychological one) to entry into a market.

6. The study confirmed the public's view that advertising was an important source of information for potential buyers.

7. Customers have too little information in general and too little independent information in particular.

8. There is a great deal more price competition amongst advertised products than is commonly supposed.

9. In some situations, competition through advertising is the alternative to no competition at all.

Those are not all the conclusions of the study but they seem to me to provide objective answers to most of the economic criticisms. The main tenor of the book is that advertising expenditures would have to be considerably more significant than they are in the economy to have the persuasive evils accredited to them by the minority.

There is one other criticism that has been well answered by Lord Cole: it is the criticism that advertising is wasteful in that money is spent on promoting the merits of identical products under different banners. Lord Cole has said: 'If those who accuse us of spending money on advertising different products which are essentially the same would do the research which we do, they would find that to the customers they are not the same.'

Of late, the whole concept of advertising has been under renewed attacks. These have been more damaging than previous ones, for they have taken the form of direct Government action against selected products in specified media. This is based upon the argument that it is wrong to mould people's opinions in favour of socially undesirable products and/or habits. Unfortunately, it is not as easy to mould people's opinions as the opponents of advertising suggest: they credit consumers with even less intelligence than advertising men are supposed to attribute to their public! Meanwhile, the moral argument that advertising puts up the cost of goods continues.

It is undeniable that accounting convention regards advertising expenditure as a cost; however, it is a cost incurred to generate more volume, greater turnover and therefore more profit. It is a discretionary cost, not an obligatory one. Why then do businessmen spend it? It can only be because they make more profit that way. As we have seen in the chapter on Pricing, it is not invariably the case that a reduction in price leads to an increase in sales; it can often be the other way round. The oft-used (and not inaccurate) justification that advertisers lower prices in the long run by creating levels of demand that justify long production runs resulting in economies of scale is only a partial answer which ignores the concept of psychological pricing and value added by advertising.

The real case for advertising is that you will make more net profit with it than without it. If manufacturers are as altruistic as the opponents of advertising suggest, and if advertising is ineffective (as they imply, although it contradicts their argument about ethics!), then the alternative to advertising is not reducing price – it's increasing profit! Why don't we use this argument? Because many businessmen are more ashamed of admitting that they are in business to make a profit than they are of admitting that they advertise.

Suggestions for Further Reading

Advertising – A General Introduction by R. S. Caplin (Business
Publications, 1959) is just what it says it is and little the worse
for its age. The same is true of a book on what to do with the
money when you've got it: *Campaign Planning* by Olaf Ellefson,
also published by Business Publications (in 1960). Three highly
readable books whichever side of the fence you may be on are:

  A History of English Advertising by Blanche A. Elliot,
  published by Business Publications, 1962.

  Confessions of an Advertising Man, David Ogilvy's classic,
  published by Athenaeum, 1963.

  Advertising for the Advertiser by Eric Webster (an advertising
  agency man!), published by John Murray, 1969.

Then, on the workings and ethics of advertising:

  Advertising in Action by Harris & Sheldon, published for the
  Institute of Economic Affairs by Hutchinson, 1962.

  Advertising and Human Memory by R. P. Kelvin, Business
  Publications, 1962 (a slim volume of great importance for it
  reminds us of simple facts we frequently overlook).

Chapter 17

Sales Promotion

I could have given this chapter any one of several titles like 'Merchandising', 'Below-the-Line Activity', 'Non-Media Advertising'. All these – and more – are used to cover a whole host of alternative ways of encouraging the trade or the consumer or both to buy your product. Let me then define my terms. I am talking about those items normally budgeted for the promotion of sales other than:

Advertising in conventional media (Press, TV, etc).
Public Relations.
Published discount rates.

Inevitably, this definition takes us into some shadowy areas. My definition allows for the inclusion of free circulation magazines full of advertisement and money-off coupons: an advertising agency regards them as commissionable media and may include such magazines as 'above the line'. Standard discounts for quantity are out; extra discounts above those published and generally available to the trade are in. Exhibitions come into my definition. So does bribery! We should recognize at the outset that within this category are promotional devices which are regarded by certain companies and even by whole industries as the prime medium (other than the salesman) for promoting their wares. At the other end of the scale are those who find the techniques of sales promotion a secondary or an ancillary medium and some who make no use of them at all.

To the advertiser, what he regards as total advertising expenditure is probably considerably greater than the amount his advertising agency sees or perhaps even knows about. Certainly it will include all the sales promotion items, sometimes (wrongly) the sales force and frequently shops where they are regarded as display sites (several television rental companies regard their showrooms as part of advertising expenditure, taking the attitude that their shop window is a sort of poster and an alternative to other kinds of promotion). It is this 'now you see it, now you don't' that has been the root cause of wildly fluctuating and immeasurably inaccurate statements about the size, growth and proportion of total promotional spending accounted for by sales promotion in all its forms. This situation has been fostered by advertising agencies who feel that they are getting a smaller share of the cake. I am convinced – and I know many Marketing Directors who would support me in this – that the share of the total accounted for by media expenditure amongst the sum total of all those who spend money on both media advertising and sales promotion activities is *greater* not less than it was twenty years ago and enormously higher than it was pre-war.

I can't quantify that statement. I defy anyone to produce any figure for sales promotion activity with any remotely acceptable standard of error. Firstly, we can't agree on what to include. Secondly, it is physically impossible to monitor all the visible activity. Thirdly, there is an enormous amount of invisible activity and, fourthly, how do you value promotions (like self-liquidating premium offers and the gifts received for cigarette coupons) which theoretically cost nothing? It is, in fact, this invisible area that causes all the confusion. Anyone who measures the amount of sales promotion activity is looking at the tip of an iceberg from afar and judging its height. He has no real idea whether it is growing or not, how much is below the surface or whether the ratio between the visible ice and the unseen part is remaining constant. It is not all that long ago that most sales promotion expenditure was devoted to selling to the trade, not through the trade. 'Movement will be created when the retailer has so much stock that he can't open his bathroom door' went the theory. Salesmen were given pound notes: goodwill allowances, display payments, advertising assistance. Call it what you like, it was bribery to stock more. As the Brand Management concept grew, the profit-responsible manager could not allow such indiscriminate, uncontrolled expenditure and he swept it into his advertising appropriation. It is the magnitude of this movement from sales controlled funds to brand controlled moneys that convinced one that a higher proportion of total promotional expenditure passes through the agencies than was formerly the case and certainly there has been no diminution in total of above-the-line expenditure.

There is still a tremendous amount of sales promotion money spent that we will never track down unless companies are forced to declare it in their accounts. There is no checking of doctors' wastepaper baskets, for example. Every professional man or woman receives a great deal of unsolicited sales promotion material. There is no systematic check of retailers' dustbins for all the display pieces that never appear in the store. We can't discover much by raking the ashes of the salesman's Sunday bonfire although many of them regularly burn unplaced material. Companies will not admit to the amounts they spend on cash inducements given to retailers to get them to cut prices, extra discounts for exceeding an agreed datum figure, gifts in return for displaying special offers . . . one could go on and fill several pages before even mentioning drinks, dinners and trips to the theatre and special sporting events. This sort of item features heavily in the budgets of many highly sophisticated Marketing companies so they can't be all that ineffective, although there is a danger that they might become part of the way of life of selling to a particular trade.

Trade Promotions

Promotions aimed solely at the trade have, as their prime aim, the task of influencing the retailer to change his attitude about your product in a positive way or a more positive way than in the past. Thus they may vary from promotions aimed to persuade him to stock for the very first time, to increase the size of his order, to do so more permanently by agreeing to hold a

higher level of stock or to throw a competitor out. Various combinations of these tactical objectives are also obviously possible.
Acceptance by most trades of promotions aimed solely at them
and not either through them to the final buyer or simultaneously with consumer promotion (whether in media or not)
is dying fast, and rightly so. Retailers have been slow to come
round to the importance of minimum stock and maximum
stockturn but not only is it now widely accepted that non-
selling space is wasted space but the more sophisticated
multiple retail organizations run to computerized stock control. Companies with such firmly held views are usually only
prepared to change their planned stock levels if a promotion
appears to promise absolute – and ideally continuing – benefit.
The modern retailer is prepared to welcome with open arms
anyone who can show him how to make more profit, not just
on your product but for his operation as a whole. Thus the
trade-only deal that appeals most is something which boosts
his profit by either reducing his buying prices or by rewarding
him for exceeding agreed, realistic targets. Either can be done
on long- or short-term bases.

Short-term price reductions I shall call paid promotions. It
is expected by the manufacturer that the retailer will actively
promote the brand and progressive retailers know they stand
to benefit more by doing so. Whatever the purpose for which
the money is ostensibly offered, it is invariably used as a contribution to (if not the whole of) a price cut or the creation by
the store of special advertising and promotional material.
Whether the money is actually used for the purpose intended
or goes straight into the retailer's (or wholesaler's) pocket
depends upon a number of things such as:

His honesty.
The deal he is getting on other competitive products.
The elasticity of demand in the particular market.
The amount of discipline in his organization.

The first two are self-explanatory, the latter two require
some explanation. In a static market, a promotion will not

increase overall sales but simply rearrange brand shares or shop shares. If all stores are getting the same kind of deal, it is likely that only brand shares will change. A retailer on a good deal for exceeding datum of the brand leader will need a substantial incentive from a lesser brand to make it worth his while to detract effort from the number-one brand. In a market which appears not to respond to price changes, the manufacturer is foolish to put money in the retailer's pocket, for that is where it will surely go. Discipline is the greatest problem. Carefully negotiated listings do not become directives to stock at store level, promotions agreed at Head Office are not communicated to branch level, price cuts don't reach the public and special deals are pocketed to swell profits. One very frequent source of complaint by manufacturers is the all too frequent practice of 'buncing': every store has a problem of 'shrinkage' – which includes pilferage. Store managers seek to offset this by adding odd pennies to products or passing on only part of a price cut. We must realize, too, that there is a large number of individual retailers, especially in the grocery and chemist businesses, who are loosely tied to some form of voluntary grouping. One may negotiate a deal with the Head Office of that group and they may try very hard to encourage their members to take part but, in the last resort, the members are in the group as a way of preserving their individuality but on terms much closer to those enjoyed by the multiple organizations. Many of them are just not going to accept being told which product to feature and when. Moreover, especially in the grocery trade, members of voluntary groups (like Spar, Mace and Vivo) do not buy all their goods through that organization and frequently belong to more than one such group.

Many paid promotions are opportunist in the event although they may well represent many months of effort. Often the initiative comes from the retailer. Under either or both circumstances, there is a danger of this expenditure being extra money and difficult to control. Many companies use the erroneous concept of marginal costing (referred to in the chapter on Pricing) which presupposes that all promotional sales will be extra sales. Elasticity of demand and the possibilities of both total market and brand growth come into this. There is an alarming tendency for such promotions to move trade around from one store to another. There is a danger, too, of offers being continued more or less regularly. There is a great deal of evidence both in this country and the USA that excitement is an essential part of any promotion and that price-features with monotonous regularity begin to pall whilst permanent or near-permanent cuts tend to denigrate the image of the product.

Other major trade promotions include such things as thirteen to the dozen (officially frowned upon in the grocery trade), free gifts for certain levels of purchase, trade-only competitions, vouchers in the outer package which can be exchanged for gifts or cash, and mystery-shoppers who hand over cash prizes if a certain product is in stock or a display piece featured. However, it is obvious that any trade deal is ultimately designed to influence the consumer and that the days of the manufacturer relying on the retailer to move goods or the retailer accepting that as his responsibility without help from the supplier are almost gone.

Consumer Promotions

This is the visible tip of the iceberg that all the discussion has been about. Why have they become so important? To answer this, we must go partially back to the question of how advertising works. Although we know little, there are two assumptions that can be made and which bear heavily upon the need for and the value of promotions:

1. For most heavily advertised established brands, advertising works mainly by reinforcing existing attitudes held by people who have already experienced the product. Advertising either strengthens existing favourable attitudes or reduces unfavourable ones.
2. Gaining new users from a competitor is difficult and likely to be rare.

It is the second of these (which follows from the first) that is so important to the whole field of consumer promotions. New users will be more influenced by some 'extra' reason for trying another brand: reasons like product improvement, personal recommendation, sales pressure and the whole panoply of sampling and promotional devices. (It should be emphasized that these assumptions about advertising do not deny its effectiveness for launching a new brand. Newness is in itself an 'extra' and whilst it will not be sufficient to cause brand-loyal

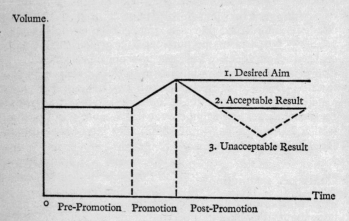

Figure 16. Aim of Sales Promotions

users to try, there is in any market a largish body of people who are quite prepared to experiment.) The place of advertising for a new product is put in sharp perspective by Jeno Pallucci in a book called *How to Make $100,000,000 in a Hurry*, when he writes: 'Profoundly important as advertising is, it still runs poor second to product quality. Please don't forget it. Ads will sell the *first* package of damn near anything, but if people don't dig your product you've dug yourself a grave.'

The object of a consumer promotion is to lift sales to a new plateau. Figure 16 shows this as the desired aim. Unfortunately such results tend to be the exception rather than the rule and an acceptable result is one where the total sales exceed what they might otherwise have been by the amount of product sold during the promotion even though sales settle back to their original plateau. Regrettably, the more frequent occurrence is represented by the third line, where the height of the peak is equalled by the depth of the trough and total sales are unchanged from what they would have been without the promotion, although profits may well be less. This situation is so frequent for two main reasons. The first is that there are too many ill-conceived promotions mounted at insufficient strength or with too little impact to persuade people to try more than once. (Competitions are notorious attractors of once-only buyers who are almost professional entrants.) The second is that manufacturers will promote long-life products or those with established franchises. In both cases you are not lifting the sales curve, you merely encourage forward buying. This is followed by a dip in sales whilst the promotional stock is used up. Subsidizing existing buyers is a very unprofitable thing to do and the more buyers you have the less effective will be any promotion unless there is a good chance of increasing the frequency of use. This is one of the most difficult tasks in Marketing.

There have been many generalizations about the amount of money spent on the various kinds of consumer promotion. Such generalizations are like averages: not much comfort to a man who drowns in a river with an average depth of nine inches! In a contribution to another book, I have dealt at length with this whole subject and quoted case histories. The conclusions are worth repeating:

1. There are no really valid generalizations because every case is treated on its merits and the good Marketing man is continually testing and analysing which parts of his total advertising and promotional mix work best under what conditions.

2. Sales promotion expenditure is partly a function of media expenditure. The first aim of most Marketing men is to secure adequate reach, coverage and frequency of their

advertising message. Advertising expenditure tends to be relatively constant in cash or ratio terms and therefore the proportion spent compared with below-the-line activity tends to increase as the total budget goes down until the point where it no longer produces an effective campaign. At this point, either expenditure will cease or trade and/or consumer promotions will be the only methods of product promotion used. (If the advertising/sales ratio produces more money each year, the tendency again is for the above-the-line proportion of the total to increase until diminishing returns set in, when total expenditure will be fixed irrespective of ratios.)

3. The part that sales promotions can play is recognized, especially in gaining new users, but long-term they are no substitute for a solid consumer franchise built up by consistent, informative and authoritative media advertising.

Some Types of Activity

I will not attempt to catalogue all the possible areas of either trade or consumer promotions. Rather, I shall follow the established pattern of Part 2 of this book by dealing only with particular points about certain categories which appear to me to be ignored, misunderstood or wrongly used. Firstly, self-liquidating offers.

A self-liquidating premium looks good because it theoretically costs nothing. You give the customer a bargain by buying at high-level quantity discount rates and everyone is satisfied. What research is available is old but it shows that consumer satisfaction with such offers is high. However, four per cent of all housewives accounted for half of *all* redemptions and ten per cent for over three-quarters.[1] This is a vital finding which can be substantiated by examination of redemption records related to sales volume. Even a very high level of response (the same is true of competitions) seldom accounts for a very high proportion of packets of product sold. It is the total activity and excitement built around the offer which produces beneficial sales results. There is a very considerable fallout between the number of people who pick up a product because it has an interesting offer (or competition) and the number who actually do anything about it.

Three other points are worth a reference. Firstly, although it is *usually* better, it has been demonstrated many times that close association between the product and the offer is not vital (e.g. a scouring pad offering a saucepan). Secondly, high-priced offers *do* sell. Indeed, they move better than ever as the savings they show are so much more attractive and because the saving on a low-priced item can so easily be swallowed up by the minimum postal charge. Thirdly, pricing. Psychological pricing applies to premium offers and it may pay you either to give a small subsidy or take a small profit to achieve a psychologically satisfactory price. Don't forget, too, that most people pay by postal order and the price should be one that can easily be handled using a postal order: one sees many prices that need a postal order and more stamps than one can add to it or that need two postal orders *plus* stamps on each.

It is clear that the manufacturer and the trade are closer together in their objectives today than they ever were, although they frequently differ in how they achieve them. It is abundantly clear that many premium offers today are designed on the basis of 'What will appeal to the trade?' (which often means, 'What would he like as a gift?') rather than any consideration of the consumer. This is recognition that the display value and associated price cut are of more importance than redemption *per se*. Perhaps this situation would change with more pre-testing of possible offers (however, this will only tell you which is best liked of a list offered, not what the housewife would *most* like).

Finally, let us not ignore the value of a premium offer to a salesman. It gives him a new opportunity to talk about the product. Few salesmen sell only one product; even if they did, they would find it hard to say something new every time. An offer gives the salesman an excuse for getting his product in a prime display site, gives him the excuse for a price cut and the opportunity to steal an advantage over his competitor.

Display Material

Point-of-sale material is meant to persuade the ultimate buyer. A calendar of spectacular nudes may do that for a buyer in a garage; it doesn't have much buying effect when it is hung for the delight of the mechanics in the lubrication bay. It doesn't work when it goes straight into the dustbin or on the salesman's bonfire. The rules are simple: display should have something to say to the ultimate buyer, it should say it simply, it should stand out from the ruck. Next to 'Free!' the best message is still 'Buy one *now*!' Display material can stand out from the ruck in many ways, by just being different (one of the most successful pieces in my Lyons experience had a black background when everyone else used white), by featuring movement, by actually showing the item offered instead of an illustration. The retailer should want your material because he can see immediately that it will help increase his sales: his space is too precious to fill with pretty pictures or wasted words.

In any trade, the number of display sites is limited, the competition for them is high (in the grocery trade between 600 and 700 salesmen may be competing for twenty possible sites), yet the allocation is haphazard. By far the most used method is a standard allocation per salesman. A sophisticated company may recognize the fact that Jock in John o'Groats will not need twenty, so ten of his can go to Bill in Balham. Any greater sophistication is rare and usually done arbitrarily by local Management or even at the request of the salesman. There is a simple remedy. Presumably you have store records. Why not class each store according to the availability of display sites and the chances of getting a display? You probably need no more than first, second and third category stores. When it comes to allocating material you can first decide whether you are going for blanket coverage or only certain categories. The second advantage is that you can allocate to salesmen more precisely and avoid both over- and under-supply. Finally, you can modify the estimates by a little use of subjective quantification to assess the probability of placing any given number of pieces in any category of outlet and you can even take this down as far as salesman level. If your sales records are computerized, these basic categories can be part of store information and a quick print-out will give you a theoretical optimum number of pieces of display material. One company into which I introduced this system now saves an average £65,000 a year and claims negligible wastage and few demands for extra material. Retailers welcome this approach, so tell them about it and discuss their category with them. Some companies permit no manufacturers' material; others will print an agreed message in the company's own style. All, however, have one thing in common. Space which is not selling is wasted and reduces return on investment.

Direct Mail

Two factors affect this medium: the message and the address list. I have in front of me a letter addressed to me as Marketing Manager, Lyons Tea Division (which I haven't been for some years), which begins, 'Dear Mr Willsmer, As a major manufacturer of furniture ...' It happens all the time. At home I still receive circulars for the last three occupants of my house. Absolute accuracy is difficult but polling lists, professional registers and so on should enable both manufacturers and mailing-houses to be much more accurate than many are. The standard of creativity in mailing-shots is not always what it might be. If it is worth using a direct and, therefore, potentially persuasive medium it is worth spending enough on production costs to make it fully effective. But 'creative' must always be 'relevant'. A doctor wants solid information, not gimmicks. Grocery retailers receive many gimmicks which they do not appreciate, for they too want information, but with something like 3,000 lines to choose from they will feel favourably towards the company which sent the mailing-shot that excited them.

There is a tendency in certain professions and businesses to regard direct mail as both a prime and obligatory medium. Its effectiveness can be tested to a certain degree by including a reply-paid coupon for further information, a personal call, a

sample or an offer. However, the response rate will include
people who are inveterate coupon fillers whilst your mailing
may well have influenced people who do not respond. However, just as there are industries who have come to use direct
mail unthinkingly (some of the glossiest, most expensive, mis-
directed and uninformative is put out by media owners, of all
people) there are many companies with a large mailing list
ready-made who do not use it and often use more expensive
media and media less effective for their purpose.

Tailor-Made Promotions

Stores frequently complain that the way to maximize their
profit is not to have the same promotion that every other retailer is being offered at the same time but to have something
specially designed for them. Unfortunately, it is not economic
for manufacturers to prepare a set of individual promotions
which add up to anything like the impact of a national effort.
However, they can be of value either throughout a whole store-
group or in selected individual stores of certain size. Although
we are looking at this, for the moment, from the manufacturer's point of view, there is no doubt that the best 'tailor-
mades' are the stores' own efforts where the theme is set by the
store, the layout decided by them and manufacturers are invited to participate. (Naturally they pay for the privilege!)

A promotion with a store-group will have a common theme,
perhaps a competition run only through branches of Fine Fare
and therefore with entry open only to their customers. Because
of difficulties of administration, a competition is the easiest
promotion to run. Self-liquidating offers are difficult because
the quantities will be relatively small except with high-turn-
over items through large store-groups. A price reduction
through one store-group only is not really in this category for it
is quickly matched by another store with or without manufacturer assistance. A true 'tailor-made' may be repeated in
format with another store but the competition and the prizes
will change so that each has something special. This is the
problem: although stores argue that they want one-off pro-

motions, they are down on you like a ton of bricks the moment you arrange one with a competitor and not with them. There are two safeguards. The first, and most important, is to attach firm conditions (offtake, period of promotion, price, etc) to any such deal so that you can fairly say to anyone who complains, 'You can have a deal with pleasure – on the same terms as your competitor.' The second is that you have a selection of alternatives up your sleeve so that you can quickly honour that statement.

The other form is not tailor-made for a company but for any shop of a certain potential in any company. Well done, retailers will queue up for these in-store units if they are demonstrated to be proven store-traffic builders. Examples are houses full of desirable household items with a box of keys as a lucky dip for anyone making a qualifying purchase. If the key fits, the winner takes any present. There have been Easter-eggs full of packets of product (the nearest to the correct number wins), name an animal and so on. They can be tremendously effective and can be used selectively. However, the cost of operation (transport, someone standing by the unit both to sell and guard against abuse, keeping the unit fresh and clean . . . and so on) can be high. It certainly needs someone to administer it. Finally, watch the legal implications!

Exhibitions

Exhibitions still offer a wonderful opportunity to contact important buyers economically in certain industries. However, in the wider sense of exhibitions aimed at the general public, their effectiveness has diminished steeply, more and more are closing or running at less frequent intervals and fewer companies exhibit. Despite rising costs of stand building, this is one area where expenditure by manufacturers *is* falling. It is widely felt by many Marketing men that the people who get most out of the majority of exhibitions are the people who run them and the stand builders.

The first rule for participation is that it should fit your overall objectives. Too many companies take part for what they believe to be prestige reasons: they usually dispense more drinks than order forms. Many are almost blackmailed by threats of what their competitors will achieve by being there. Some businesses still exist where it is thought bad to be conspicuous by your absence, but this is no way to seek out a competitive advantage when you are forced to operate right under the nose of your direct competitors. If an exhibition fits in with your defined objectives and is an efficient and economic way of achieving them, then take part. Otherwise, ignore all threats and blandishments and stay out. If exhibitions fit your strategy then they cannot be looked upon as isolated events. You will stay with them until your objectives change, the effectiveness of the exhibition diminishes or it becomes an uneconomic way of promoting sales. (Many trades have not a single exhibition but a series throughout the country in any one year. The same criteria will be applied to deciding how many of these to participate in.) Prestige alone is not sufficient reason for appearing at an exhibition; however, you can easily suffer a loss of prestige by exhibiting badly. Better not to do it at all than do it on the cheap.

Perhaps two of the most direct results that can be expected from an exhibition are sales to customers who otherwise would not have bought and extending distribution by a medium which can be more economic than direct cold-canvassing by salesmen. Both are more applicable to smaller companies with either few direct outlets of their own or limited distribution. However, exhibits can have a good deal of advertising benefit which can manifest itself either in future sales or an increase in sales effectiveness. Greater distribution, more orders per call, orders for a wider range of goods – all lead to a reduction in the unit cost of selling.

The effectiveness of exhibiting is enhanced by a Marketing appreciation of consumer needs. At a recent Motor Show, a young German-speaking colleague asked on every stand for a German-speaking salesman and multi-lingual sales literature. No British manufacturer could provide either. I have been to a catering exhibition where an exhibitor told me that he had no personal knowledge of the machine that interested me but he could give me the card of a salesman who knew all about it. (Perhaps he had heard the typewriter salesman story!) Pretty girls may attract buyers to your stand but they perform no more than a decorative function unless they are well trained. Most buyers want information anyway and they want to talk to the people best able to give it. (This remark applies mainly to trade exhibitions: the situation may be different at consumer exhibitions where demonstrators and salesgirls are required.) In short, consider an exhibition with as much care as you consider your campaign objectives and specific advertising and promotions. Then if you don't feel that you can afford the sort of money on space, stand building, staffing, demonstrations and samples (or whatever is appropriate), don't do it.

Use the task approach when considering exhibitions in just the same way as you would when considering the total advertising budget.

Attitudes to Sales Promotion

We have already noted, briefly, that housewives' reactions are generally favourable to self-liquidating offers and very few have felt any dissatisfaction with any offer they have ever sent for. There are many aspects of sales promotion which are directed straight to end-users – medical literature and samples, speculative offers from book and record clubs, exhibitions and others – but I want to consider briefly the manufacturer/ retailer relationship.

Let me repeat: the attitudes of each side are coming closer together. Which influenced the other is debatable. However, only the dregs of retailing and manufacturing concern themselves with anything other than movement *through* the trade (although the rates of movement still vary enormously). But whilst both sides are in pursuit of profit they do it in different ways. The manufacturer by single-minded devotion to his product range; the retailer by fostering more store-traffic. Just as it is easier to get more people buying than more buying more frequently through the techniques of advertising and sales promotion, so the same is true of retailing. Thus store-traffic and the number of times stock is turned over are the keys to retail success.

The Persil salesman expects his promotion to sell more Persil; the retailer will be just as pleased – perhaps more so – if people come into his store attracted by the Persil offer but leave with something else. The retailer's ideal is fifty-two weeks of traffic-building promotions and his interest in any one (except in an assessment sense) ceases the day it is pencilled in on the promotional calendar. The longer ahead that is filled, the more he likes it. He can always throw a relatively weak promotion out if a red-hot alternative comes along later. This is practically the only effective distinction left among sophisticated manufacturers and retailers between 'trade' and 'consumer' promotions. The retailer doesn't mind if he has twelve different soap powder promotions in a year as long as they fit his store-traffic/profit-building criteria.

That's one point for manufacturers to understand. The other is the concept of the 'besieged retailer' (which I have referred to elsewhere – see reading list). The average retailer in every trade is offered more products than he can stock, more new products than he can make space for, more promotions than he can mount and more display material than he can place. The manufacturer *must* accept that he faces very long odds – even without considering a counter-offer by his competitors – of obtaining one of these limited promotional or display sites (at least in a good selling position). Any manufacturer considering an offer should really ask himself this question: 'What right have I to occupy valuable space in stores with this promotion?' If you answer that objectively and honestly early on, you may save yourself a lot of money, for the retailer will question your promotion in those terms and he has two advantages over you: he knows the value of his space and he knows the competitive bids for it.

Whilst retailers and manufacturers are close together in theory, they remain apart in practice. I make three suggestions how that might be remedied:

1. To repeat that manufacturers must adopt greater realism

in the offer of promotions. Too many try to jump on what seems to be a profitable bandwagon without realizing that a ticket has to be earned, it cannot just be bought.

2. Greater realization by retailers of the obligations of accepting a promotion and their only doing so if the support of the organization can ensure that the manufacturer is not just pouring his money down the drain (or into a fat wallet).

3. Realization by retailers that there are some promotions they can do better than manufacturers and some that work the other way round. To rigidly reject all manufacturer offers is frequently to slam the door in one's own face.

The future, however, must be one of both fewer retailers and a lesser number of groupings, although it must be wrong to suggest a future of only a very few, very large, multi-product stores. Those store-groups will wish to preserve their own identity and look more like a store with a common theme than a well-laid-out stockroom of multifarious products of innumerable manufacturers. I therefore expect stores to dictate to a far greater extent the design of promotional material and to give the prime sites to promotions of their own choosing even though they may well feature – and be subsidized by – manufacturers' products. This will be a better solution all round than one suggested alternative (which is actually practised in some trades and stores) of paying for display sites. Apart from being unsatisfactory from the manufacturer's point of view, it could be nose-cutting for the retailer: the best bidder may not be the best profit earner!

Reference

1. MIS with Burlington Marketing Associates, 1965–6.

Suggestions for Further Reading

At the risk of appearing vain, may I suggest my own contribution to *New Ideas in Retail Management* entitled 'Promotion in Retailing', published by Staples Press, 1970, which gives a fuller catalogue of items plus some original research findings. All exhibitors should get hold of a copy of the Institute of Directors' booklet *Exhibiting for Profit* by H. M. Carter and M. E. O'Keefe Trowbridge (1969).

Managing the Marketing Effort

Introduction

In Part 1 we considered the meaning of Marketing and how it equates with the philosophy of modern business. Part 2 looked at just a few of the techniques used by Marketing men to consider potential gaps in knowledge and gave a brief distillation of personal practical experience that has been helpful not only to myself but to companies I have worked with and numerous students I have written for or lectured to.

Part 3 is closer to home for the Chief Executive, Marketing Director and embryo Marketing Director. It deals with practical operational questions of planning and control and thus relates closely to Part 1. It also deals with the peculiar management problems of running a Marketing organization, a hybrid assembly of specialists and generalists, extroverts and introverts. No man who has never had full control of a total Marketing organization can grasp the complexities and anomalies involved. Let's hope the later chapters open a few chinks in some doors!

The main areas of activity for the Marketing Director are:

1. Product planning.
2. Short-range planning.
3. Long-range planning.
4. Organizational planning.

In Part 3 we shall deal with the last three items.

Chapter 18

The Short-Term Marketing Plan

From practical experience, it is a valid generalization that most Marketing men are more concerned with making plans than controlling and assessing them. Good Marketing men are as much creative people as are artists and writers; every Account Executive in an advertising agency knows that there is a happy balance between the amount of time required to permit a good creative solution and a longer period of time which often leads to a new solution every day. This is true in the Marketing department too. There comes a time when you have to cry, 'Halt: this is the plan we will follow.' Not only must one decide which plan to follow but for how long it seems reasonable (other things being equal) to tread that path. Many, many companies who pay lip service to three- or five-year plans in fact produce a new three- or five-year plan every year. Unless there is some very good reason, year two of this year's plan should not look too different from what is now planned when it in turn becomes year one of next year's mid-term plan. This is especially important for multi-product, multi-divisional companies who frequently find themselves on a treadmill of new investment plans involving fresh outlays in excess of the returns planned from the last investment plan.

The Problems of Multi-Product Companies

The difficulties of short-term planning are best illustrated by the problems of a multi-product company and are even more complicated in a multi-divisional company where each division has several product ranges. Since the majority of companies do, in fact, market more than one product or service, the sequence of planning is well illustrated by considering this kind of company.

The importance of advertising in many companies and the fact that it is looked after by specialist staff can easily lead to the damaging situation of advertising being seen as an end in itself. Obviously, this is dangerous but it happens more frequently than common sense would lead one to suspect. For promotional effort to succeed, virtually all the resources of the company must be employed. One has experienced too many situations where the sales estimates of a brand manager have been regarded as 'pie in the sky' by the production department who promptly substitute a figure that seems more sensible to them. Often they are right! Often they might have found the estimates acceptable if they had known the evidence which backs them and the plans made to achieve these forecasts.

No sane company regards the annual Marketing plan in isolation but rather as part of an annual operating plan for the whole business. This acknowledges that various resources within the company have alternative uses (especially time and money), that these alternatives frequently conflict and must compete with each other, and that the whole organization must be pursuing the same aim and matching resources to agreed investment or opportunity areas to be attacked without investment. This overall commitment area is where the Chief Executive exercises the ultimate Marketing role; the Marketing Director presents the best opportunities for the business to follow.

At the stage where departmental plans come together, the Marketing department is in the peculiar position of recommending the direction the business should follow but also asking for the funds to achieve certain ends (by selling, advertising and other forms of promotion) whilst also requesting a budget to cover departmental expenses. It is both the prime mover in setting the business course and just another department begging for money. It is the role of the Chief Executive (with whatever supporting group is appropriate to his company) to sort out conflicting demands for a limited supply of cash or factory space or whatever it might be. This can only be done within the framework of agreed overall objectives. Only selling (in its widest sense) brings in cash; there is a limit to the amount it can bring in given the market opportunities and agreed support levels. Almost invariably something has to give. Sometimes it has to be agreed profit levels. (The classic case of this is where a larger market opportunity exists, more promotional money will be necessary to attain that goal but the factory will need more plant. One without the other is totally wasted.) The Chief Executive, therefore, is faced not merely with a Solomon-like decision between alternative investment requests from different areas of the business, but the possibility of forgoing profit today for greater profit and security in the longer term. (The Chief Executive of a multi-divisional firm faces this problem greatly magnified.)

The Sequence of Planning

One of the things that has surprised me in working for and with many very different companies and hearing students describe their own operations is how many companies have separately and intuitively (perhaps 'by trial and error' is a better description) arrived at very similar policies. What follows is thus a sort of 'amalgam ideal' based upon the methods of several sophisticated companies, but I trust the reader will forgive me when I use terms appropriate to my own operating experience. I should make it clear, too, that although the case has not yet been argued, I assume a Marketing Director with overall control of both brand and sales functions and all ancillary services (like PR and market research).

The guiding principles in this sequence of planning are:

1. The need to achieve an agreed profit objective is paramount.
2. Money is limited.
3. Sales-force capacity is limited.
4. Sales objectives cannot be achieved unless all other departments receive early warning of what is required of them.

Although there is an apparent rigidity in this system, it will be seen that a great deal of interdepartmental discussion *must* take place even at times when, theoretically, no plans are required from other departments.

Given knowledge and acceptance of the overall divisional and/or company objectives, the planning sequence *must* start with the Marketing department. Their prime function is to identify opportunities, project trends and recommend the areas for attack. Thus, in this system, each brand manager works out the ideal strategy for his particular brand – ignoring (unless company objectives decree otherwise) all other products. Each brand manager will work out with his advertising agency counterpart the strategy for his brand for the coming year. He should start with a fairly wild, overall, long-term objective and refine it down to a fairly specific direction for next year. The wild statement has its place. It may seem futile to set a long-term objective of twenty per cent of the market, nationally, for a brand which at the moment sells only in Tyne-Tees and has only a two per cent brand share there! Nevertheless, in formulating a divisional strategy, as distinct from a *brand* one, it is important to know what a brand's ultimate pretensions are.

The Brand Strategy document would also have a sales projection for the coming year, based upon recent trends and the suggested advertising and promotional strategy. The advertising strategy should propose the copy strategy for 'theme' advertising; the promotional strategy would suggest the platform for 'scheme' (i.e. non-media) advertising. One more thing (in what is designed to be a very short document): the consumer proposition for the product. What are we selling? What is in it for the consumer?

Now the basis of the divisional strategy is that one cannot do everything one wants. There is no point in brand managers working out detailed plans, alerting other Management, spending money outside and so on, when their plan may be invalid simply because some other brand with a higher priority is going to utilize all the sales force's capacity during the period. Thus, when all the individual strategies are in, the Marketing

Director should sit down with the senior brand and sales people to decide the divisional strategy. What can you afford to do? What is it realistic to aim for? Who should have priority and when and where? Only then should brand managers be given the authority to develop their plans.

When the Brand Strategies are approved, they can become not only a statement of intent for the division's activity but also a framework of reference by which creative work and promotions can be judged. Advertising can be judged not on subjective approval of words and pictures, but the validity of the theme in terms of the agreed consumer proposition and advertising objectives. The same goes for consumer promotions: premium offers, price-off packs, etc. We shall refer to this possibility later when we consider responsibility levels and limits.

It is extremely unlikely that a brand manager will have got thus far in his planning without consulting the buyers of raw materials, the production department, distribution and anyone else – say, the accounts department – whose opinions and participation may be important. The good Marketing Director will also have questioned other departments affected by the plans to ensure that they are aware of what is planned and have been consulted. However, once the total Marketing organization feels sure of its directions and has agreed on the way it will recommend resolving the conflicts between brand demands (by deciding who should have investment priorities, whether the sales force needs strengthening, how many promotional periods will be allocated to each brand and so on), it is time to fire a more formal shot across the bows of production and buying than will have been done before. Now the functional heads of other departments can be told, 'These are the figures the Marketing department feels are feasible and they will form the basis of our Marketing plan.' They may not be approved, but in most organizations where this sort of discipline is conducted against a background of stated objectives the chances are high that they will become fact. This formal shot will be called something like 'Planned Sales' and, assuming that we are preparing plans for the next five years, budgets are prepared for the next five years on the assumption that funds will be available to meet the final annual plan. These figures will assist Production, Buying and Distribution in planning resources and budgeting expenses so that, a little later in the time span, the Chief Executive can look at all the plans of the business simultaneously. Sales for year one will be broken down by appropriate sales or fiscal periods with annotations to account for planned peaks of activity. Years two to five will be in terms of annual totals only.

This business of indicating peaks and troughs is very important, for they can have significant repercussions on staff engagement, stockholding and labour utilization, all of which affect profit. It provides the production department, for example, with the opportunity to ask for a special promotion to iron out a trough; this can be a valid use of promotional activity where the diseconomies of a promotion at a 'wrong' time are less than those of employing people to do nothing or have a factory shut down. Remember, too, that production programming and distribution schedules have to be discounted for time. The Marketing plan begins by assuming periods when consumers will buy and then introduces a short time lag to allow for selling-in to the trade. Distribution introduces a further lag to get the goods to the salesmen, and the factory is programmed to produce further back in time ready to build up adequate stocks. Thus, these 'planned sales' must be produced well in advance of the period in which production is actually required.

In many companies, managers responsible for production scheduling prefer to have these figures as a range indicating the highest and lowest possibility for each period. Obviously this can be taken further and probabilities assessed as to the chances of being nearer the top of the range than the bottom. If the chances are high that the factory will be asked to work for most of the year near the top of the range, they may take very different decisions about manning, for example.

Finally, we are ready for the Annual Marketing Plan. I propose to devote a whole section to types of plan and what I consider to be the best under most circumstances. I want merely to consider for the moment whether annual plans are a good idea.

They vary from a few pages to several volumes. Some are so long as to be virtually unreadable. Much is usually repeated from last year with figures updated. One internationally famous company in fact prints a standard booklet with blanks for the appropriate figures; it features statements like:

Sales last year increased/decreased by   (   )%
Total market volume increased/decreased by   (   )%
Our share increased/decreased   (   )% to (   )%.

This is printed in many languages but the same information is to be found on the same page number whatever the language! I do not quote this example disparagingly: it fits the need of that mammoth business and makes central international control far easier than allowing anarchy. However, that company believes in the absolute rigidity of an annual plan and I do not.

To me an annual Marketing plan is a good opportunity to take a couple of paces back from the trees to look at the wood, to escape from everyday involvement and expose your thinking to independent witnesses. It is no excuse for abandoning creativity and objectivity for the rest of the year or neglecting interdepartmental contact. The discipline of the annual plan, however, has the disadvantage of creating a search for something new to do or say: Marketing men are, in general, too ready to change horses in midstream, to believe that a year-old advertisement must be a stale advertisement. Some of the most successful Marketing ideas and advertising campaigns have pursued identical themes over a large number of years.

The annual Marketing plan should be no more than a longer-term plan with the first year spelled out in detail. Because it is an essential part of the annual operating plan and financial forecast of the company, it will represent recommendations and a request for formal approval of those courses of action, a formal request for the necessary funds and a 'promise' of the profits that will result from following this course of action with the requested funds. However, the business wants to know what is in store for it in the future and one will normally be indicating the likely sales trend and profit forecasts for up to five years ahead (the actual figure will depend on the business). Whilst prediction over such long periods is clearly hazardous, every effort should be made to ensure that when you present next year's annual plan it should not come as a complete surprise but should represent what was year two this year, modified only by circumstances and experience. The best way to avoid shocks is to produce 'rolling plans'. Thus, if the business makes a formal review of its financial position every quarter, the sales and profit forecast should be amended for five years ahead. At the end of the first quarter, the original forecast will become a set of actual figures. The rest of the year will be amended in the light of what has actually happened and a judgement made as to what effect this will have on the next five years. This is shown diagrammatically in Figure 17. Each shaded area represents the actual figures for a completed quarter and we can assume that these will be reflected in changed forecasts for the year if necessary. Changes in forecast for the remaining years may be done less rapidly but will certainly reflect any well-established alterations in trend. At the end of the first quarter of year one, a forecast is added for the first quarter of year six and so on until years two and six become years one to five of the new annual plan. This 'rolling plan' does not preclude changes of direction: frequently it makes their necessity even more apparent. It does, however, indicate to the company, both for individual products and the company as a whole, what is the best estimate of the future if present trends are continued.

The computer allows for greater sophistication. It is possible, for example, to substitute actual sales for estimates by any appropriate period. Thus, if at the end of four weeks sales are below forecast, the plan for the quarter and for the year (and for the following years if required) will automatically be adjusted downwards. (The opposite if forecast is exceeded.) The brand manager, however, may regard this change as a temporary phenomenon which will be recouped in the next period.

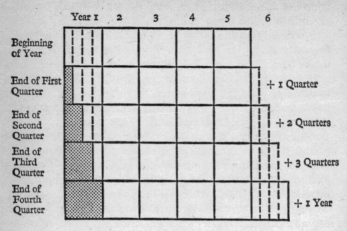

Figure 17. Rolling Five-Year Plan

The discipline is that he has to initiate a change to write-out the computer correction. If he fails to do so, he is agreeing that what actually happened is the basis for a new forecast of the future. An almost infinite number of variations around this theme are possible. There are three great beauties of the rolling plan, computerized or not:

1. Nasty shocks are avoided as each new annual plan appears.
2. Action is prompted more rapidly than in those companies which wait for the annual plan (unless something of disaster proportions is apparent).
3. All departments have adequate forewarning which enables them to plan materials buying, plant investment, labour and cash needs well ahead.

The ideal is, of course, a rolling plan for the whole business. This is a theme I shall return to later, but clearly a false picture is being shown if only sales and receipts are incorporated without using the same disciplines on all the other cost and expense variables that affect final profit.

The discipline of a rolling plan, especially where computer print-outs can produce results by quite short periods, is a fundamental tool of Marketing management. The task of producing all the required control information by hand is lengthy and costly and the time for action may well be past by the time it is received. However, even with the growing use of computer bureaux, not all companies can afford computer analysis. Nevertheless, rolling plans still force attention on what is happening and demand prompt action or reasoned comment for non-action, either of which is better than the normal expectations of managers that 'this is just a temporary set-back; things will come back on trend'. Sometimes they do; most times they don't, and it can be more expensive to run over-budget than below it.

Writing the Plan

Every company has its own ideas about the format of its plans. The variability between plans basically concerns the extent to which the past should be examined and how far back, the extent to which alternatives should be mentioned (even though some may be barely worth mention) and the detail required about actual tactics: is it enough to say that there will be four promotions or must you say what they will be? To a considerable extent, the length and detail of the plans will be conditioned by the complexity of the organization, the number of individual plans to be considered and the extent to which the Chief Executive is prepared to delegate. In many organizations, the Chief Executive wants only to see the total operating plans of the company as a whole. He will delegate decisions on individual Marketing plans to his Marketing Director, who will make those decisions within the reporting limits assigned to him. Doubtless he will have to report to his Chief Executive any plans for new or changed products, alterations in prices and trade terms and any other variable which affects the measurement of the Chief Executive's own performance. However, two things may be said to be common to all companies:

1. No senior manager wants to be presented with plans which leave him to decide between too many alternatives.
2. Every senior manager wants to know how much profit he is being promised, over what period and with what certainty.

The ideal plan is, thus, one which presents a reasoned recommendation in the most succinct way and points to relevant appendices to support it. The number of levels within the Marketing organization normally determines how detailed the content is to be and who checks it. Such a plan should ideally be of medium length containing enough information to provoke action but devoid of superfluous padding. For the busy manager, it will have a terse summary of what is planned, what is required and what the results should be. There should also be certain appendices which are common to all plans (which does not exclude the possibility of others as required) so that the responsible manager knows that he can extract the meat of the recommendations by reading the summary and, say, the first three appendices. Only you can decide which appendices are appropriate to your business but they will probably include: sales this year compared with last year (and possibly further back), detailed sales and profit forecasts for this year, summary plans for the next five years, and the requested promotional appropriation and its recommended breakdown compared with the same detail for last year. (In the past, I have found it useful to include, as obligatory appendices, sales-force targets by region by bonus period and regional profitability figures – a topic we shall consider later.)

The danger of the short plan is that it becomes a catalogue of events without adequate explanation and therefore misses out a great deal that is of importance. If the short plan is a catalogue then the long one is an encyclopaedia: too long to read and with important facts frequently concealed amongst irrelevant trivia. I want to put forward the following list of items that might be included in an ideal plan. Some always will be, others only when appropriate.

1. Market Background.
   This section will include all the salient features of both the market's and the brand's development which have affected the position since the last plan was written and show how they affect both the current situation and the Marketing plans.

2. Current Situation.
   This follows on logically from the first section and is basically a review of actual against forecast performance. It should be an analytical examination and should point up lessons learned and any strengths and weaknesses which have emerged in the total Marketing effort for the brand.

3. Marketing Objectives and Strategy.
   A short outline of major objectives for the coming year in particular and for the longer term in general. Wherever possible, objectives should be stated in precise and measurable terms and include statements on the way results are to be assessed.

4. Profit.
   Although this will be detailed in the appendix, a short section quoting the bottom-line figures arising from achieving the objectives should be stated, compared with previous performance and any significant factors causing variations (like raw material costs) noted.

5. Advertising.
   How much money is required and why (if at all) it differs from previous years. If any major change is proposed, it will be justified here. Creative and media strategies will be presented in outline and the reasons for any changes noted. The detail will come later in the form of specific agency recommendations. If the sequence of planning recommended earlier is followed, there will be no surprises in this section.

6. **Promotions.**

The same is true of this section too. To the detail provided for advertising will be added a review of the effectiveness of last year's promotions and a broad-brush picture of the *type* of promotions proposed and their objectives.

7. **Research.**

A statement of new data urgently required and the action planned to obtain it, plus a budget estimate. This is also a good place to make a general review of all gaps in your knowledge and your market and the costs of filling them.

8. **Product Development.**

This item occupies only a low place, on the assumption that it relates to an assessment of the results of changes made or a review of changes planned and either under investigation or where funds are being requested for that purpose. If a new or reformulated product is a major feature of this year's plan, it will be featured in the 'Objectives' section. If dealing with the past, this section will review the reasons behind the changes and what has been their effect. When considering the future, proposed changes will be set out with the reasons why, proposed timings, and cost and benefit estimates.

9. **Packaging.**

10. **Pricing.**

Both packaging and pricing will be treated in the same way as product development.

11. **Appendices.**

Enough has already been said about these but one should perhaps add that the temptation to use pages and pages of appendices as a substitute for encyclopaedic prose should be discouraged!

Consider the Marketing plan like a set of railway lines. There should be just enough of the right gauge and reaching far enough to achieve the objective of acquainting senior Management with your intentions and gaining their consent. Too few rails, the wrong width between them and an abrupt termination will lead to a derailment before the goal is achieved. Too many rails will send your train off in all sorts of directions until someone skilled is put at the junction. That is a waste of everybody's effort.

There is one adjunct to the Marketing plan which I have personally found to be enormously valuable. Invariably, the plan enjoys only limited circulation either for security reasons, because there is much that does not concern certain managers, or because of sheer indigestibility. However, there are many items in the plan which require action and commitment. It is extremely useful to produce a 'Plan and Commitment Summary' which details events, action required, when and by whom. Although there can be no excuse for not discussing such activities with the responsible managers before the event, there is a world of difference between the kind of discussion where ideas are just being tossed around and the final planned activity. Functional managers do not always understand the distinction, especially in organizations where the rule is to follow the last thing said by the most senior manager present. This summary says, in effect, 'If my plan is approved, this is what will be expected of you'. If it involves capital expenditure, it is too late but it will then record what managers have accepted as their commitment if the plan is finally approved – as it should be if the correct sequence has been carried out against a background of set objectives.

The Marketing Director's Role in Planning

The task of the Marketing Director is more than simply checking and judging the technical feasibility and creative dynamic of the plans. Much of this could be delegated to specialists. His primary role is to present to his Chief Executive plans which will achieve the division's profit objective (which obviously implies providing sufficient funds to cover all budgeted costs and expenses of the business). His second, and complementary, task is to show how further profitable growth is to be achieved. Additionally, he must act as a self-accounting functional manager, budgeting and allocating his resources and submitting economic and practical cost estimates. Frequently, he may have to tell his Chief Executive that the present objectives are unattainable and must either be modified or a period of retrenchment or investment must be followed.

This is one of the most difficult tasks of a Marketing Director responsible for a number of profit-responsible brand managers who will have products in various states of economic repair. How can judgement be made easier? Firstly, a company paying full attention to the product life-cycle concept will know which products to back, when and for how long. It will also have a series of replacements (either new products or product improvements) in the pipeline. Secondly, decisions between brands can be simplified if every manager presenting a plan for consideration is obliged to present not just the one he considers ideal and recommends but also one which *will* achieve his share of the profit objective. By doing this, it frequently becomes very clear that a plan to achieve objective is a plan to condemn the product to death: it may well be better to accept less than the objective in order to provide a higher contribution to the total costs and expenses which the company has to meet. You may find that the difference between the plan which just achieves objective and the 'ideal' is so minimal as to put the 'ideal' plan out of court.

Fortunately for most Marketing Directors, there are in the majority of product mixes brands which can easily exceed their objective. There are two ways of playing this situation: either you can offset the excess on one brand against the shortfall on another, or you can allocate the overall objective on an actual cash basis before the plans are prepared. Most companies start by costing on some form of ratio (percentage, cost per lb, etc). However, under this system, a minor unadvertised brand may show a handsome excess over its profit aim simply because it adds the money it doesn't spend on advertising to the profit it makes. Taking the total contribution required as a cash sum and sharing it out among brands can be a satisfactory way of overcoming this difficulty. It overcomes a lot of fiddly juggling on the part of the Marketing Director (which can often lead to a cut-back in sales forecast if advertising budget has to be reduced and will thus be self-defeating) and it also seems highly regarded by brand managers who operate this system. Cash sums are more tangible, one can see one's progress towards them and they are less open to manoeuvre (as we shall see later) than are ratios. If every individual product is required to achieve its specified objective on a ratio basis, there is a grave danger of penalizing developing brands and those that have the best opportunities, whilst apparently favouring lesser products. However, when allocating cash sums to brands as objectives one must not be over-kind to brands. As we shall see in a later chapter dealing with financial considerations, all brands must be capable of standing on their own two feet at some time and when they are not doing that, it must be as a result of a conscious decision which can be reversed when the necessity arises.

Chapter 19

The Role of Marketing in Long-Range Corporate Planning[1]

Early in this book we highlighted the importance of every business accepting that it might have to become a very different business in the changed circumstances of the future. More recently, we have identified long-term planning as one of the tasks of the Marketing Director. However, long-range planning for new markets inevitably involves the whole enterprise and all departments must be involved in such a way that all the complementary activities come to fruition at the same time. To ensure that this happens, all departments must be involved to some degree in formal planning for various possible futures rather than be passive recipients of information.

I want to make it plain that I shall concern myself solely with the role of Marketing (either as a department or in the case of a small business a single person). I am not concerned with the increasingly esoteric techniques that are being used by Corporate Planning departments. However defined, the end result of all corporate planning should be an increased rate of profitable growth in the long run. As that wonderful pioneer of so many automobile and aeronautical developments, Charles F. Kettering, once said: 'We should all be concerned about the future because that's where we will all have to spend the rest of our lives.'

A business must be prepared to look beyond the lives of its present goods or services, beyond the lives of its present Management, even beyond the lives of its present owners. None of these 'deaths' must be allowed to disrupt the business. Hence my own favourite description of corporate planning: 'It is not

... a process of making tomorrow's decisions today, but rather a process directed towards making today's decisions with tomorrow in mind, and a means of preparing for future decisions so that they be made rapidly, economically, and with as little disruption to the business as possible.'[2]

No successful Marketing man lives only for today. He is accustomed to looking forward in order to maximize profit opportunities. He is continually dealing with the situation where he has to decide between bread and jam today and only today, or bread – and no jam – for a good few years to come. He is no stranger to long-range planning, but the period of the plans and their comprehensiveness have varied according to the situation of the company, the business it is in, his own outlook and that of his colleagues – especially his superiors. However, too often he has ploughed a lonely furrow into the sky-blue yonder. The introduction of long-range corporate planning will mean that the commitments the Marketing man makes today will be accompanied by a much greater awareness on the part of the rest of the enterprise in the future.

How Long is 'Long'?

Just as a brand has a life cycle so, too, there is a corporate life cycle which is the summation of the individual volume and profit curves. We have already considered the importance of keying activity on individual brands to the forecast life cycle of the brand and of ensuring a succession of product developments and new products coming forward to maintain corporate growth. All this forms a back-cloth to the role of Marketing in this area of corporate planning. To a considerable extent, the share and profitable time span of the corporate life cycle of profits determine the length of time for which plans must be made. Clearly, the situation will vary from company to company. Many companies would regard a five-year plan as a long-range plan. There is a not unnatural tendency to keep regular plans down to short periods. With the pace of technology and fashion, to say nothing of competitive pressure and developments, profit plans tend to be restricted to periods offering the best possible chance of accuracy. (The rolling plan is an attempt to lengthen the period considered and give the longest point greater accuracy.) An obsession with accuracy (which is seldom achieved even over comparatively short periods) leads companies to question the need to plan for longer time spans. We need to look further ahead simply because the profitable life of the results of management decision (whether it be a product, an investment policy, a factory) is becoming shorter and shorter whilst the complexities of taking the decision are becoming much greater. The brand manager's five-year plan can be positively dangerous for his company if his absorption with accurate prediction leads him (as it must) to merely project what was and what is. To take the product life-cycle concept to its ultimate, he will eventually succeed in telling his Chairman when his company will go out of business!

This is where life gets difficult for the company Marketing man. Of course, we all know that the conventional response to the plateau on the life cycle is to find new markets for the product, to produce product variants, improvements, new sizes, etc to create a new growth period above the plateau. But somewhere he'll have to think of a completely new product.

Perhaps even a new market!

Now we really do have corporate problems. Where is the technical expertise for the new market going to come from? How long will it take to site, build, equip, and staff a new factory? Is there sufficient capacity in the sales force? Do we need to call on different types of outlet? What distribution system do we need? These, and many more, are the *corporate* complications of a new product/new market recommendation and they're often difficult for people to take. They seem so remote from day-to-day reality and so much in conflict with the normal operations of the going business that they often become 'spare time' planning jobs or are relegated to the people who can best be spared.

As with all areas of Marketing, there are no simple answers. I prefer, as apparently do most experienced corporate planners, to set my time limits by a landmark approach rather than a rigid adoption of a set number of years. Thus, if you are selling well-established staple products it might make sense to regard five years as the 'short-term', the period over which you can satisfactorily project current business. The 'mid-term', which might well be five to ten years, could be seen as a period during which the business would remain within its existing areas of expertise, but the variation in life cycles of individual categories will cause profitability to swing between those areas in ways which might dramatically change the employment of resources (especially machinery and labour). With this kind of landmark approach, the really 'long-term' (perhaps ten to twenty years) would encompass the possibility of finding no more profitable growth in existing markets and therefore being forced to search for new ones. You will only get to stage three if your objectives are couched in terms of returns on resources employed and not in terms of something like 'We are in the bread business': there may not be a viable business in bread in twenty years' time.

Every business can work out, though possibly rather arbitrarily, such landmarks and produce two or three segments as I have indicated. In some rapidly developing businesses where technology is advancing rapidly, the 'long-term' can be shorter than a relatively staid market's 'short-term'. The 'short-term' in producing a new aeroplane or car may seem insufferable to the brand manager who can put a new food product on the market within three months of the word 'go' (but this may have ended its profitable life before the first aeroplane is in flight!). It is ironic to me that fashion changes often occur with much greater rapidity in product fields with a long gestation period: I suspect that product obsolescence is in inverse ratio to development time. It is strange, too, that product changes seem so much more traumatic in many companies with short development times and low capital intensity!

Reverse Profitability Analysis

There is a great deal of current talk of 'gap analysis' in the context of long-range planning. This is the topic I call 'Reverse Profitability Analysis'. Basically, one defines the long-term objectives of the company and plots the trends of existing business against those objectives. Eventually, there must come a time when there is a profit gap, a point where the objectives exceed the forecast attainment. Expressed this way, every part of the company can be made aware of the need for action to prepare for dramatically changed circumstances – circumstances which must be met by:

1. Improving the performance of present products or services in their existing markets.
2. Discovering new markets for the existing lines.
3. Developing new goods or services for present markets.
4. Developing new goods or services for new markets.
5. Acquiring a company active in present markets.
6. Acquiring a company active in new markets.

Those, singly or in combination, are some of the answers. Let's look more closely at the analysis of the problem.

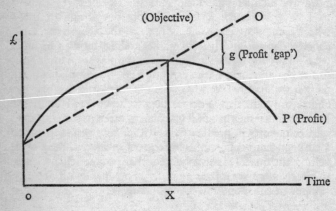

Figure 18.

Figure 18 sets out a very simplified picture of the way the profit gap arises. The forecast sales of the enterprise result in a long-term profit forecast (P) which shows the familiar decline pattern. (Each of these diagrams assumes a going brand with a start-point where objectives are just achieved.) This eventually falls below the objectives (O). Point X is the position where, once again, the profit generated is only equal to that required and, thereafter, a 'gap' (g) will appear which can be filled only by the profits created by one or more of the six methods mentioned a little earlier. We can now introduce a little more refinement into this simplified model with a more realistic one

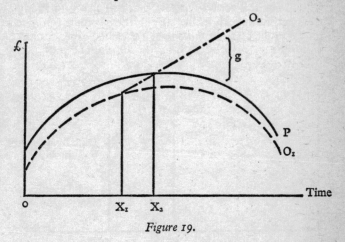

Figure 19.

(Figure 19). On the previous diagram, we saw the profit objective increasing as a straight-line progression. A sophisticated company will normally have two sets of objectives. One will be the minimum acceptable profit objective defined in terms of return on capital employed; the other will be an acceptable growth rate over and above the minimum. Thus a company may express its objective as: 'To earn an adequate return on the capital employed and increase profits by a minimum of five per cent per annum.'

This is sensible because a good Marketing man will arrange things so that he nearly always achieves the minimum objective even though volume and profit are declining. (I say 'nearly always' because, when sales of a product fall very low, fixed

costs and overheads assume increasing proportions and make
the attainment of profit objectives difficult if not impossible.)
You see this situation illustrated on this refined model. O_1 is
the minimum objective, O_2 is the growth objective. On this
model, the company falls behind its growth objective from X_2
in time, but on the ratio of actual profit to growth objective
shown here the warning shot is fired at point X_1.

'Reverse Profitability' comes from the need to work backwards. Using this sort of analysis, you will give your Product
Development team a brief like: 'By X_2 (time) produce products
with £P profit with not more than £C capital expenditure.'

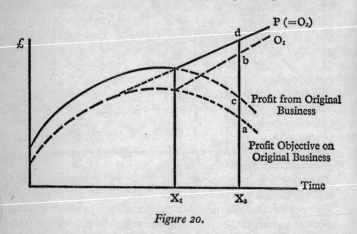

Figure 20.

The effect of achieving such a brief is seen by this third
chart in this series (Figure 20). From the point where a line
drawn from X_1 meets the minimum objective curve O_1, profitability (P) increases and coincides with the old line O_2. O_1
similarly increases in proportion to the extra capital employed.
The whole business is on a new course. If we look along the
line X_2, the distance 'ab' is the measure of the extra profit to be
earned upon the extra capital employed in the business; the
distance 'cd' is the extra profit attributable to the new business.
The margin represented by 'bd' is the extent to which the

enterprise succeeds in bettering its new minimum profit performance requirements.

I should, of course, point out here that my model is a very stylized one. The relationship between profit achieved and a profit objective based upon the capital employed in the business is not constant as my graphs show, even in a highly successful business. Capital is employed in real assets (plant, property, etc), in stocks (of raw materials and finished, unsold goods) and in net debtors (debtors less creditors). Expenditure on real assets progresses as a series of plateaux, as new plant is put in and new factory sites are purchased. Stocks and the net debtor/creditor position are much more directly variable with output. Thus the distance 'bd' will vary at different points of time as the proportion of fixed assets employed in the total capital structure varies.

The great value of this analysis should be in highlighting the need to achieve certain ends by specific dates. (I've talked about products, but the objective could just as well be the achievement of, say, certain production cost savings.) It is this sense of urgency, involvement and commitment that the corporate planner is trying to create. The difficulty of creating this sense of urgency has been, historically, one of the greatest problems of Brand Management.

However, many a company has invested money in machinery and bricks and mortar on the pipe-dreams of a brand manager! The opposite side of the coin to the decision to invest in new plant at a point on the life cycle where a product is in decline, is to invest in machinery for a product that isn't going to make the grade. Long-range brand plans can lead to unnecessary investment in management time (if not in plant, etc) if there is no review procedure built in. Whilst other functions need the longest possible notice of the chance of something dramatically new happening, they need swift notice that a project *isn't* coming to fruition even more urgently. It is in this area that network planning with clear 'Go/No Go' check-points is needed. This takes us back to the chapter on New Product Development.

These forecasts are only as good as the sales projections upon which they are based. Whilst inaccuracies in working out the profit figures will obviously affect the absolute accuracy of the projections, they are of lesser importance at the early stage. If I have been derogatory about the degree of technical mystique and jargon entering into corporate planning, I should redress the balance by saying that a tremendous amount of valuable work is being done, particularly in the field of Operations Research, on refining the accuracy of forecasts and considering relevant interrelationships between product projections and environmental studies (the population trends, economic forecasts, technological predictions and so on). What I object to is the amount of *technique*-orientated work which is being done instead of work directed at producing information which will allow – or even force – managers to take decisions.

Clearly the short-term rolling plan can provide a more reasonably accurate base for the longer-term plan than any procedure which relies on less frequent updating. As far as the long-term plan goes, however, this automatic review will do no more than define the likely contribution from existing products. The projection of what different products might exist or what new markets one might be in, for example, will be revised by continual examination of economic, sociological and technological circumstances, by the use of the forecasting techniques and information available, by the techniques of new-product research, all backed up by some form of network-plan review procedure for all the likely runners. Thus the input to the long-range corporate plan from the Marketing Director will be the summation of long-term projections of the present business plus the likely contribution from new ventures if they arrive on time. The latter projection will, ideally, be backed up with a series of network plans (one for each product under development) in which the truly critical dates from the corporate point of view are the decision dates when resources normally employed on the present day-to-day business have to be diverted and where new investment costs are incurred in those areas.

Human Problems

I want to say a few things about the very human problems of real, creative, long-range planning by the Marketing man. Since he is faced with predicting what will sell, when, and in what quantities, his head is seen as being clearly on the block! Faced with a sickening responsibility and experienced enough to know that his predictions will be wrong at least as often as they are right, he will be inclined to find reasons why longer-range planning than he is used to should stay near the bottom of his work pile! To this, all I can offer is that it is the very uncertainty of prediction that makes some form of long-range preparation all the more necessary. After all, your prediction that your present product will go on selling for twenty years is only a little more probable than the surmise that you might be selling a completely new product in an entirely new product field in twenty years' time! Any good corporate planner will tell you that it is the *process* not the *plan* that is important. The detail of the plan could well be obsolete almost as soon as it's written: the *process* which created it shouldn't be. Hence the importance of review techniques.

Another very real problem is that of day-to-day pressures. There is profit to be made *now*, a commercial by next month, a new premium offer to be found, and so on. A very healthy company may find fewer problems in devoting a high proportion of Marketing talent time to the very long-run plan. Companies with problems today need to solve them quickly – tomorrow if not today! As we have seen earlier, the first task of Management is to run the business it has; the second is to ensure its future. There is no reason why the two should not run closely together.

More and more companies practise 'management by objectives'. These are usually short-term objectives. After all, you don't want to wait five years to see if a brand manager is capable of doing his job! But how do you assess a planner? Most of his plans will not come to fruition (witness the many confusing statements on the very small number of new product ideas which ever reach the market, let alone succeed). So you judge him by the quality of his plans – which could produce a completely 'ivory tower' detachment!

Earlier in this book, we considered the question of whether one man should be responsible for all new product development and concluded that he should. Because of the importance of new products and/or acquisitions, this man often becomes the 'Brand Manager, Long-Range Planning', in effect if not in fact. It is worth repeating some of the human problems we considered earlier if only because some companies see these two titles as meaning quite different sorts of men. The basic problem is that of a man who does all the donkey work and hands it all over just as it gets exciting. And who will everybody remember when the brand is a success ? Your 'Planner' is only human; he wants to grow up with his plans, he wants promotion, and he is only too aware that results are most often judged by profit, volume and brand share. In terms of management appraisal, he must be assessed by the quality and practicability of both the plans and the process he creates to achieve them.

Comparatively recently, corporate planning departments have grown up, usually headed by a senior man reporting direct to the Chief Executive. These are all in very large companies and must therefore be considered in the light of whether the Chief Executive is able to fulfil a Marketing role at a level low enough and detailed enough to be of value to the planner. The answer must be 'no', and neither would it be desirable for him to try. His job must be to balance all the items in the mix and it may be more important to the immediate solving of the problem of the profit gap to speed up, say, debt collection than to search for new products. Not all the contributions to solving the gap arise within the Marketing function.

To me it seems not to matter at all who does the planning job – it might be a very arduous chore which the Marketing Director will be glad to be rid of – as long as it is realized that the contribution of the Marketing department is fundamental. Cost saving exercises are once-and-for-all, short-term, or at the best a continuing reduction of variable costs. Generally speaking, the more continuing the reduction in cost, the less the amount. Remember, until a business has customers it has only costs. Even if the forecasts of present business are prepared elsewhere, they should be passed to the Marketing Department (and thence to the Chief Executive) who will question assumptions, solicit remedies, query developments. Specialization is found in the central organizations of many multi-divisional companies. This can create difficulties (in human terms especially), but the companies who work this way reason that the advantages of avoiding duplication of effort outweigh any disadvantages.

Many Marketing men seem to fear the corporate planners, perhaps because they see them as becoming the guardians of the long-term success of the enterprise – a role coveted and jealously guarded by Marketing Directors and by brand managers for their specific products. I believe there is an unreasonable fear of the concept of corporate planning and especially the role of the corporate planner, and that the Marketing man should welcome any assistance towards reaching total commitment to common goals. However, in the last resort a great deal depends upon the way top management use corporate planning. It is a means not of *supplanting* Marketing plans but of ensuring their success.

The Role of the Marketing Department

It has already been said that, in their role of direction finders, the role of the Marketing department is the most important single one. However, they can achieve nothing alone. There are other basic roles they can perform. The most fundamental is to introduce the concept of corporate commitment to a longer term (even if, in the first instance, no corporate plans result) in companies where this is not yet accepted – and this is still the majority. The Marketing department, with its eyes always towards the far horizon and generally more inclined towards risk attitudes than other functions, is in a very good position to initiate the concept of corporate planning – but don't expect it to happen overnight. My own experience is that it takes a good deal of time to effectively introduce longer-term plans than the

Management of the business is used to. I don't really find that surprising. It was not so long ago that many of us first persuaded our Boards to think in terms of three-, four- and five-year plans, and there are still many companies who have only the very sketchiest idea about their overall plans for more than a year ahead. Even when you have convinced everybody that a longer-term plan for the business is meaningful and you have secured their involvement and commitment, there is a good deal of spadework still to be done. The longer the planning period, the more rigorously must you examine the conventions used. You may, for example, be able to ignore the possible effects of inflation in the short run but this may be a vital factor in a ten-year plan. You can't set up a rush programme by putting all your top brand managers on the job for six months. Quite apart from the dangers to existing business, remember the old adage that making nine women pregnant simultaneously won't produce a baby in one month!

The area of maximum contribution from the Marketing department is being both the creative and practical antidote to the necessarily theoretical thinking involved in long-range corporate planning. By attracting first-class brains from many disciplines, many companies have fallen into the trap of making their planning heavily technique-orientated and it is a difficult trap to escape from. In particular, more use will be placed on OR techniques and the computer, and the Marketing man can perform a valuable function by assessing the practicability of the models that are being built to ensure that they offer the best possible chance of meeting the ultimate test of profitability. Unless this test is met, the whole process will quickly fall into disrepute.

There is, finally, one absolutely fundamental role which the Marketing man must fulfil. The more 'programmed thinking' there is in forward planning and the more companies make use of mathematical prediction, the greater the need for creative thought. The computer enables a far wider range of likely variables to be considered with great speed. This, combined with growing conventionality in the responses of large companies to certain stimuli, inevitably increases the chances of different companies coming up with the same idea. You can see evidence of this growing, week by week. It is becoming harder and harder to make the sort of breakthrough that gives you a healthy solo spot in a new field. This is where the questioning mind of the Marketing man comes in.

The greatest contribution the Marketing man can make to the long-range plans of his company is the use of real *Creative* Marketing!

Conclusion

Once an area of business activity gets itself a name it becomes a 'technique'. It then surrounds itself with jargon and mumbo-jumbo, is magnified out of all proportion and ends up by becoming yet another tyrant cult. Corporate planning has attained that status although healthy scepticism seems to have set in earlier than with other similar cults.

In its most grandiose form, it is a technique for large companies only. Stripped to its essentials, it combines the concept of the profit life cycle with the identification and attainment of objectives and ensures the full commitment of all parts of the business to those plans. Expressed that way, it is a common-sense management tool for every type and size of business to achieve. The small business, in fact, has many advantages, for it usually has the commitment of everyone in it and the aims are not so complex that it is difficult to reconcile the odd conflicts that arise. Whilst it is harder to separate the future from the intense involvement with the day-to-day, most managers of small businesses can feel the hot breath of expectancy down their necks as people wait for them to steer a new course and act. Additionally, a wild idea is more easily followed on a small scale than on a large one. The basis of corporate planning is for everyone, then; the extremes are for the very few.

Because it is allied to a technique, the word 'plan' can attain a sanctity it was never meant to possess. A plan, whatever kind it may be, is a good servant. It is a terrible master. Remember that it is the process of planning – actively considering the future – which matters, not the plan itself. That will be outdated many times before any part of it becomes fact. The long-range plan is an indication of likely directions: unlike the annual operating plan, it is not a promise of results. Use corporate planning as a set of signposts: you may change your direction along the way but at least make sure that everyone takes the same road. Marketing men have had a history of being pathfinders with others following grudgingly and belatedly behind, sometimes even turning in the opposite direction. With long-range corporate planning, the Chief Executive will lead the column; the Marketing Director will recommend the tunes the troops should sing.

References

1. I am grateful to the Marketing Society Ltd for allowing me to reproduce a considerable part, including the original diagrams, of a paper I presented at their first annual conference in April 1967 and published in the proceedings: *The Role of Marketing in Corporate Planning*.
2. *Long Range Planning – The Executive Viewpoint*. An excellent short work by E. Kirkby Warren, published by Prentice-Hall Inc, 1966.

Suggestions for Further Reading

The best-known work is H. Igor Ansoff's *Corporate Strategy*, first published by McGraw-Hill in 1965 and now available in a paperback edition by Penguin. *Corporate Planning – a Practical Guide* by A. J. A. Argenti is just that, by a prominent British practitioner. Industrial companies are catered for by *Strategic Planning in Industrial Organisations* by R. Ackoff, published by the University of Lancaster. We have to go to America for *Long Range Planning for Small Business* by R. M. Hass, published by Indiana University. An analysis of *Long Range Planning in 45 Industrial Companies* also comes from the USA and is by Harold

W. Henry, published by Prentice-Hall in 1967. *Multi-national Corporate Planning* is an area of great interest to the larger international companies, and this is by Steiner & Cannon, published by Macmillan in 1966. Finally, *Marketing Planning: a Systems Approach* by E. Mark Stein, McGraw-Hill, 1966.

Chapter 20

Profit and Cash Control

'Profit' is one of the most frequently used words in Marketing. It features in every formal definition, our objectives are set in terms of it, brand managers are expected to be profit-responsible and profit-conscious. At the same time, it is one of the most frequently misused, misplaced and misunderstood words in the businessman's language. In our definitions, we qualify it. For every one brand manager allowed *real* profit responsibility, there must be a hundred to whom the term is a fiction. For every one brand manager with that real level of responsibility, there must be fifty who really don't understand what it means and are incapable of exercising it. Frequently, one is misled into a belief that one is profit-responsible and profit-conscious by adherence to (and achievement of) company objectives which are themselves living evidence of a lack of understanding of what profit is all about.

What is it all about? Surely everybody knows what 'profit' is. It is the difference between income and expenditure or revenue minus costs. Sorry; that's too easy. What revenue, which costs? Remember the case of GEC and AEI (Chapter 9) and how one company's 'profit' became another's 'loss'. The Pergamon-Leasco episode of the latter half of 1969 showed how the way stocks of books were valued could influence the 'profit' of the company. By valuing these stocks at wholesale price (a perfectly legitimate thing to do) Pergamon were showing a profit that had not been made and possibly might never have been made. Alternatively, they argued, to have valued them at nothing at all (or their value as pulp) would have distorted profits in the years in which the books were sold – possibly a year in which the only costs directly attributable to the sales would be minimal since they would exclude production.

I must emphasize again that there is nothing illegal about these manoeuvres and in terms of strict accountancy practice it is almost impossible to say who is right and who is wrong in these cases. The valuation of assets is a very good point. A year-old machine which cost £100,000 when new may now be valued after allowing ten per cent depreciation at £90,000. If the company went bust tomorrow, how much could you get for that machine? You might have trouble giving it away. Many large companies would suffer dramatic falls in net asset values if these were at calculated break-up prices.

The whole point of these examples is that 'profit' as most managers know and use the term is nothing more than an accounting abstraction, often close to being a myth, arrived at after making a series of unrelated or interrelated assumptions. In all the examples quoted, it would have been possible for a company showing a book 'profit' to actually be in a loss position if the measure used was available cash and quick resources. More large businesses than one might think live on a knife-edge: one company which has regularly been in the top twenty companies on all the conventional measures of profitability had to stop paying its bills a couple of years ago. It held off for two weeks until it had generated enough cash to get over its problems. It lost a few prompt-payment discounts, but it was (and is) a very large company so no one instituted dunning procedures. Most prompt-payment discounts were handled automatically by the computer in any case. The manoeuvre was well worth while. Compared with the cost of borrowing it was a stroke of genius, but the most important thing was that the company refilled its coffers with cash.

CASH!!

A profit which does not result in cash availability is no profit. The important ways of making profit are cash-generating sales and cash-saving cost exercises. The rest are accounting devices, many of which have considerable merit.

Many invite disaster if not approached with understanding.

In this chapter we shall consider the ways in which a company may frame its objectives and several areas of cash-saving exercises which the Marketing Director should carry out. In doing these things we shall inevitably dwell on the dangers of regarding profit and return on capital in the abstract sense. The Marketing Director should see his profit-responsibility as the generation and retention (at least until they become dividends) of the maximum amount of cash and quick resources rather than the manipulation of assets to produce book figures. Try running a very small business and see which you would rather have at the end of the week, a handsome book profit or enough cash to pay the wages!

The Framing of Objectives

The word 'framing' has more than one meaning, one of which implies a trumped-up affair; we shall see that this meaning can have particular significance if the rules for achieving company objectives are not considered with great care. The dangers already referred to and those yet to be mentioned are attributable to partial and growing sophistication. However, we must never forget that the vast majority of companies in this country are small businesses: little over two per cent of British manufacturing companies employ more than 1,000 people; the highest number of companies occurs in the group employing more than twenty-five but fewer than fifty people. Thus it would not be unreasonable to assume that – despite my earlier cautions – the *majority* of companies *are* aiming for cash profits and for more profit this year than last. It is the larger, 'more sophisticated', quoted public companies who get themselves into trouble over accounting conventions affecting return on capital and earnings per share. Return on capital is increasingly becoming either the sole objective or part of the objective of a company.

To make a point, I shall inevitably pour ridicule on the concept of return on capital, but let me put the case in perspective: return on capital is a valid part of any company objective. After all, why invest your money in running a business with all the attendant risks and problems if you can make more money sitting in your armchair and putting your money in Unit Trusts? The fundamental difficulty with return on capital is, which way do you achieve an improvement, by reducing capital or increasing profits? Most companies will find it a great deal easier to concentrate upon reducing the amount of net capital employed, a technique which can lead to the high book profits/no cash situation already dramatized.

One problem which has to be faced is, what is capital? As we shall see, some people look for return on equity capital, others on total assets. Ignoring for the moment the problem of what to include and what to leave out, here are some of the ways of manipulating the denominator (capital) in the fraction without altering the numerator (profits), and making the return on capital look good. You can probably think of more.

1. Reduce the value of stocks.
2. Sell wherever you can and lease instead; it's more expensive but it takes items off the balance sheet. (Sale and leaseback of property is a common way of raising working cash without diluting equity holdings and reducing return on capital.)
3. Depreciate capital equipment as rapidly as possible (which usually means as fast as the Government will allow).
4. Build your factories in development areas where the Government or the local authority will give you investment grants of up to fifty per cent.
5. Rather a borrower than a lender be! Never let people owe you more than the total of your own debt.
6. Never pay for your goods until you have sold them – the resultant return on capital tied up in stocks is utterly confounded by your having sold more stocks than you have paid for and valued.
7. Why buy a new factory when you can rent; buy a new car when you can use contract hire?
8. Increase your overdraft and deduct it from net assets.

9. Examine the effect of selling machinery and using labour instead. You will reduce the denominator this way and produce a more favourable return on capital as long as the increase in labour costs does not lead to a commensurate reduction in profit.

10. Try to move into areas of business where people are prepared to allow you the interest-free use of their money. (Good examples are cigarette coupons, trading stamps and dividend stamps where the company has the use of the cash until the coupons or stamps are redeemed.)

If you do all these things – and some more you can easily think of – you have a very good chance of producing a fantastic return on capital and simultaneously going bust or being taken over!

Obviously the situation must never reach such farcical circumstances. Many of the things considered are quite sound areas for investigation and improvement. Of course you should chase up debts: this is part of sound cash control. There is equally obviously no point in holding larger stocks of raw materials or finished goods than the circumstance demands. One company which is a heavy user of a basic commodity was able to reduce its average stockholding by over £1m without any adverse effect on the company's sales, with no adverse effect on profits (the advantage of buying futures was the claimed justification for the high stock-level), but with a significant effect on its return on capital and thence on its share price.

Then, too, there is the question of what is 'capital'? Many companies mean the ratio of return on owners' (or equity) capital; others have a concept of total assets employed. When we look at the operating ratios of a business we shall see again how many variables can affect the measure other than an increase in profit. Some companies regard bank overdrafts as part of capital employed and thus close one avenue of manipulation. Such companies may say that they measure the return they get from assets set against the money put into those assets, and thus they include all creditors, bank overdraft, loans and advances (the latter arising mainly when talking of a division or a subsidiary). Thus a company which regards net indebtedness in its return on capital calculations will find no joy in any manipulation which turns an asset into an offsetting liability. A wide definition of 'capital employed' is to be encouraged. Any method which restricts the definition of an asset and thus disguises changes in the composition of total assets (in the ways described) is a bad system.

A simple way of avoiding the worst excesses of the simplified return on capital system (which is widely used among so-called sophisticated companies) is to take the following short list of assets:

Real Assets (property, plant, etc).
Stocks (raw, finished goods in stock and transit).
Net Debtors (debtors less creditors).

One will probably seek a different rate of return on each and the final desired rate will be produced by an amalgam of the separate returns weighted by their importance in the total mix. My simple list ignores working levels of cash (which are often included on the basis that they could otherwise be invested) and does not include surplus cash (which is usually earning interest) and investments: these are customarily omitted from any list of assets when calculating both required and actual return ratios.

This still leaves the doubtful areas of valuation of assets, what is an asset, depreciation policy and so on. These are running sores that are likely to plague us for some time to come. One man who tackled this problem of manipulation by bookkeeping earlier than most was Forrest Mars, whose basic principles have remained unchanged. He calls for a defined level of 'return on total assets' and he values his businesses by the amount of money that went into the purchase or leasing of those assets. In meeting these targets he takes no account of depreciation at all: the critical ratio is sales income minus the cost of doing business divided by the real funds put into the business and expressed as a percentage.[1]

We can't finish with return on capital easily and we have other objectives to consider. Earning an adequate return *is* important but be careful how you frame the rules and don't cheat. Whilst cost reductions can have significant effects on profits, real money profits are earned by Marketing. All the major efforts of Marketing must be to increase cash flow. Keeping capital to a minimum and turning it over fast is the best way of improving the return. For example, if a business makes only one sale a year at £X profit, it can earn the same return on the same capital by making two sales at £$\frac{X}{2}$ profit. The principle of high turnover/lower profit is the bedrock of modern grocery trading.

Let's stop fiddling. We are now honest traders presenting our shareholders with the best possible picture of our return on capital. We have shareholders who are people like ourselves: willing to take a risk to make a profit. An equity holder wants to see either his dividend go continually upwards or his share value rise steadily or both. Thus, we should add to our profit objective a factor to allow for the distribution of profits and bear in mind any capital needs we may have which will require either fresh borrowing or generating enough profit to retain sufficient to fund our investment and enough to distribute to shareholders.

This brings us to earnings per share. As a measure of Stock Market performance, this is so widely used that some companies frame their objectives entirely in terms of earnings per share (public companies, that is) whilst few ignore them. Unfortunately, earnings per share and price/earnings ratio (the latter is but a logical extension of the former) are subject to the same problems as return on capital. Questions one must ask oneself include: to what extent is the psychology of the market or the performance of the market category an important influence; were profits the result of better trading, better cash control, changing conventions or what; is the trend a well-established one; how are R & D costs treated; does a company use realistic rentals in arriving at profits; how are raw material stocks treated; how are finished stocks valued? One could go on. Again, however, the earnings per share and P/E ratios have value whatever their inadequacies. Their greatest value is in indicating a performance trend which enables one to forecast the likely future. A sudden unexplained jump is a pretty clear indication of a change in accounting convention.

What do we end up with? A composite objective which takes account of acceptable rates of return on different classes of asset, allows for the effects of taxation, considers the problems of necessary ploughback and future borrowing, and sets an acceptable growth rate for the future which will reflect upon the company's earnings per share and P/E ratio. At the same time it will be utilizing its capital to the full, controlling its cash flow effectively and Marketing aggressively. Such a company will have happy shareholders and few bidders – the price will be too high.

The objectives, once framed, should be seen by the Chief Executive and the Marketing Director as a minimum to be achieved. The Chief Executive must beware of those sectional manipulations which may look good from the narrow view but are in conflict with the long-term corporate goals. On the other hand, expense budgets should be regarded as maximum figures to be exceeded only under the most exceptional circumstances – and I include advertising appropriations here too!

Management Ratios

Different comparative measures and various consultants use their own lists of management ratios. Comparison of these ratios may, subject to the qualifications mentioned already, give a clue as to why overall performance is not as good as the average for your industry. The ratios in most common use relate cost elements to sales but, although they include assets by type, there is no measure of the return on capital employed in various departments. In Figure 21 I have used 18 ratios, all stemming from operating profits divided by operating assets – a return on total assets employed concept. This is yet another way of hammering home the point I have made repeatedly:

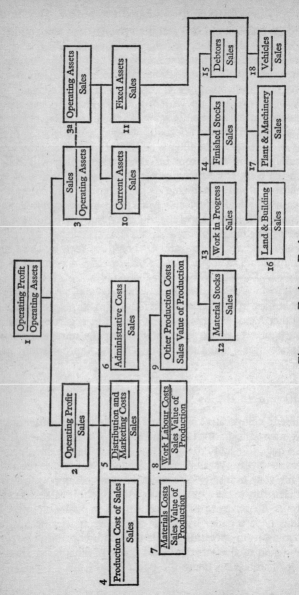

Figure 21. Business Ratios

that return on capital calculations can be affected – manipulated if you like – by many other relationships and manoeuvres.

The two prime ratios relate sales to profit and sales to assets; in order to keep sales on the bottom line throughout for maximum comparability, the ratio of sales over operating assets is inverted. This inversion (3a) reflects what assets will be required for every, say, £1,000 worth of sales. Thus changes in ratios 2, 3, and 3a are the main determinants, for they show the profit margin (2), the number of times total assets are turned over (3) and, as we have seen, assets required per £1,000 of sales (3a). Each of these ratios, however, can be influenced by a change in any other ratios in the two main streams.

Marketing Uses of Break-even Analysis

We have already considered a stylized model of break-even analysis when considering price-fixing. Additional uses include analysing customer and product mix, sales force expansion or contraction, advertising and promotional expenditure, regional profitability analysis: in fact, any calculation of the volume needed to achieve required profit rates. The stylized model (so called because a true plotting would usually reveal plateaux and downturns in place of the straight lines depicted) is a rather long way round the problem and shorter ways can be used by employing the right formula. Let's start with the ratios we have already used. In Figure 21, ratio 1 can be arrived at by multiplying ratios 2 and 3, thus:

$$\frac{\text{Operating Profit}}{\text{Sales}} \times \frac{\text{Sales}}{\text{Operating Assets}} = \frac{\text{Operating Profit}}{\text{Operating Assets}}$$

– since 'Sales' cancel out. We could express this another way by saying that:

$$\text{Profit Margin} \times \text{Stockturn} = \text{Return on Total Assets}$$

e.g.   Operating Profit = £100,000
             Sales   = £1,000,000
             Operating Assets = £400,000.

Therefore:
$$\frac{£100,000}{1,000,000} \times \frac{1,000,000}{400,000} = \underline{\underline{25\%}}$$

or

$$10\% \times 2 \cdot 5 \qquad = \underline{\underline{25\%}}.$$

As with any equation, one can measure the effect of any change. For example, what operating profit must be earned on the same sales and assets to increase the return to thirty per cent? Let operating profit be the unknown P. Then:

$$\frac{£ \quad P}{1,000,000} \times \frac{1,000,000}{400,000} = 30\%$$

$$\equiv \frac{£ \quad P}{400,000} = 30\%$$

and therefore P = £120,000: to raise the return by five per cent, profits must increase by twenty per cent if sales are unchanged. Obviously this is a very simple model capable of much greater sophistication up to the point of computer simulation of changes in all the management ratios.

Having established the principle, I do not wish to go through every possible area in which the basic techniques of break-even analysis may be used, but I do want to highlight some areas in the Marketing department's sphere where the techniques can be employed but seldom are. I want first to look at the concept of regional profitability. Suppose, for example, we know that we can make our target net profit only if we keep to an advertising/sales ratio of five per cent. We may be doing this handsomely nationally but are we achieving the desired ratio in each region? Is it even important that we should? An unfortunate tendency in the majority of markets is for sales in promoted areas to go up and those in unsupported areas to go down. It often happens that the areas with rising sales are bolstered by a high advertising/sales ratio partly funded by the underspending in other areas. If the sales in the unsupported areas fall dramatically – or even disappear – you could find yourself unable to support the high expenditure levels necessary to maintain sales in the stronger areas. Not only are you likely to be spending above the allowed rate in certain regions but you will probably find that inordinate sales and promotional costs are being incurred in the same areas. If the sales manager has his own paid promotion budget, he is highly likely to spend most of it behind the most heavily promoted brand (he is seizing his opportunity!). Tot it all up and you may get a shock. I once discovered that the *total* promotional expenditure on my lead line in one area exceeded the gross profit – a fact that had been concealed by low advertising and promotional effort in other areas. Short-term these may be valid decisions but in the longer term every brand has to stand on its own two feet without help from other sources.

Most companies shy away from regional profitability analyses because of the arbitrary assumptions that have to be made. I would argue that decisions based upon arbitrary assumptions are better than ignoring possible problems. The first step is to arrive at a regional Marketing contribution. The formula can be adapted from company to company but a suggested basis which will be appropriate to most companies will look something like this:

Gross Profit

Dr Discounts
Dr Share of Advertising
Dr Share of Sales Expenses
Dr Share of Promotional Allowances
Dr Share of Marketing Department Expenses
= Regional Net Marketing Contribution

Many of these can be measured precisely, some with a mixture of arbitrariness and precision, and some only by the adoption of some standard rate such as cost per lb sold. This exercise in itself may be enough to throw up valuable ideas

about the allocation of resources to areas. You can take it
further and look at the return on regional investment.

Let's imagine that Birmingham shows sales of £100,000, a
net Marketing contribution of £10,000, and there is £50,000
invested in the region (in warehouses, offices, equipment, cars
and so on). The formula is only subtly different from that for
examining company return on total assets. It is:

$$\frac{\text{Regional Net Marketing Contribution}}{\text{Sales}} \times \frac{\text{Sales}}{\text{Regional Investment}}$$
$$= \text{Return on Investment}$$

or   Profit Rate $\times$ Stockturn $=$ RoI.

Thus: $\dfrac{£10,000}{100,000} \times \dfrac{100,000}{50,000}$ $= 20\%$

or

$10\% \times 2$ $= 20\%$.

Again the warning that these calculations provide tools
which should only be placed in the right hands. They generally
pose more problems than they solve: questions like, does the
potential of the region justify the investment; should it be
more or less; are there too many salesmen; is advertising and
promotional support out of gear with sales? All the ingredients
that go to make up the almost too simple ratio calculation need
examining. Personal experience has shown that the number
and location of regional offices and depots and the allocation of
discretionary funds to local managers can be improved
dramatically by this kind of analysis. If regional profitability
summaries (stopping short of RoI calculations) are done by
product, damaging conflict can be avoided. This is a valuable
discipline on local sales management which is a refinement on
simple sales cost per unit – although that too is a measurement
of great value not in general use.

Similar calculations can be done on increasing the size of a sales force or part of the force, although the problem of determining what contribution an individual salesman should make to fixed costs and profit is usually more difficult. When we employ a new salesman, we want to know if he will sell enough to pay for his own salary plus all the ongoing variable costs associated with the extra sales. There is no return on the investment in new salesmen until they are paying for their keep in this way. Let us assume that we employ a new salesman at a total cost of £4,000 and we expect him to sell £30,000 worth of goods. On each pound, he makes a contribution (after allocated variable costs have been allowed for) of twenty per cent. We can measure the return on investment by applying the contribution from the new salesman beyond the break-even point to our basic formula. The real contribution from the extra man will be:

$$
\begin{aligned}
\text{Sales} \quad &\times \text{Contribution Rate} - \text{Cost of Salesman} \\
= £30,000 &\times 20\% - £4,000 \\
= £6,000 &- £4,000 \\
= £2,000.&
\end{aligned}
$$

The return on this extra salesman will be:

$$
\frac{\text{Net Contribution from Extra Man}}{\text{Sales}} \times \frac{\text{Sales}}{\text{Cost of Extra Man}}
$$

$$
\frac{£2,000}{30,000} \times \frac{30,000}{4,000} = 50\%.
$$

Again, we can 'play' with this in various ways, adjusting various items whilst holding other elements in the mix constant. This is a lesser-used formula, for the sophisticated companies have established break-evens per call by work-study and use these as yardsticks. However, it must be remembered that sales costs feature in the list of management ratios (No 5) and salesmen earning low returns will show up in the final results.

One other example is important both to retailers and those

who want space in their stores. Retailers don't actually charge you rent for a place on their shelves, but the better ones calculate precisely the return they require per square foot, linear foot or cubic foot and rate products accordingly. The retailer can seldom vary his fixed investment with any great rapidity and therefore he is primarily interested in his investment in stocks and how often and how rapidly they move out. Thus, the calculation for the retailer is:

$$\frac{\text{Profit}}{\text{Sales}} \times \frac{\text{Sales}}{\text{Stocks}} = \text{RoI}$$

or

Rate of Profit × Stockturn.

This is what he will look at when deciding to stock a new line or give an existing product or brand more space. The wise salesman will be prepared with profit-times-stockturn calculations. The return on investment becomes all the more attractive if the goods don't have to be paid for until they are sold (a basic attraction of rack-jobbing). The retailer, of course, will look upon profit as does the manufacturer, i.e. after deducting all directly attributable costs. The salesman usually can only do his calculation on gross margin and bear in mind that any special storage and handling problems, for example, will worsen the profit picture he presents.

Enough examples have been discussed to make it unnecessary to go through all departments to examine their individual return. Perhaps especially interesting to the Marketing Director are considerations affecting channels of sales and methods of physical distribution. The techniques are the same and, again, the results are more likely to pose relevant questions than provide solutions. Similarly, we can provide break-even analyses to such questions as changing the product mix, adding new products and changing promotional emphasis. The technique is the same in each case.

Marginal Cost – Again!

The theory behind marginal costing is that a company should expand sales up to, but not beyond, the point where marginal costs equal marginal revenue. In fact, that would be an unsatisfactory position, for the company would be making no profit. If marginal costing is to be used it must be used properly and that means accepting that there are few businesses where marginal revenue equals price. Thus, for practical business purposes, the strict economist's definition of marginal revenue as that revenue resulting from the sale of one more unit needs amendment. What the Marketing man must be concerned with is the revenue accruing from the sale of an extra unit after taking account of the effect that that additional sale may have on market price. The nearer one is to the margin, the more likely it is that extra units can be sold only by price reductions or special incentives which almost always have to be offered across the whole of the business in that product or service. Thus one is normally facing a situation in which the gains from the marginal sales have to be offset against lower profit rates on existing business. Only under conditions of perfect competition is marginal revenue likely to equal price. Where a marginal costing approach is used for pricing, one must consider the elasticity of demand both for the product and the market as a whole and the likely response of competitors.

In a multi-product company, there is a danger that arbitrary allocation on a standard cost basis may lead to the misuse of the marginal costing approach we considered in Chapter 12. Two systems are widely used. One says that, say, the standard cost for selling is £1 per ton and is therefore applied to all sales. The other says that the cost of the sales force is fixed and already paid for on a standard rate basis and therefore any extra sales or new products incur no sales cost. Both have their dangers. The first approach may prove very profitable but only if your competitors are not taking a more realistic approach: if they are, they may change their Marketing mix in some way disadvantageous to you – like reducing price, increasing promotion or increasing the sales force. I have actually experienced a situation where this standard rate basis was applied to a product which initially showed a loss. Sales were increased dramatically, the factory was able to produce more economically, no more salesmen were employed, yet, because the high standard costs of the original loss situation were still being applied, this particular product actually showed a bigger loss the more it sold. The benefits of these extra sales were not being attributed to the brand but as a bottom-line variance (and a very favourable one) on divisional profits. Had this situation not been recognized, a very successful brand might well have been taken off the market.

The other approach suffers from all the dangers of the free ride. We are all envious of the airline employees who travel the world with their families at absolutely minimal rates. However, they only get their cheap travel if there are spare places on the aircraft. The analogy is close. A product only gets its free ride if the sales of the products paying the costs are up to budget. If they aren't, the company will fail to reach its objectives. Very few companies really can use the marginal cost approach and I prefer to coin the term 'Direct Attributable Cost' (DAC) approach. Mass-market companies can apply the DAC approach to promotions, the anticipated return from exceeding the budget, pricing own-label products and even new products if they wish (although I oppose this). The DAC approach can start with a price or end with it. The method is to assume that all standard costs are met and that the only new costs incurred are those directly attributable to selling in excess of budget. These will be things like the promotion to generate the sale, the cost of physical distribution, perhaps extra clerical work. Using the DAC approach you can measure the extra profit from the extra sales and gauge how much you can afford to spend to get those extra sales. Care must be taken to consider the odds of the sales in which DAC is used being genuine extra sales, for this will affect both the number of attributable cost items and the rate at which they must be charged.

In the longer term a brand must stand on its own feet, and therefore one must consider carefully the effect of extra sales this year becoming continuing sales next year *but at a rate which may not make an adequate contribution to overheads.* Wherever possible, the long-term solution should be to re-allocate standard costs over all brands at rates appropriate to the new volume (whether that is higher or lower than before). If a man is truly responsible for the profitability of his product he must have the most up-to-date and accurate cost information; there must be no bottom-line variances which prevent him from making the best possible Marketing decisions for his product or service.

We have strayed slightly from marginal costing and it becomes logical to consider a comparable situation: that of 'milking' a brand. When people talk of milking a product they usually mean taking away all promotion and special attention, leaving the brand to find its own level. This means that certain allocated items – like advertising – will not be used, thus swelling its profit. This is a sound tactic over a short period, for lower sales times higher profits without promotion may make a greater contribution – but for a lesser period, possibly – than higher sales times lower profit. The danger of milking a brand or an area is that of diverting funds to supported brands which they could not otherwise afford. Eventually the milked brand will die and the supported brand must stand alone. Such diversion of funds may be entirely satisfactory during a short-term investment period but most experienced Marketing men can point to brands and services that could not hold their previous levels within the costing allowances made for them: once the element of subsidy was withdrawn, their sales fell. By all means subsidize, but only if you are sure your brand can stand alone. By all means use DAC, but only if it is paying its fair whack and will not either make it harder for the brand to pay its way as a whole because the forecast sales are not all extra, or start a price or promotional war which will lower profits on existing business.

Conclusion

Every Marketing man should have a deep understanding of finance and should make a firm ally of his accountants. The number of companies in which there is mutual distrust and misunderstanding is alarming and this situation must be harmful to any business. Whilst there may be initial resentment on the part of the accountant at making changes and producing new analyses and on the part of the Marketing man at the apparent intractability of the accountant, one usually discovers a close affinity between the two sides. It would be surprising if this were not so, for the preoccupation of the one with generating sales and the other with having adequate supplies of cash and quick resources amount to one and the same thing. My own preoccupation in this chapter is with the point that the only profits that are meaningful are cash profits, and the temptation to produce book profits by manipulating accounting conventions must never become an end in itself.

There are aspects of financial control we have not considered: discounted cash flow, for example, and the alternative techniques like net present value, and internal rate of return. One would normally rely on one's accountants for those calculations. It is enough to know the simple bases of these methods and follow them up in more detail if required. Traditional methods of investment appraisal have tended to concentrate on average annual rates of return or how long it would take to recover the original outlay. The newer methods realize that the further one gets from the present the greater is the risk of being wrong and thus they attribute greater value to the early years.

Discounted Cash Flow (DCF) can be applied to any investment project and allows for the way in which the value of money alters with time (present money is worth more than possible future money) and for taxation and investment grants and allowances where appropriate. Although there are many who argue strongly against DCF in favour of other methods, the majority of modern accountants accept it as the most effective technique of project appraisal. Net Present Value (NPV) is another way of arriving at the same decision about the profitability of a project by calculating how much the company should be prepared to pay for the chance of investing in any given project allowing a constant rate of interest on borrowing and lending money. All outlays and incomes are discounted in terms of present value, hence the description. Internal Rate of Return (IRR) also ends up at the same point since all three methods share a common theoretical basis. It is the more easily understood method, since the criterion is return on investment, but the most difficult to calculate. The calculation depends upon deciding the maximum amount of money that could be paid to a bank lending the same amount and shows the acceptability of the project when the calculated IRR value is more than the cost of financing the investment. Leave the calculations to the expert: simply appreciate that cash promised tomorrow is more probable than cash promised in five years' time and these are techniques which help decide which is the more likely to produce quick returns.

The study of management ratios merely illustrates the importance of coordination and awareness of the effects of the actions of one department upon another. A manager looking at his own departmental performance and return can easily do something which is damaging to the overall objectives of the company. The common denominator in all the contributory ratios is the cash value of sales. Whilst every effort must be made to use capital efficiently, keep costs to the minimum and not spend up to the limit because the standard costings allow it, the prime duty of the Marketing Director is devising plans to see that the cash keeps rolling in at ever-increasing amounts above a minimum acceptable level.

One word in conclusion about the problems of multi-divisional or holding companies with central services which have to be paid for. The objective of a division or a subsidiary must include a figure to cover a contribution to these central services. There is a growing tendency to allow subsidiaries greater autonomy in the way they achieve their objective, which can lead to corporate nonsenses. For example, a very large company has a highly efficient market-research company with an excellent field force of interviewers. Because it does little outside work, the overhead cost of retaining those interviewers is relatively high and the interdepartmental charges are higher than the prices demanded by competitive companies. Divisional managers can make their profits look better by buying outside, but the company overhead remains. This is a frequent source of conflict in holding companies and those with many separate divisions and often leads to the unwise closure of a service department. The selfish views of any department or division or company must not be allowed to detract from the overall corporate objective.

Reference

1. 'The Sweet, Secret World of Forrest Mars', *The Sunday Times*, 21.5.67.

Suggestions for Further Reading

An excellent book for all who would understand cash control better is *Managing Money and Finance* by G. P. E. Clarkeson and B. J. Elliot, published by Gower Press in 1969. Peter Kraushar (op cit) also deals with the subject briefly but more fully than I have.

Chapter 21

The Marketing Organization

Whilst the Marketing philosophy may have been adopted intuitively for generations by successful entrepreneurs, organized Marketing departments staffed by experts in various key areas of customer identification and the ways of exploiting opportunities arrived late in this country via the USA. By 1939, the number of Marketing departments in manufacturing companies could have been counted on the fingers of one hand. Procter and Gamble, the earliest American company with anything we would now recognize as a Marketing department, had introduced the idea into their UK company Thomas Hedley. Unilever, their leading competitor, was quick to respond. These two companies have been the 'universities' of generations of Marketing men. The most ardent advocates of Marketing techniques and the employment of experts in the company were, however, to be found among the leading advertising agencies, with the J. Walter Thompson Company setting a very hot pace. In the immediate post-war years, it was again the advertising business that spread the gospel.

Why have a Marketing organization at all? Let me immediately say that there are many businesses where a separate department is an unnecessary luxury and the Chief Executive fulfils the Marketing role, buying in such services as he needs on an *ad hoc*, task basis. Marketing departments are just one phenomenon of the managerial revolution which has separated the Boardroom from ownership of the business and has taken top Management off the factory floor and brought them in from the field. The need for a Marketing department stems from the complexities of modern business: there are relatively few businesses – even small ones – where General Management can be deeply involved in the detailed day-to-day running of every department. We do not normally expect a Chief Executive to work a machine: why should we expect him to draw up a research sample or plan an advertising campaign? We tend to single out the Marketing department for special attention and questioning partly because it is one of the newer manifestations of departmental organization and partly because so much of its work is concerned with subjective, unquantifiable matters. Thus every manager is an advertising expert but only the brave claim to understand the workings of a computer. I was once accused by a fellow manager of only getting my job because I was 'the best guesser'; actually, I was very flattered, but it does rather illustrate the point.

The normal, simplified pattern of growth of a company starts with an act of intuitive Marketing which either is production orientated ('I can make this, let's see if it will sell'), or rapidly becomes so ('This is what we sell because this is what we make'). Gradually, the influence of the sales force is felt: 'Our competitors sell nuts and bolts as well as screws; so could we if we had them.' These ideas may be encouraged by the fact that the original product is getting harder to sell as it reaches the peak of its life cycle. Panic diversification or undisciplined expansion tends to set in so that growth can be maintained. If our hypothetical company continues to develop logically, there will come a stage where the number of lines becomes too many for the Chief Executive to give detailed attention to each one, or they simply become an embarrassment and a policy of variety reduction becomes necessary: 'Everyone knows it must be wrong to carry this number of lines, but if we drop some how do we make up the profit?' A fairly rudimentary Marketing organization may be set up to study the problem with the danger that the function may be placed too low in the organization to carry the authority necessary to take the Marketing job right through the enterprise. This is a criticism I would level at the current state of Marketing organization in many service industries today, especially in banking and insurance, where the necessary authority of action runs contrary to established management traditions in many old-established businesses.

More recent businesses tend to find the impetus to create a Marketing organization in the need to search for new profitable areas as the spread of management education and knowledge through the many excellent professional bodies, courses and journals warns of the dangers of the old-style progression of my hypothetical firm. Often the suggestion comes from a management consultancy firm or from the company's advertising agency acting in an advisory role.

Just a handful of companies have become truly Marketing orientated (as exemplified by my Petfoods anecdote in the very first chapter). Such companies are aware from top to bottom that they are in the business of satisfying customers. The example comes from the very top where the Chief Executive actively preaches the Marketing philosophy; the handling of the techniques, the consideration of alternatives and the management of the specialists is delegated to the Marketing Director. The traditional company is the sum of the parts; the Marketing-orientated company pursues a common objective which is broken down (*vide* the management ratios) into component parts. That may sound pedantic, but the difference is fundamental and vital.

The normal pattern of growth is circular unless the Marketing philosophy predominates throughout. A successful new business has – perhaps intuitively – recognized a latent consumer desire and satisfied it with an acceptable product or service (or it wouldn't stay in business). As it grows, it becomes too complex to adhere to a single aim and to be firmly controlled by the original entrepreneur. When it becomes so large that it approaches the point of maximum risk, the need for total Marketing orientation is again apparent.

The Brand-Manager Concept

If Marketing is confused with individual techniques, it is even more confused with individual people. To many people the marketing organization is a group of brand (or product) managers. This is often, sadly, true but the effective Marketing organization is more than just that.

The Brand Manager concept is all part of the necessary divorce of top Management from entrepreneurial activity on individual goods and services. He becomes the Chief Executive's personal representative on that one product whilst, at the same time, safeguarding the customer's interest in that product. This concept has led to what might be called the 'Managing Director theory of Brand Management'. It is widely contended – especially by brand managers – that he is the Managing Director of his brand. This is nonsense. He is basically a coordinator, and whilst he may have much of the delegated responsibility of a Managing Director, he has none of the authority or power. Rather than elevate him to an impossible position, I prefer to regard the brand manager as the lowest-ranked man in the organization who should know everything to do with the product or service he is responsible for. Above him are people who know the profits, the costings and the sales; beneath him are people who know how to operate the machines. The brand manager is the man who coordinates all the activities, assembles all the information and makes recommendations. He has no power to instruct, he doesn't replace anybody; he acts through other line managers.

This is frequently a source of internal conflict, for the brand-manager concept is an organizational anomaly. Apart from managing any moneys allocated to him, the only person he manages is himself: 'manager' is a courtesy title to give him the status to carry out his job effectively. He does, however, occupy a unique position: as the only man totally committed to a particular aspect of the business, he tends to have more frequent and direct access to the corridors of power. He must be a tactful and persuasive communicator if he is to secure the goodwill of those he works with and through, if he is to convince them that he will not abuse this special position.

In any large organization brand managers will be essential, otherwise the overload on the Chief Executive is to a large degree transferred to the Marketing Director. One of the most difficult tasks of the Marketing Director is to decide how many brand managers he will need. This will vary from time to time. In a situation where there are too many products needing urgent attention, more will be needed initially than will be required eventually. Frustration will result as the solutions become clearer, and it is a valid generalization that the people who see the light most rapidly and leave first are the people you don't want to lose. There is a strong case for starting slowly, possibly with the help of a small task force of consultants, until you feel ready to make a long-term investment in staff. In more complex Marketing organizations, it may be necessary to break up the brand organization into groups, perhaps common-interest groups, under a Group Marketing Manager or some similar title in order to relieve an overload on the Marketing Director.

The Sales Force

The most important single ingredient in the total Marketing mix is the part that actually brings the revenue in. Advertising, promotion, packaging – all these may be essential prerequisites, but it is the final clinching of the deal, the taking of cash, that keeps the company in business. For most businesses, this will be the sales force; in many, the 'sales force' will operate over the counter, or door-to-door, even (as with Avon Cosmetics and Tupperware) in people's homes. How can a Marketing Director possibly weigh up the most effective total deployment of resources if he has no control over this absolutely vital area of activity? The majority of Marketing organizations do not give the Marketing Director ultimate control of the sales force, although there is a growing tendency for this to happen. Thus, most companies consider advertising increases and sales-force expansion simultaneously and often accept both when the answer may well be that they are alternatives. Certainly the small and medium-sized business ought always to look first at the size and disposition of their sales effort before considering advertising at what are almost certain to be minimal levels of doubtful effectiveness.

The alternative is to have both Marketing and Sales Directors. In such a situation, the Chief Executive is not only the ultimate Marketing authority but also the executive

authority acting as a departmental manager, allocating resources between the two and reconciling conflicts of interest.
Especially the latter. It is a rare organization where a harmonious relationship can exist between apparent equals –
which is assumed to be the case where Marketing and Sales
organizations are split this way. The very nature of their jobs,
which puts the Marketing Director in very frequent contact
with the Chief Executive whilst the Sales Director is out in the
field, is itself a source of conflict. One is seen to have (and
almost certainly does have) more of the ear of the boss, whilst
the other has to go out and achieve the forecasts. It can be
argued that the right choice of men, good management and
effective communication can overcome these problems, but
this throws an unwarranted work-load on the Chief Executive,
who really has much more important tasks to perform.

Organizations are frequently a function of the people available. Since Marketing departments and personnel are relatively
new, they have been added to companies where sales departments with often Board-level management already existed. The
reluctance to downgrade senior sales managers is understand-
able and commendable from the human relations point of
view even if it may prove less profitable than the alternative.
The impetus to coordinated departments is probably due more
to a natural wastage of older sales management than to a deep
conviction that total coordination of all the elements in the
Marketing mix is right.

I want to leave for the moment the question of who should
be the dominant personality, but one must recognize that there
are businesses where selling is practically the only technique of
real importance and the Marketing organization might consist
solely or mainly of the sales force. Again, if it consists *solely* of
the sales force (as is frequently the case with insurance companies, who tend to equate Marketing with selling and nothing
else), all the innovation and identification of opportunities,
pricing policy and so on will be laid at the door of the Chief
Executive, probably aided by specialists whose training does
not habitually encompass the Marketing philosophy. (To continue with the analogy of insurance, 'pricing policy' will be

recommended by actuaries and accountants.) Which is the dog and which is the tail will vary from business to business but the tail must never wag the dog. Selling is not something apart from Marketing any more than advertising is: they are all ingredients in the same cake. The same cook should bake it. How he employs his *sous-chefs* is a matter of discretion and will vary according to both the business and the personalities available.

Whilst there is frequently a case for the sales force being the major factor in the Marketing organization, there is a danger that it will continue to adopt traditional selling methods and not apply the Marketing philosophy to its business. We have already expressed this simply so far as the sales force is concerned as selling *through* the trade, not *to* the trade, and the transition to this latter approach is being helped and hastened by the fact that retail traders at least are well aware of the importance of giving customers what they want and fast. However, the average sales force has several levels of customer and it must satisfy those it sells *to* as well as using them as the means of reaching the ultimate consumer. In some businesses, especially those selling raw materials and components, the chain can be very long.

What about those other sales forces, the ones that don't fit the conventional pattern? By this I mean shopgirls, bank tellers, showroom attendants, demonstrators and so on. They are an even more fundamental part of the Marketing mix than the grocery sales force, for to the buyer they are often seen as the product. The Prudential Assurance Company saw this many years ago and sold 'your friendly man from the Pru'. An unpleasant salesgirl may put you off a shop for ever. They are an essential part of your Marketing mix: face to face contact can be a boon or a disaster and smart, courteous, efficient service (and continuing after-sales service) is part of the Marketing of your product if you are in one of those sorts of business. Philosophy is more applicable than technique, but whilst the Marketing Director may not control these people he must be allowed to recommend how they should behave and be given the authority to influence their behaviour. You may fill hotels using great advertising, but the things that strike people most when they get there and which are a major determinant of whether they ever come again are the welcome they get from the receptionist and the manner of those who conduct them to their rooms. These people are part of the sales force of a service industry.

The theory is one thing; practice is another. To run a co-ordinated Marketing organization is rather like sleeping on a bed of nails: not very many people can do it, some actually enjoy it, but it is asking a lot of a person who normally sleeps on a spring mattress. We'll come to that in the next chapter. For the moment let us accept that Marketing uses sales as one – usually the prime – technique and to talk of Marketing and sales as two separate things is absolutely wrong: the latter is part of the former.

Advertising

Where a company employs brand managers it normally charges them with the responsibility for advertising. They carry out the normal everyday contact with their advertising agency and are held accountable for the funds allocated. However, again the principle of responsibility without authority is paramount, for the brand manager is seldom allowed ultimate approval of the advertising he is held responsible for – a situation that can lead to acute management problems as we shall see in the next chapter. Some companies, however, have advertising managers and others impose intermediaries called something like Advertising Content Manager either between brand manager and agency or as a sort of internal ultimate deterrent to be employed either against the brand manager, the agency or both! It is extremely rare to find an advertising manager in a company employing the brand-manager concept – other than for purely historical and humane reasons.

Advertising managers tend to be found most frequently in non-consumer goods and service industries. They are, however, found in very large companies where the advertising is either corporate or concentrated on a narrow range of product streams, thus making the conventional brand-manager system of lesser value. In such circumstances, however, often it may well be simply a case of a rose by any other name.

My own inference from personal experience and the exchange of information with many students on Marketing courses would be, firstly, that many advertising managers are misnamed and that they frequently perform at least the brand-manager function if not that of a more senior member of the Marketing department and, secondly, that the term is correctly used where the manager has direct control of studios, technical writers, PROs, etc. In the latter case, the Marketing gap has to be plugged in just the same way as in those companies where only a Sales Director exists whose sole concern is control of the field force.

The subject of advertising-content managers perplexes me. I am convinced that it is wrong in almost every conceivable circumstance and is a tacit admission of the inability of the brand manager to understand and critically assess advertising content and/or an admission that the company concerned is never going to allow the brand manager to have real responsibility for creative content. I am perplexed because some very highly regarded companies with large Marketing organizations employ the system. For the life of me, the only justification I can find is where group policy is involved. A company marketing a range of competitive biscuits, soap powders, teas, pet foods or cigarettes (as examples only, for in only one of those fields is this concept used) might find such a need. Only a very minute number of companies do employ the system. I have no real practical experience of the system, for the only time I ever worked with a client using this kind of man we never met nor was I ever aware of his influence. I can, therefore, only register that advertising-content managers or their like do exist and I, personally, find them even more of an anomaly than the brand-manager system. Departmental and product conflicts are normally resolved without the creation of this extra layer who either has to be in on all the relevant discussions, thus duplicating the work of the brand manager, or may be tempted to put his contribution in without adequate background information in order to be seen to be doing something. If such a person exists, he should in my opinion be regarded as a staff functionary reporting to the Marketing Director and acting purely in an advisory capacity: he should have no line responsibility for, or authority over, anyone else.

The Marketing Accountant

Few companies have Marketing accountants; that is, an expert in the various aspects of costing and finance necessary to the achievement of profit promises *located in the Marketing organization.* Access to cost and management accounts is normally given and taken (often grudgingly on both sides) but it is my experience that there is no substitute for at least one accountant on the Marketing team in a company of any size or financial complexity. We can expect brand managers to know of the types of project appraisal, the reality of the return on capital concept and all the other cost and profit items we have considered. We should not expect him to be an expert in their calculation and application. He will get the best service from someone unencumbered by the tyranny of producing quarter-ending and year-end reports, items which are normally the signal for all new work to stop. The Marketing Accountant can be especially valuable in the area of new product development and the consideration of alternative demands on scarce resources. Where the computer is widely used, he should have a high level of knowledge of its capabilities, preferably extending to the ability to write at least simple programmes and understand how to specify the information necessary for reaching the best decision.

It has also been my experience that accountants thrive in the creative and exciting atmosphere of the Marketing department and the natural affinity I mentioned earlier rapidly becomes apparent. However, the Marketing Accountant must not become divorced from other central and functional accountants. If he reports to the Marketing Director, this close liaison with the main stream of company accounting is also necessary to keep the Marketing Accountant in line for the greater career opportunities which will almost certainly exist in the main stream and for which he should be exceptionally well equipped after some years with what might be called the 'revenue-earning division'. I regard it as far more important that the Marketing Director and his staff should have the uninterrupted use of at least one accountant familiar with the aims and objectives of the department than that he should actually report to the Marketing Director for pay and rations.

Brand Administration

In a large Marketing organization, the brand manager can easily become overwhelmed with detail at the expense of his valuable creative time. Caring for existing brands and promotions, devising new ones, liaising with other departments, spending time out in the field – all these and more will suffer badly if he becomes desk-bound. In a medium to large organization it is not only more efficient but also more economic to split the more creative functions of Brand Management from the administrative chores. By this split, brand managers can handle an extra product (maybe more than one extra) and the administrators can similarly operate on several products.

The function exists in most of the larger, well-established Marketing organizations. There is also a very strong case for such a person in the small company. Companies vary in attitude between those who regard the function as a combination of super-clerk and part accountant and those who regard it as a stepping-stone and part of the training of a brand manager. Whilst I would never preclude the possibility that anyone anywhere in the organization might become a brand manager in time, I personally favour the concept of continuity. Part of the reason is simply the value of continuity to a product in a management situation where there is a strong argument for changing the products brand managers handle from time to time. Data books and fact books are all very well as hand-over documents and valuable in their own right as works of reference, but they are no substitute for personal involvement at a detailed level over a long period.

What a Brand Administrator might actually do will depend

on the other support services and people already available.
Areas normally found in their job description include budgetary control, clearing invoices, placing orders, arranging delivery
and dispatch of point-of-sale material, data collection for
major reports and plans, checking voucher copies of printed
material, and routine clerical and possibly financial contact
with advertising agencies and other service suppliers. Whilst
they might be involved fairly heavily in brand accounting,
their level of involvement (and, indeed, ability) will be quite
different from that of the Marketing Accountant. The organization of the administrators is an internal matter related to the
size and complexity of the business and the total Marketing
organization. Some companies will allocate brand administrators to brand groups, others will have them work on groups
of similar products, whilst others again may prefer to make
contact with advertising agencies the focal point, having each
brand administrator work with only one agency. In a large
organization, it may be necessary to have a Brand Administration Manager for precisely the same reasons that any other
function or sub-department needs management or supervisory
control.

Market Research

It goes without saying that market research should be under
the control of the Marketing Director. However, it should be
remembered that in some industries the market-research man
is far more important to the business than the traditional brand
manager trained man. A problem is frequently found in placing
the Market Research Manager within the complex kind of
organization I am describing. Traditionally, he is either out on
a sprig on the organizational chart and placed as a staff functionary to the Marketing Director or he is placed under, say, a
Marketing Group Manager for pay and rations although used
by the other groups too. I prefer to class market research as a
common service partly to emphasize that no one man or group
has a particular lien on that service but mainly, and as a corollary, to demonstrate that market research is as applicable and

available to the sales department and public relations as to anyone else. Sales managers ought to think of techniques like retail audit as their research tools, not figures rammed down their throats by brand managers.

In the large multi-divisional company, there may actually be a large operational market-research department. Even the large companies normally find the cost of a permanent field force of interviewers an expensive luxury unless they can guarantee a demand for regular work, such as conducting their own retail audits (to overcome the problem of wrong weighting for their particular commodity in syndicated research) or where there is a predictably regular demand for ownership and usage surveys. The number of such departments has fallen dramatically and many become subsidiary companies to enable them to do outside work to recoup their high overheads.

The normal function of a market-research manager in a company Marketing department is that of skilled buyer and interpreter. Easy to say but difficult to be. Skill in buying means knowing the right techniques (which presupposes you know the right questions to ask), knowing who can provide the services, what their level of competence is, obtaining quotes and helping to frame the questionnaire, and being in on the briefing of fieldworkers. (This is an ideal list which it is not always possible or practical to achieve.) Skilled as good research companies may be in interpreting the figures they produce, there must always be areas where they have insufficient knowledge to comment intelligently and areas whose importance escapes them because it has never been revealed to them. This extra level of perceptive interpretation is best provided by a skilled man in the commissioning company who will relate the relevance of the replies to the importance of the question and the reason behind the question. It will also be the company market-research manager's job to make sure the research is free of all technical bugs before it gets into the hands of anyone less skilled than himself.

The market-research manager has one other vital function to perform: that of prompter and prodder. He should be looking at the products of his company continuously to see what

information gaps exist which if plugged would increase the
efficiency of the total Marketing effort. This will become vital
input into one of the sections of the annual plan.

Public Relations

In terms of methods of organization and function, the role of
Public Relations Manager within an integrated Marketing department in which his is not the dominant role is very similar to
that of market research. Public relations may be managed on a
company or divisional basis, handled entirely from within or
bought-in by employing an agency or consultants, or possibly
hired off into a subsidiary company. Unlike market research,
there is often some confusion in that the public-relations
manager may work on corporate matters only, probably reporting to the Chief Executive, whilst product publicity is handled
like advertising by brand managers. Really creative public relations comes from close integration with the brand stream and
is not merely a matter of exploiting opportunities arising out of
already scheduled activities but of planning events of direct
relevance to the products and making news happen. Again the
analogy with the market-research manager is close. In a
Marketing organization with many products and a large number of brand managers, even keeping abreast of what is happening is difficult enough. It would be easy to produce a wildly
extravagant system whereby market research and public relations people were allocated to brand managers in the same way
as brand administrators might be. Thus it is normally better
for a public-relations manager in a coordinated department to
act as the market-research manager does and coordinate needs
and buy the operational and practical aspects of the service
from outside. However, this must never be allowed to permit
him or her to hide under a cloak of anonymity. A public-
relations manager should always be available and the company
switchboard should always know where to find someone (even
if you haven't got a PRO) at any time. Many a potential
disaster has been avoided in this way. When I was at Lyons we
were faced with a threat by a national Sunday newspaper that

one of our products (and similar products of two of our competitors) would be exposed as health hazards. The allegations were untrue and easily disproved but they were published naming our two competitors, not us. Why? Simply because the Lyons switchboard was able to give a reporter my telephone number and that of my public-relations manager late at night. The reporter could not contact anyone at either of the other two companies before the story went to press.

Other Services

One can produce a list of almost infinite variability. Some companies include the physical distribution function as part of selling and thus, by my definition, it would become part of the Marketing organization. Actually, I don't favour it for the kind of complex organization I am describing. The burden of problems of depot stocks, warehouse location, servicing of vehicles, capital budgets, and union problems with drivers does not mix happily with the already long list of burdens of the Marketing Director. Moreover, as I have indicated earlier, there is a need for a new breed of distribution managers capable of applying modern techniques of depot location, vehicle routing and the cost of stockholding, and this is an area of relatively new and developing skill which justifies specialization. As long as the distribution manager never forgets that his is a service department catering for the needs of the customers of the business, it doesn't matter where he is. In a small company, he might live most happily under the wing of the sales manager. Again, the positioning of the function may be as much related to the personalities involved as to organizational optimization.

I have already written at length about the special problems of the sales force. These are so special that I believe they justify their own personnel manager. Problems of location and relocation, changes of schooling, the strains and stresses on families of prolonged absence and separation pose problems not commonly experienced by normal company personnel people who think largely in terms of staff welfare, interdepartmental transfer and management development. These

needs exist with sales forces too, but again they are different. A
Marketing Personnel Manager can be regarded as a part of the
sales force or as a common service so that he can also handle
routine recruitment matters and so on for the whole department. My preference is for the latter, although he will always
spend the bulk of his time on sales force problems which means
spending a lot of time with them.

I will add one more man to my list, a Media Coordinator. I do
not believe that companies should buy or plan their own
media: that is a job for their advertising agencies. A company
with a Marketing department as complex as the one we are
considering is probably using several agencies and/or promoting several brands. Comparison of media-buying efficiency
and effectiveness in terms of research, frequency and coverage
of the messages should be standard practice and a spirit of
healthy competition engendered. The results can be most
beneficial. A man in constant contact with the media business,
aware of rates, knowledgeable about availability and when
special deals are available is invaluable to a large company. He
can help produce more messages for the same money or obtain
the required level of advertising for less money. Contracts for
continuity and guaranteed expenditure levels can be negotiated with the major contractors in all media and these can be
done separately and often in addition to any deals your agency
may be doing on your behalf.

Such a man is usually best employed on a company basis
where there are many divisions or subsidiaries so that he can
lump together total buying power. A decision has to be taken
as to whether a central decision is taken to spend so much and
the Media Coordinator or controller then allocates it amongst
divisions or brands by medium, or whether he merely collects
the individual sums together with the recommended media lists
and negotiates from that basis. Where I have operated or instituted the system into a company, I have adopted the latter
approach. It is a rare company that can say one medium is
correct for all its products. To dictate on media matters re-
moves even more authority over advertising from the brand
manager. Companies who practise this form of dictation tend

to be those who also institute several echelons to vet the advertising plans too. With the system I have used, it has very occasionally been necessary to dictate. The circumstance has arisen where, on one classic occasion, it was necessary to instruct a brand manager to spend an extra £9,000 on one television station, otherwise the company would have lost discounts of £50,000. Not a hard deal to sell!

Conclusion

This must be a rather frightening chapter to many readers. Of course, you don't have to have all these people; you don't even have to have an integrated Marketing department to practise the Marketing philosophy. However, the alternative is a heavier load on the Chief Executive, but that has to be accepted on pure economic grounds in many companies. This chapter, like this book, is primarily a distillation of personal experience. It is therefore only fair that I should summarize an organization I controlled as a Marketing Manager myself. It is not ideal – in Marketing it is seldom that anything is. I freely admit that it arose partly from the circumstances of the company, situations I inherited and the people on the team. One obvious lack is a single General Sales Manager. All I can say is that it worked very well because the field sales managers worked well as a team. My successor did have a General Sales Manager and no doubt that was right in the changed circumstances he inherited.

Marketing is a dynamic system. One cannot, therefore, have an inflexible organization. At one point of time you may need twenty brand managers. Later, you may actually have more products to manage but need less people to manage them. My advice to anyone starting from scratch is to start small and start slowly. Choose a man who can grow into the senior job and make much use of consultative task forces to establish what your long-term needs are going to be. The message of this chapter is that all the prime ingredients in the total Marketing mix should be controlled by one man and, whilst ultimate power and responsibility rests with the Chief

Executive, time alone dictates that these functions be grouped under some other senior man.

Suggestions for Further Reading

Examples of different forms of organization are given in the books already mentioned by Leslie Rodger (pages 66–69 and 128–133) and Douglas Smallbone (pages 28–42). The only British work aimed at the Brand Manager function is that already referred to by Gordon Medcalfe.

Chapter 22

Managing the Marketing Department

A man who has never actually headed a complex Marketing organization of the type described in the last chapter can only begin to guess at the kind of problems involved. To the normal management problems of dealing with different time spans – optimizing the present opportunities, and preparing for the future – comes a whole host of diverse situations which demand pure management expertise in an area where narrow specialization is common and where the qualifications, qualities and talents of the members of the department vary enormously. A typical day's problems for a Marketing Director may include approving new promotions, choosing a new regional sales manager, deciding on a new policy for removal and disturbance allowances for transferred salesmen, with the ever-present possibility of becoming involved in some complex and tragic personal affair of one of his staff. It is no longer enough to know how to choose good creative work, understand the difference between a random and a quota sample or the latest media theories. The Marketing Director must know all about taxable and non-taxable allowances, the Redundancy Payments Act, company rules about early retirement, the circumstances under which instant dismissal is possible, and many, many more aspects of pure management from which he will previously have been shielded and for which he will have received no formal training. Despite all the experts he has to call on, he will continually be forced to make new precedents and handle affairs entirely alone by the force of his own personality.

The problems are accentuated by the people he is responsible for. The salesman is generally extrovert and gregarious yet mostly alone. He is out of sight and therefore not subject to direct command. The Sales Manager will spend a lot of his time (most of it, preferably) out in the field, partly to see that field control is being exercised as it was intended and partly to reassure himself that he is in control; that delegation has not become abdication. Market researchers by and large are the opposite of salesmen and can easily become wrapped up in their specialization and take themselves off into ivory towers. At the accounting and clerical levels one does not normally expect the wild flights of fancy the brand manager is prone to; indeed, one frequently encounters intolerance of this apparent lack of practicality. Then there is perhaps the most difficult animal of all, the brand manager. The ideal is probably an ambivert – part extrovert, part introvert: a man who can coldly and dispassionately immerse himself in piles of figures until he arrives at a conclusion and then wholeheartedly go out and sell himself and his ideas to everybody from Chief Executive to the most junior salesman. It's an exciting atmosphere to work in but poses some challenging problems.

Delegation or Demarcation?

For the Marketing Director the question of priorities is paramount. The first question he must ask himself is: 'What am I now, a specialist or a manager?' The answer must be: 'A manager first and foremost.' Of course he is a specialist manager but no more so than the Production Director or the Finance Director. The work of the Marketing Director in many businesses may involve a great deal less specialist knowledge than other managers and certainly a considerably smaller amount of scientific knowledge. The next priorities are of the kind faced by all functional managers but heightened by the fact that it is unlikely that any other specialist manager will employ so many people who are all highly qualified in different skills and with quite different psychological backgrounds closely allied to their chosen field. Which problem do you deal with first when you have a brand manager waiting for a decision about an extra promotion, a queue of candidates to be interviewed for the position of Regional Sales Manager, the factory wanting to know if they should delay the introduction of a new pack because they still have large stocks of the old or write-off stocks of existing packs, and one of your best local sales managers faced with the problem of a seriously ill wife, three children to look after and his nearest relatives almost 200 miles away? This is no exaggeration: it is a fairly typical day extracted from my diary. I cannot emphasize this aspect of the Marketing Director's job too strongly: it is an area where Marketing is traditionally weak; we stand high in the application of skills but low in the art of management.

It is obvious that a conscientious Marketing Director can drive himself to an early grave or render himself useless to his Board if he allows himself to be overwhelmed with too much detail of the various sub-functions within his organization. Obviously there must be very clear lines of demarcation and defined responsibility and authority statements. Notice that I deliberately avoided the word 'delegation'. Delegation means entrusting something you are responsible for to someone else. At best, that is a short-term expedient; at worst, it can lead to abdication of the function. The better method is to so define your own job that neither you nor any other manager has to delegate. You all have clear job statements, defined and – ideally – quantified objectives and written responsibility, authority and reporting limits. Thus the job statement of any person within the Marketing department will start with the name or title of the person to whom he is responsible (which should always be his immediate superior) and will follow with a statement of objectives. The Marketing Director will normally report to the Chief Executive. His objectives may read something like this:

1. To recommend plans to ensure the long-term continuance and profitability of the company. (There may be some reference to the way company objectives are framed, for example, actually stating the return on capital to be earned and the growth rate required.)

2. To maintain an efficient Marketing organization capable of ensuring the execution of those plans.

T–O

3. To be generally responsible for the employees and other resources of the Marketing Department.

There will then follow a section detailing the plans the Marketing Director is to cause to be prepared and to whom he is to submit them. Any special responsibilities (for example, providing a company-wide service within a divisional organization) will be included here too. Then will follow a set of restraints and constraints. The form of statement of managerial responsibility which finds most general favour nowadays does not set out to list what a manager can do (with the consequent temptation to assume that anything not listed is somebody else's job) but to list only the things he may not do. The list for a Marketing Director will vary according to his overall responsibilities but might be expected to include limits on the extent to which he may make changes without reference to anyone else in such areas as:

Advertising and promotional budgets.
The product mix.
Prices.
Capital (purchase or disposal).
Trade relations, service, discounts, etc.
Salary scales (normally he will also need specific authority to change the salaries of his immediate subordinates).
Personnel policy, etc, etc.

Clearly the job statements of the Marketing Director's immediate subordinates will reflect the way his own powers are restricted.

The next thing to be done is to allocate as much power, authority and responsibility to a manageable span of senior subordinates. Normally, this will mean either a single Marketing Manager and a single General Sales Manager or as many people of equal level as may be necessary to fill these roles. Each of their subordinates will have constraints and reporting limits that reflect those of the superior. Thus, for example, the general sales manager may be able to increase salaries up to a ceiling of £2,500 pa without reference to his Marketing Director; the regional manager's ceiling may be £1,500 without reference to the general sales manager and so on down the line as far as one permits managers to hire, fire, and increase salaries. This is not a delegation in the true sense, it is establishing clear lines of demarcation. Every manager knows how far he can go without reference to his superior. If he goes beyond that without authority or continually seeks advice or ratification for things he is permitted to do, then one management decision is made a little easier for the Marketing Director!

The Marketing Director must play the game according to the rules he sets. He cannot say that the brand manager is responsible for the creative content of all advertising and then insist on all work coming to him for final approval. This doesn't stop him from seeing all new work before it appears on the air or in print: indeed, he would be very foolish if he did not give himself this power. He would be equally foolish if he insisted on approving every new salesman. Obviously, a reasonable balance must be preserved. Remember that once you have given a man a written statement of responsibility, interference is far worse than abdication, for you revoke the man's responsibilities every time you overrule him or interpose yourself between him and, say, his customer or his agency.

Many of the problems of management complexity in the Marketing organization can be overcome by using the same principles as those suggested for handling sales problems: give as much responsibility as possible to the man closest to the problem. Refer only major problems and exceptions upwards. When something out of the ordinary happens it usually needs correction rapidly: it can easily become magnified out of all proportion if it escalates too much.

Qualities of a Good Marketing Man

Before we can really consider what type of man should head up the Marketing organization, we ought to examine the qualities we should look for in a Marketing man. These are the qualities one would hope to find in the all-round Marketing man, not merely a salesman or a researcher or some specialist function within the organization. We are really looking at the qualities of a good brand manager and of a Marketing Director.

The first requirement is a lively, flexible mind which is constantly looking for new solutions to old problems, anticipating new problems and postulating solutions. Yet he must also be totally objective. He is the customer's representative in the company and his objectivity must reconcile the personal involvement and inward-looking attitudes of the company operatives with their day-to-day problems with the ever-changing attitudes and needs of the buyers. He should always strive to be positively, progressively and aggressively different in his approach to problems, products and services. If he is to preserve his creative flexibility and his objectivity, he must be prepared to distrust the obvious. Much of what a Marketing man must be stems from what Marketing itself is not. Marketing is not an exact body of knowledge whose practice is limited to people with formal training and recognized qualifications like, say, the law or accountancy. There is no dogma which once learned will stand you in good stead for the rest of your working life with only minor updating. Instead, the Marketing man needs to combine analytical ability with creative flair and think clearly and systematically about everyday things. He must recognize accurate sources of information but distrust the obvious and reject the spurious. He must look for relevant correlations and for complexities. He must always try to see in the round and full what others see in the flat and narrow. Dissatisfaction will be his lot, for he should always assume that things can be done better.

The good Marketing man is a generalist, not a specialist. He may well know more about advertising than anyone else in the company but that doesn't make him an advertising specialist. The only thing he really specializes in is his brand (or brands). Many people misunderstand the word 'generalist', interpreting it to mean a jack-of-all-trades with its inevitable corollary. A generalist is a man with a wide knowledge of many things and fairly deep knowledge of a few: a sort of 'master of some'. Thus a good Marketing man should have a questing, searching mind. Finally, I like my Marketing men to preserve the common touch: not to take themselves off into rarefied atmospheres as they progress in business life but to maintain contacts with the people who represent their market, to go into supermarkets and corner shops to shop, wander around showrooms, be generally aware of what is happening around them. For example, the phenomenon of high discretionary spending power by teenagers doesn't just offer opportunities for manufacturers of clothing, cosmetics and records: it offers untapped potential for banks, building societies and insurance companies. A good spread of out-of-hours interests (providing they are not too esoteric) is usually a good sign.

Finally, he must be a fluent and effective communicator. It is not enough to care deeply about his products; he has got to persuade others to care just as much. This means that he must be literate and fluent in speech: two conditions that regrettably impose a severe limitation upon both the intake and progress of Marketing men, for they are sadly lacking in so many candidates. He must be able to present a case clearly, concisely and convincingly in print or on his feet. He will often do so to people more skilled in professional presentation techniques than himself and he must win them over by his abilities, self-confidence, and arguments.

Notice especially that I have put intellectual abilities above technical ones. He will need some technical skills, but the same ones will not be appropriate to all circumstances and all businesses. Experience and technique can do little more for the Marketing man than define the parameters of any problem. He must treat each new problem as a new intellectual exercise and assume that the relevance of what happened in the past in any similar situation is likely to be extremely limited. Marketing is dynamic and both the facts and the reasons behind the facts change: the extent to which one can generalize is therefore limited.

All the qualities mentioned apply to the Marketing Director but for him we must add business experience, the ability to stand back from the impossible detail of the total job, and a very real entrepreneurial spirit. He also needs management ability, and this combination of professional competence, management ability and entrepreneurial skill is increasingly rare and almost impossible to create.

The Marketing Director

When Peter Drucker first wrote *Managing for Results* in the early 1960s he said (of American business): 'Not everything that goes by the name "Marketing" deserves it. It has become too fashionable. A gravedigger remains a gravedigger even when called a "mortician" – only the cost of the burial goes up. Many a Sales Manager has been re-named "Marketing Vice-President" – and all that happened was that costs and salaries went up.'

The same has been true of many British companies. However, we have learned from American experience (or so we believe) and gone the other way. That can often be even more disastrous.

Drucker was criticizing a situation in which changing the word 'Sales' to 'Marketing' was pandering to the latest management fashion. People not versed in the philosophy of Marketing were thrust into a foreign environment and the results were either disenchantment or escalating costs as highly paid specialists had to be brought in to cover the deficiencies of the head man. The situation in many leading American companies now (and in some of their UK subsidiaries) is fascinating, for the Marketing organization is frequently headed by a man of proven business and management ability rather than a man of proven sales or brand management ability.

Perhaps we in this country have paid too much heed to Drucker's warning as echoed by other leading writers on both sides of the Atlantic, for we have tended to draw our senior Marketing men from the ranks of Brand Management, creating the situation I referred to earlier of high professional skills but often abysmally low management skills. A man who may never have managed more than a couple of kindred spirits suddenly finds himself confronted with all the problems which I outlined at the beginning of this chapter. One of two things tends to happen. Either he leaves the sales side to his sales manager and concentrates on the brand and brand services stream (thus effectively destroying the coordinated Marketing organization) or he exercises nominal control without any real appreciation of the special skills needed in controlling – even through senior managers – a sales force. The dilemma is this: the sales manager is better versed in management skills but the Marketing Manager better understands the role that can be fulfilled by a fully coordinated Marketing department.

The problem is often easily solved where there is one very dominant role. If there is one skill that is far more relevant to the business than any other, the Marketing Director should be fully conversant with it. If that skill is selling, it might make considerable sense for the total organization to be created under his wing. There are companies where, important though selling is, the sales force is very small and the most important role may be market research or advertising, for example. Providing the man is right, the solution is easy. But in each of these cases, the complexities of the organization do not pose the kind of problems raised earlier. In those cases, if it is a case of turning a good manager into a Marketing man or trying to make a good Marketing man into a good manager, I would opt for the proven good manager. There is more chance of his getting good results out of the good Marketing man than vice versa. In time we shall have, as there exists in the United States, a breed of managers who have been exposed to the Marketing philosophy throughout their academic and business training. This situation allows a great deal of interchange between departments in an environment where no one is seen to lose face by moving from production manager of a very large plant 'down' to brand manager of a very small brand. He knows, and so does everyone else, that he is being groomed for bigger things. Marketing men in this country had better look out: specialist managers flock to courses on Marketing, but Marketing men are generally conspicuous only by their absence on general management courses – except for those who have already arrived at the top and aim still higher.

Problems of Training and Succession

Obviously not every man within the complete Marketing organization can be trained for succession to the role of Marketing Director. Salesmen, for example, must first earn the opportunity to attain the first stages of supervision before they can even think in terms of management within their own stream. The two problems to concern ourselves with are the training of brand managers in other aspects of the total operation (since they are in a shorter stream than the sales side their promotion opportunities are greater, plus the fact that they must understand all that goes on around them if they are to perform their job efficiently) and equipping senior managers for possible transfer between streams and eventual succession to the most senior position.

Many companies insist that new brand managers spend at least some time out on the road selling. Generally speaking, I am against this. The qualities for which you have chosen the man may not be those you would look for in a salesman and you could place valuable business at a hazard. There is, too, usually a logistic problem in giving a trainee a regular journey, which is really the only way such sales training can be effective. The practice can be especially dangerous where there is a considerable gap between the calibre required in the two functions. For example, putting a potential brand manager out on a van selling operation where he has to drive a van, hump goods, collect cash and check his van stock and cash takings can be especially soul-destroying. On the other hand, sophisticated sales forces employ people of similar calibre and background to brand managers and this particular problem is minimized. The closest parallels are between brand managers and Head Office salesmen, but you can never afford to disturb a well-cemented relationship with a buyer by substituting a trainee for a man he knows, respects and identifies with your company. Brand managers should learn as early as possible what the salesman is expected to do and what his problems are. It is, therefore, valuable for him to undergo salesmen's training courses and accompany salesmen for long enough to know the men and really understand what the job is about. And he should go on doing accompaniments (as should the Marketing Director) varying the territory or the customers to get the widest view of the help the salesman needs from him. Continuing access to salesmen is essential but this must not be abused in any way by the brand manager. The greatest abuses he can commit are interfering with the salesman's job and influencing him in favour of a particular product contrary to company policy.

How brand managers are allowed access to middle sales management is a matter of company policy: some companies leave it to the discretion of the two parties, others ban such contact entirely. Most have some kind of filtering system through senior sales management to ensure that a region does not become overburdened with visitors. Local problems are best discussed where the problem is, where you can not only look at the figures but get out together to examine the situation on the ground. These visits and invitations to address local salesmen's meetings about his product will all help to give the brand manager a greater understanding of the sales force and the problems they face and help dispel the 'them and us' attitude.

There will also be a good deal of interchange when the brand manager is preparing his annual budgets. It is at this stage that more formal relationships between Brand and Sales exist and present a valuable foundation for the management development of the more senior Marketing people. Where Marketing group managers and field sales managers sit down together to allocate priorities each exposes his problems and objectives to the other. A tremendous amount of learning can arise from this exchange provided it is approached without assuming set attitudes. The more frequently this group can meet, the better will be the understanding of the other fellow's point of view. Again, the type of business one is in helps determine the frequency of such meetings, for they must have a real purpose other than just a get-together. Many food companies operate a system whereby promotions are announced to meetings of local managers at regular intervals (usually corresponding to the sales cycle). At this meeting, the brand manager will

expose his thinking for, say, three months ahead and lay it open
for critical and constructive comment. Both sides are learning
the other's point of view. This meeting may be preceded by
another at more senior level to discuss potential promotions
with brand managers which, if approved, will be presented
with further detail and rough designs at the following month's
meeting. There are two great advantages in this system:

1. The sales force do not feel that everything is cut and dried
   before they see it. They enjoy real participation and learn
   more about the brand manager's job, pick up more knowledge of advertising, research and so on.
2. The brand manager is in a similar learning position in an
   atmosphere where participation encourages greater effort
   behind accepted plans.

Such systems are a valuable part of total Marketing planning
and control and can be applied to most businesses. The titles
of the participants and the length of time between meetings
may vary but the benefits will be the same.

At the level immediately below the Marketing Director, say
Marketing Manager and General Sales Manager, each functional head should have access to the full plans of the other's
function and preferably should debate them as a sort of Marketing Committee with the Marketing Director before the latter
puts forward the company or divisional plan to his Chief
Executive. All this follows the pattern of planning outlined in
Chapter 18. Again, it is not only a vital way of maximizing resources and obtaining full commitment to the total plan but
also a valuable part of the training process as each side exposes
and justifies its thinking to the other. At the very least, this
kind of discipline will lead to a greater understanding of the
various vocabularies that different parts of the Marketing
organization use!

This regular contact can be supplemented by formal training
in specific areas as required. Just as brand managers spend time
with salesmen, so sales managers (at whatever level is decided
to be appropriate) should spend time with the company's ad-

vertising agency. If continuous audits or panels are used, a visit to these companies should be on the schedule, followed by a detailed presentation of results. The training needs of people in the sales stream are normally more numerous because they are specialists trying to learn to become generalists. They must have some of those basic qualities we considered earlier or this sort of formal training will be wasted on them. However, the training needs of those in the brand stream may be more complex, for they have to be turned into man managers. Sales managers reach their eminence (normally) because of their man management abilities rather than pure selling ability: pure selling probably ceased to be a major part of their function a long time ago. Only in the largest brand organizations will there be much opportunity for exercising man management and even then it will be limited by the extent to which one is dealing with similar people to oneself with the same sort of qualities and business background.

The problem of management succession in a Marketing organization is an issue complicated by many factors. We have dealt quite fully with the fact that someone has to be promoted to a position where he assumes responsibility for a role he may never have fulfilled. This can be partly overcome by transfer between streams, but this is normally seen by everybody as a move leading to eventual promotion either in the stream he has joined or in the one he has left. One has to be fairly certain that one has chosen the right man, that the opening will occur in a predictable time and that the man himself knows he is in an up-or-out situation. If you don't fulfil these conditions, the man will probably move out in any case: few men will readily accept reversion to their old position after such a change and those who do may be rendered less effective by disillusionment. Perhaps the most difficult factor of all, however, is that the kind of balance between personalities required in an effective Marketing organization may not create any one single natural successor.

The larger the team, paradoxically, the greater may be the problem. Teams of brand managers may be picked for their complementary characteristics. This one is a good digger for facts; this one is a superb ideas man but weak on detail; a third is great at execution and follow-up but not the world's best ideas man. In a multi-product company, there is not only room for such various characters, there is need for them. There are horses for courses in selling too, and under one set of circumstances you would choose one man for promotion but you would pass him over given different circumstances. The good Marketing Director may find his hardest problem to be that of choosing and training his successor, for he will have chosen his immediate subordinates as a team. The team as a whole would make a perfect successor and that is often the reason why a Marketing Director is *not* replaced by a single man but by two men, a Marketing Director and a Sales Director.

Conclusion

It is a sad mistake to believe that a complex Marketing organization will run itself. Nor can a man be the titular head of the organization and totally abdicate responsibility for whole sections and avoid contact with them. Salesmen, in particular, resent the Marketing Director who is a sort of unseen *éminence grise*. The man chosen to run this kind of completely integrated Marketing department must be chosen primarily for his man-management ability and only secondarily for his technical ability.

Chapter 23

The Coordinating Role

It has already been emphasized that the Marketing man does not exist to replace anybody, he is primarily there as a co-ordinator with particular expertise in identifying and seizing profitable customer opportunities. It would be foolish to pretend that bringing a Marketing man into an organization will create willing cooperation and total commitment where none existed previously. Resentment by other functional heads and the wrong choice of man for the Marketing job frequently create quite the opposite effect. Inevitably there will be some repetition between sections of this chapter and previous ones for, throughout this book, I have either encouraged or assumed close contact and a regular exchange of information along the shortest possible lines of communication. I want to look at some of these situations again, and some new ones, as they affect the Marketing Director. His role is a special and difficult one, for he must be careful how he handles relationships upwards, downwards and sideways: he must both set an example himself and also be responsible for seeing that his subordinates go through not only the necessary formal motions but also those of pure courtesy.

Production

All Marketing men recognize the fundamental importance of close cooperation with Production. This is not always reciprocated and we probably all know of instances where something has been done in the factory for purely departmental reasons without any consideration of the possible effects on the buyer. However, even where close cooperation does exist it is frequently altogether too one-sided with Marketing the dominant role. An early appreciation of what the factory can do and what would be the ideal method of operating if it had only to consider its own departmental situation should be compulsory for all Marketing men. There is, as we have already seen, a great deal of reconciling to be done between the desire of the consumer to become a buyer and the ability of the producer to be a supplier. Similarly, the existing capabilities of the production department and any special expertise it has usually provide a firmer foundation for success than shooting off immediately in new directions without optimizing existing opportunities in present ones. Areas where Production should speak up and where Marketing may be able to help concern seasonality and over- or under-employment of resources. Break-even analyses may reveal that the overall good of the company is best served by trying to iron out peaks and troughs even though the insular view of the brand manager would be to spend against the time of peak opportunities. Any calculations of this sort must look for differences between the short-term solution and the longer-term one. Loss of profit is highly likely through irregular employment of total resources in the short run; in the longer run lost opportunities may be more important. It is probable that too few production departments raise the question and that too many Marketing men assume the answer without doing the sums.

It may seem strange to expect a brand manager, say, to want to know how the Production Director would like to run his part of the business if it weren't for the perversity of the customers. However, this is an excellent way of discovering the economics of production, its flexibility or the extent to which it is tied to doing certain things, and the kind of change that is going to cost money. It is the beginning of an understanding of what short-term demands for something out of the normal run of things will do. The expected value from extra sales by attaching a dish-cloth to a packet of detergent must be set against the problems the factory will find in using hand operations, slowing down the packing rate, using special sized outers and so on. Problems will be created for other departments too but we can consider those later. The Marketing Director should constantly be saying to his brand managers, 'What does the Factory Manager say about this; can he do it; how will it affect his costs; what will it do to timing?' and whatever other similar questions may be appropriate to your business. The Chief Executive should be able to rely on his Marketing Director to ensure that these checks are carried out. Many companies who rely upon brand managers to make final recommendations insist that wherever another department is committed in any way their signature should appear in a special column alongside the appropriate item, or alternatively that a list of appropriate managers should signify their approval to the commitment and figures applying to them by initialling and dating an appropriate box at the end of the document. This is a useful formality, but an atmosphere should be encouraged by both the Chief Executive and the Marketing Director where frequent face-to-face contact occurs without pressure being brought to bear on either side.

Perhaps the biggest problem in interdepartmental communication arises from the kind of people Marketing men are. They are basically ideas men, interpreting opportunities and turning them into realities. Production men, especially, are practical men dealing with possibly scarce and expensive resources. They must be made to understand clearly the difference between 'pie in the sky' ideas and those with enough substance to justify work and probable interruptions to existing production from the factory. Friction between the two departments is frequently due to brand managers starting too many wild hares. In a large organization, procedures will probably exist that make it necessary to seek formal authority for new work. The greatest dangers are in the small and medium-sized companies where the brand manager may have – or act as though he had – much more power of command.

The production department is responsible for the manufacturing aspects of the total Marketing effort of the company. (Substitute 'service' for companies in the service business: here your 'production' department may be pilots, technicians, air and ground hostesses, or actuaries, brokers, agents and door-to-door collectors.) Good coordination with Production is not merely a matter of brand managers talking over ideas with factory managers: it is also very much concerned with letting people on the shop floor know what is going on, why this product is going to be replaced by another and so on. There are several ways in which this can be done. They are of very different levels of effectiveness but even the worst is better than none at all. The most frequent methods, where such communication is regarded as important, are product show-cases, notice-boards for advertisements and bulletins, and articles in the company magazine. Better than nothing, but no substitute for actually talking to each shift and explaining what is happening and why, perhaps showing them the advertising before it appears. This was the secret behind the Petfoods anecdote in Chapter 1. Showcases quickly get tatty and out of date, notice-boards don't always get changed as often as they should, and magazines appear at the wrong times for many of these events and are in any case meant for a wider and often less closely involved audience.

The importance of detailed and early discussion with Production and Programming has already been considered when we examined the planning sequence. Once that plan is under way it should be continually amended. However, Production should be asking Marketing from time to time how much credence it now places on its plans, what is the probability of targets, say, being exceeded in August when holidays will cause labour problems. The Marketing man, for his part, should intelligently anticipate these vital questions. The majority of companies *do not* employ rolling plans, and make amendments at intervals which are too long for effective remedial action to be taken in terms of taking on or putting off labour. This makes a continuing dialogue all the more important.

Buying and Programming

Here I am no longer concerned with formal early-warning systems such as we considered when looking at ways of formulating annual plans. I merely want to emphasize the kind of day-to-day early-warning systems and checks that are necessary to ensure that the right product is produced at the right time in the right quantities. Obviously, this must also mean that Production produce to defined quality standards and Distribution have the right stocks in the pipeline.

One of the first things the Marketing man must understand is the degree to which buying, programming and production are linked in his business. It may be that changing the blend of tobacco in a cigarette will make no difference to programming or to production. On the other hand, it may be that a coarser or finer blend could have very significant effects on Production who would have to run extensive machine trials and perhaps have to change the length or thickness of the cigarette or cigar. This situation would clearly affect programming and the launch date of the changed blend. Apparently insignificant changes (so regarded because they are not discernible to the consumer nor significant to the accountant) can often have quite dramatic repercussions in the factory, and serious delays can result if planning does not take trials into consideration.

There are three main areas where close contact is necessary between Marketing and the buyers of raw materials or components (remembering that to the package-tour operator, for example, the buyer is the man who charters the aircraft and books the hotel rooms):

1. Buying needs the longest possible warning of long-term changes in demand.
2. Marketing needs the earliest possible warning of changes in raw materials (etc) prices.
3. Marketing needs early warning of changes in buying standards so that their effects can be measured.

In the first of these, we are again talking mainly about those companies where the rolling plan is not in operation. One of two things tends to happen: the buyer rings up the brand manager and asks whether sales are going to stay at this level because, if so, he needs to go into the market hurriedly (and perhaps uneconomically) or try to sell off some stock or get the best price he can for his 'future' (promises to buy at a fixed price at some future date). It will depend on how good or bad prospects look. Stocks of raw materials usually occupy a significant place in the total assets of a company. They can play an even more important part in the fortunes of the company where shrewdness in buying can itself be a profitable activity. Companies in the confectionery, coffee, sugar and tea businesses – among many others – have frequently made large profits and losses on market operations quite independently of their selling of converted product. Bad forecasting, reluctance to change forecasts or – far worse – sins of omission through lack of contact can result in employing too much cash in raw materials stocks (or more aircraft than there are passengers for, more shops than there are customers for, more beds than there are occupants for, etc, etc) or reduced profits through having to buy at times of high prices. Worse still, lost sales through lack of stocks. It should not be necessary to spell out the resultant problems of having insufficient raw materials on the one hand or full warehouses on the other.

I think I may safely generalize about the second point from personal experience of dealing with a number of companies and from intensive questioning on the second point among managers attending courses at which I have lectured. My generalization would be that there is usually early warning (most often up one side of a triangular structure to the Chief Executive and down the other side to the brand manager) of an impending price rise or shortage. However, favourable variances are pulled out with a 'look what a good boy am I' smirk at the end of the financial year. This is due partly to bad communication, partly to interdepartmental jealousy and partly to distrust of Marketing who are frequently regarded as likely to rush out and spend the extra profit. If that is likely to happen, the Chief Executive should change his team, and quickly. No good Marketing man will ever sacrifice tomorrow for today but that is precisely what may happen if important cost facts are sat on either by the buyer or the Chief Executive. The Chief Executive has every right to say, 'We are making this extra profit through advantageous buying: I propose to keep it – unless Marketing can make a good case for any better course of action.' There are other options available to the Chief Executive: if the buyers are feeling 'bullish' (that is, if they expect prices to rise again), there may be a case for increasing the capital employed by filling the warehouses. The Marketing man must know of this and, preferably, be a willing part to the decision. It may mean that the required return on total assets will have to go by the board this year in the expectation of a much more favourable result next year. All the questions of elasticity of demand and likely competitive reaction must be studied in such situations.

The third area concerns the role of the Marketing man as custodian of the customer's standards. If the buyers are going to use a lower proportion of Assams in your tea, how do you know whether the fact that the tasters can't tell the old from the new means that your loyal customers can't either? If your booking agents are going to use Don Carlos's hotels this year instead of El Pedro's, will your regulars be put off; how can you sell them the advantages of the new deal? This problem is acute both where science is conspicuously absent (as with products like coffee, tea and wine) and where highly scientific standards are used (as in heavy industry). The first case, where skilled judgement is used, needs little expansion. The second seems clear-cut, yet there have been absolute disasters with aircraft components which have passed all their tests on the ground yet failed in the air. Perhaps no known form of test could have avoided such disasters, but Chief Executives would do well to recall what we examined in Part 1: that customers do not always buy the product for the use you intended when it was made. Close contact at the stage where changes are under consideration should help cover all known eventualities.

Programming seems to have received little attention in this section other than a mention of the way that over- or under-stocking of raw materials, ingredients or components can disturb scheduling, affect warehousing and lead to uneconomic and inefficient production. It is difficult to single out Production Programming because it is treated in so many different ways from company to company. Sometimes it is housed in Production, sometimes with Distribution and, more rarely, sometimes exists in its own right. One especially valuable thing that the production programmes can do is to accurately log all batches and code all outgoing products. This is vital if complaints are to be tracked down, faults rectified, below-standard products kept out of distribution and tabs kept on the acceptance (or otherwise) of changed product formulations. One very famous company received a significant number of complaints about a particular model of an expensive domestic appliance. Because it had no way of telling whether all the complaints related to the same batch, it withdrew all available stocks and advertised extensively for people to take their machines back to the shop where they bought them for check-ing. All the faulty machines (both from the initial complaints and those discovered as the result of the free check) were found to have the same fault. A simple system at the factory which could have tied in with the guarantee card that customers re-turned on purchase could have saved that company some £200,000 – the difference between the cost of contacting the right people less the cost of unnecessary checks and the cost of advertising. Doubtless the advertisement didn't help the image of that company which fell from leading innovator and thus brand leader to a minor share of the market within two years. Another example of the extent to which everyone in the busi-ness must have the interests of the consumer at heart: an in-plant system could have resulted in speedy action at the least cost to the company.

Other Departments

We have already dealt extensively with Research and Develop-ment and Finance. There is no need to consider relations with the sales department for we have already put it under the wing of the Marketing Director and considered the coordination of brand-stream and sales-stream activity there. Two areas we may have missed by assuming them to be in departments already considered are quality control and technical research.

It is the Marketing man's job to ensure that quality control is carried out against consumer standards, not production standards (ideally, the two will become the same). He should be a frequent visitor and pass on first-hand all new information he has gathered about the buyers of the product. He should also see all complaints investigations and look for any patterns that may reveal new things about consumers' attitudes. (For example, complaints about the product often increase after a pack change even though nothing else has changed. Incidentally, the customer is always right: you never tell them that you could find nothing wrong with the product!) With technical research, it is a matter of applying the creative input of the Marketing man, based upon deep study of buyer behaviour, to the technical skills of the experts. This combination, as we saw in the chapter on new products, can lead to new uses for existing materials or previously unthought-of uses for new materials.

What is of great importance is that the Marketing Director should not only maintain close contact with his opposite numbers on detailed points but that he should create general contact with *all* his colleagues. The results of the Marketing Director's activity are visible and thus open to comment in a way which a machine breakdown (unless widely publicized) is not. This combination of direct relevant contact and general information sessions can prevent conflict at the Board table, a situation which must cause the Chief Executive to doubt the word of someone if not several members. The Marketing Director should invite his colleagues to view new advertisements before they appear, invite them to attend sales conferences as guests, ask them to come along and talk to members of his team about their job, their programmes, what makes life difficult for them and how they think the Marketing department could help make it easier. The Marketing Director should inveigle reciprocal invitations to address factory managers, works committees and so.

Below Board level (or executive or whatever it may be called in your business) direct contact between operational managers may usefully be supplemented by informal committees. These should meet only when decisions can be made and upheld at the level of the participants, or they should be purely exchanges of information and problems. They probably ought not to be standing committees or they will be held whether there is any real reason for meeting or not and status problems will creep in and a useful meeting between four men will become a useless one between fourteen. Much more useful and practical (although not removing the need for these informal committees) is the 'project system' where a mixed team is given a specific problem to solve and recommend on. The leader of this project can come from any branch of the business and no one department should enjoy a monopoly of project leaders. It will, however, normally be a good idea to pick a man who will be both a good team leader and learn a lot about some function other than his own. The principle should be carried upwards with a member of the senior management team having authority for controlling any expenditure, prodding and pushing and making the final recommendation or giving it his seal of approval if the project leader is to present it.

No man is an island but in business senior managers frequently behave as though they were. Whilst it is the Chief Executive who must ultimately bear the blame for this state of affairs and remedy it, the Marketing Director must realize, and must make every member of his team realize, that effective coordination is essential if the business is to achieve its goals. The Marketing department expects, and has a right to expect, a great deal of information and willing cooperation from other departments but they must realize that the managers of these departments have objectives to achieve which leave little time for providing inessential information, attending unnecessary meetings and chasing hare-brained schemes. The Marketing department has a complex relationship with other departments: it can either ask them to do things or get the Chief Executive to instruct them to do them. There is no doubt that a shared commitment based upon common agreement of the need is the surer way to success.

The Advertising Agency

Most Marketing Directors will have come up through Brand or Sales Management. In both cases, it is difficult to loosen the grip on the reins one has previously held so tightly. Since everyone regards himself as an expert on advertising, it is particularly hard to sever one's connections with the advertising agency or at least reduce them to an absolute minimum. If the Marketing Director is seen to reserve the right of final approval to himself, the advertising agency will be tempted either to by-pass the brand manager or present to him and his Director simultaneously. The problem is magnified if the Chief Executive also has to set the final seal of approval.

It would be easy to give brand managers absolute power of acceptance or rejection of all advertising material and thus remove the gibe that they have responsibility without authority. However, many brand managers are inexperienced and few have received any sort of training to judge creative material or accumulated enough experience to make snap decisions. Those who have are usually in more senior roles. The problem is thus one of giving the brand manager authority in his dealings with his advertising agency yet imposing disciplines and checks to safeguard against inexperience.

The biggest danger for a Marketing Director may be that of granting the power to say 'no' to too low a level in the organization. The power to say 'yes' is less harmful: you can always see the results and, late in the day though it may be, there is still time to stop or make changes. The great idea to which some young, inexperienced brand manager has said 'no' will never see the light of day and may result in lost opportunities. This fact first struck me when I was walking round one of my agencies and saw what I thought was a great advertisement pinned on someone's wall. When I asked when I could expect to see this presented formally, I was told that it had already been rejected by the brand manager concerned. I reinstated it into a piece of creative research and it won by a wide margin and was a major factor in the successful re-launch of a brand. I went back to my office and sat down with my two Marketing

Group Managers and we evolved a system which worked very satisfactorily from everybody's point of view.

The basis of the system was the Brand Strategy, an outline of how the customer was to be approached through both advertising and promotions arrived at jointly by the brand manager and his agency counterpart. Once agreed internally, the basis of judgement of creative work was 'How well does this fit the agreed strategy?' Brand managers were asked not to give immediate decisions – other than ask for factual corrections – at the first presentation meeting. The agency had put a great deal of thought into the work and it was only fair that the brand manager should pay it the same compliment. The next stage was that he would make a recommendation to his Marketing Group Manager to accept or reject the work. If they both agreed, that was the decision the brand manager would take back to the agency. If they disagreed, the senior of the two would discuss the matter with me. (The reason for the senior coming alone in the first instance was to avoid the possible embarrassment of deflating a senior manager before his subordinate.) When the two of us had reached our decision (or I had given a ruling!) the brand manager could have a go at changing our decision if it had gone against him. If the two of them had decided to go ahead, I would see approved scripts, storyboards or rough artwork at the appropriate time.

This may sound like a very formal and inflexible way of working but it operates very smoothly when approached in the right spirit and with a conspicuous lack of formality. There would be occasions when an agency wished to present something which was such a radical departure that it wanted to sell its ideas to the full decision-making group simultaneously: sometimes a brand manager would ask his immediate superior and myself to attend a special presentation. Rather than rules, these were a set of guidelines which would normally be followed.

They had three great advantages. Firstly, it took at least two people to kill an idea (which is far safer odds than one!). Secondly, the agency, having been involved in setting the strategy, knew that they were unlikely to have their ideas re-

jected *in toto* if they fitted the agreed strategy. Thirdly, and
most important, the agency did not feel they were dealing with
an echelon of command. When this happens, there is a temptation either to present to the top man or to have a series of
separate and often conflicting contacts at each level on both
sides. The Brand Manager-Account Executive direct relationship, each with his own internal disciplines, was the bedrock
of the system.

Although we tried – and I think we succeeded – to use this
system as informally as possible, it can be even less rigid for a
less complex organization. It is merely one way of solving the
problem of who has the authority to approve creative work
and with what constraints. In other words, what is the point of
having dogs if you are going to bark for them: it is better to tell
them when not to bark. In many companies, the problem is the
Chief Executive who insists on approving all advertising, which
is rather like sampling all the products before they leave the
factory. In smaller organizations the Chief Executive may be
the last-resort man in the same way as the Marketing Director
is used in the system outlined. I submit that this is only justified if he has both the necessary experience and time to do the
job properly.

One final point: in the system outlined the agency had the
right of appeal. It was hardly ever exercised because the basis
of assessment was a subjective judgement (quantified wherever
possible) of how well the work submitted fitted the declared
objectives. In view of the way the strategy was set, there wasn't
a great deal of room for argument in the majority of cases.

I do not make a case for the Marketing Director abdicating
from all contact with his advertising agency. He is a very busy
man and he must ration that contact. It will be primarily concerned with communicating high-level policy decisions, discussing staffing problems, overall agency/client relationships
and involvement in major presentations of special campaigns
or major departures from previous campaigns. What I strongly
make a case for is direct contact at the smallest possible number
of decision levels – ideally only one – on each side. This will
give the brand manager greater job satisfaction, give the

account executive greater respect for him and make everybody's life easier. In practice, the brand manager will probably say something like, 'I like this very much, it's smack on our strategy; I'll go away and sell it to my boss. I can't see that we are likely to argue about more than the odd word.' Even with only limited experience of this system, he will probably be right. From then on, it's his baby.

I do urge Chief Executives and Marketing Directors to consider seriously, not only in the area of advertising but in all other areas, whether they may not have put themselves in a potentially dangerous situation by giving inexperienced managers at relatively low levels in the organization the right to say 'no'. The corollary, however, is not that only the Chairman has the right to say 'yes'!

Recommendations

The end results of coordination are recommendations and action. Recommendations must be framed in ways that make suggested action clear and ease the path for their acceptance. Whilst different companies have their own formats for recommendations, the underlying principles should be the same: no busy manager wants to wade through masses of paper trying to find a suggested course of action or sort out alternatives for himself. He wants alternatives spelled out, evaluated and rated. All that should remain for the recipient to do is to indicate his approval or rejection. The good Marketing Director says, in effect, 'I have considered all the alternatives and I recommend this plan because . . .' The bad one presents half a dozen carefully worked out plans and almost seems to say, 'You're paid to take the decisions around here. You choose.'

This principle applies both upwards and downwards: the Marketing Director should expect to receive recommendations from his staff in the same way. There will be one big difference, however. As part of the training role of the Marketing Director and as a tribute to his expertise and experience he will more readily accept that his subordinates may sometimes ask for help, for they will more frequently encounter new situations.

Except in the early days of the working association between Chief Executive and Marketing Director and where precedent may be concerned, the latter should always advise the former what to do, not ask him! Even in the cases mentioned, it will normally be better to consult other line managers rather than worry the already busy Chief Executive. Two other aspects merit attention: one is the preparation of documents to go out under another person's name, the other is the preparation of rough discussion drafts. None of us likes the idea of doing all the work for someone else to sign but it frequently has to be done: when the Chairman writes to the Managing Director he expects the same man to answer; he isn't bothered where the facts come from. In such situations, the ideal letter or memorandum is one which is so completely thought out and well expressed that the man it is written for indicates his approval merely by signing it. He may ask for a rough draft first. There is no excuse for a rough draft including ideas just for kicking around; the Americans have a lovely phrase for this kind of behaviour in word or print: 'Let's run it up the flagpole and see who salutes'! A discussion draft should have all the finished thought that one would hope to see in the final document; it will lack only polish in physical presentation. The one valid respect in which it may vary from the final version is that it may include all possible alternatives whereas the final document will concentrate on the most viable and merely indicate the reasons for rejection of other alternatives. Even so, one course of action should be spelled out in the detail and form in which it should ultimately appear: a draft is not a vehicle for shifting the burden of decision between alternatives.

The greater part of this philosophy derives from an article believed to have first been published in the American publication *Army–Naval Journal* some time prior to 1943 and reprinted periodically in the *Daily Administrative Bulletin* by the US Bureau of Ships at regular intervals well into the 1950s under the title 'Completed Staff Work'. The last three points (numbered 7, 8 and 9 in the original) bear repetition:

1. The 'completed staff work' theory may result in more

work for the Staff Officer but it results in more freedom for the Chief. This is as it should be. Further, it accomplishes two things:

(a) The Chief is protected from half-baked ideas, voluminous memoranda and immature presentments.
(b) The Staff Officer who has a real idea to sell is enabled more readily to find a market.

2. When you have finished your 'completed staff work', the final test is this:

(a) If *you* were the Chief, would you be willing to sign the paper you have prepared?
(b) Would you stake your professional reputation on it being right?
(c) If the answer is in the negative, work on it further, because it is not yet 'completed staff work'.

3. The above applies to each individual for each of his work assignments. In pursuing an assignment, discussion of the assignment with a supervisor has a proper place. An improper application of this discussion is avoidance by the individual of the responsibility for 'thinking a project through' in all its phases.

Substitute the appropriate words for 'Chief', 'Staff Officer' and 'Supervisor' and you have a system of tremendous value for all levels and all functions but, above all, a working method which should be absolutely sacrosanct in the relationship between the Marketing Director and his Chief Executive.

Conclusion

The Marketing man does not exist to replace anyone but to co-ordinate the various activities of the business to achieve the company's desired goals. Although it has been necessary to make some of these relationships sound exceptionally formal, coordination is greatest where people meet and talk freely because they share common goals and commitments to those goals. Whilst this is both primarily and ultimately the responsibility of the Chief Executive, the Marketing Director (or whatever may be the title of the man fulfilling that function) has an absolutely critical role to play. Indeed, many an ineffective Chief Executive has been shielded by the sheer professional competence and pride of his next level of management.

One must always remember that the new management techniques that spring up with monotonous and frightening regularity often have very short practical life cycles and, like the lives of products, they are getting shorter. The questing creative mind of the Marketing man should act as an antidote to outmoded thinking and adherence to obsolete theories. The more thoroughly he acts as a coordinator, the more opportunity does he have to keep the company young in outlook, fresh and vital. If he retreats into an ivory tower and plays with his theoretical toys or tries to do the Chief Executive's job, he runs the grave danger of being obsessed with habit and deterred from fresh thinking about existing opportunities and creative delving into future ones. A Marketing Director locked up in an ivory tower is an exceedingly insular and exceptionally useless animal. He must never forget that he is a business manager among business managers even if, as in some companies, he is treated as rather more equal than the others!

Appendices

Appendix A Data Questionnaire

This is the example mentioned in Chapter 6. The questions have been broken down in such a way that they can be answered by department. Only the more general questions have been included and anything which might enable the company concerned to be identified, or concerns problems too specific to this particular problem, has been excluded.

If the questions seem exceptionally wide, it must be remembered that this was the beginning of a consultancy operation. The answers could have been found in the Marketing area or they might have been found in poor credit control or bad sales-force utilization.

The questionnaire was carefully presented to the people directly concerned and their immediate subordinates and explained in just the way it was in Chapter 6.

Section 1. Basic

1. What is the company profit objective and on what basis is it calculated?
2. In what form are company and management accounts kept? (Specimens please.)
3. What are general overhead and departmental budgets – for the current year and last year? Which areas have shown the biggest changes (up or down)?
4. How are these kept and reviewed, how frequently are they reviewed and who is responsible for reviews?
5. What is the current business strategy?
   (a) Overall.
   (b) By major lines (i.e. which are chosen for development and why; which are to be allowed to decline and why.)
   (c) Which are profitable/unprofitable? (Justify.)

(d) Which have/have not growth potential ? (Justify.)
6. What plans exist to develop the business over the next five years ? How firm are these and what do you estimate are the probabilities of success and the degrees of risk involved ?
7. What 'ideal' capital investment schemes exist or have recently been under consideration ? If rejected, why ? If deferred, why and for how long ?
8. What limitations exist on expansion of your current sites ? How recently were these checked ?

Section 2. Accounting

1. Is there a standard costing system integrated in the Management Accounts ? Describe, show specimens, describe review procedures and any other relevant detail.
2. What is your invoicing system ? How many invoices are there each week and who raises them ?
3. What are credit terms and what is the credit sanction procedure ?
4. What is the dunning procedure ?
5. What is the average level of bad debts ? Have these shown any variation from norm recently ?
6. Are there any cash collections; if so, how are they controlled ?
7. How are sales dispatched reconciled with sales invoiced ?
8. What is the cost of direct selling and how does this split between channels ?
9. How are new products treated in your costing system; are these costs segregated ?
10. How are overheads allocated to new products and is any adjustment made to existing products ?
11. Are any products costed marginally ? If so, which ? (Justify.)
12. What overhead recovery do you look for on own-label brands, catering packs and export lines ?
13. Are target net profits (or contributions) set by product ? If so, how ?

Section 3. General Administration

1. What is the cost of general administration ?
2. What is the total clerical organization ? How is this split

between departments? (Number of staff, by grades, in each
office, work done by each office, etc.)
3. What bonuses are paid and how?

(Note: Many other questions were included in this section
relating to details of mechanical accounting and payroll handling
at various factory and office locations.)

Section 4. Product Details

1. Give a brief description of each brand with main ingredients
   and product pluses or negatives. (Please state whether these
   are subjective opinions or backed by consumer research.)
2. For each brand: number of packings, packing materials, net
   and gross weights of pack unit and outer unit.
3. Give shelf life for each product. What meaning do you give
   the term and what factors determine it?
4. Full costings for each packing of each product.
5. What is the basis for product costing? Is a target gross
   profit (or contribution) calculated for comparison with
   actual?
6. Which costs are regarded as prime? How are prime cost
   differences treated?

Section 5. Sales (Figures, etc)

1. Copies of all regular sales statistics supplied to senior
   management.
2. For each individual brand (home sales, own-label, catering
   and export versions and broken out by packing where
   appropriate):
   (a) Annual sales (volume and profit) for the last five years;
       budget for next year and as far ahead as you plan.
   (b) Sales by quarter, by sales area and total country, for last
       two years; budget for next year.
   (c) Sales by trade channel, last two years.
   (d) Brand share of total market and market segment (includ-
       ing year-ago position, comparison with any points where
       significant changes occurred and indications of longer-
       term trends if known).

(e) Shop and sterling distribution figures, national and by area (including year-ago position, comparison with any points where significant changes occurred and indications of longer-term trends if known).

(f) Comments on any especial selling problems.

(g) Comments on any especial seasonality.

3. Where significant events took place outside the periods mentioned above, please supply sufficient information to indicate trends and changes in trend (e.g. we believe one of your lead lines reached its peak eight years ago).

(Note: The time periods chosen were, in general, appropriate for the business concerned. This section indicates the type of question: the precise wording will vary by industry.)

Section 6. Advertising, Promotion, Research

1. Full details of total media advertising and all forms of promotion for the last five years, budget for next, by brand. Wherever possible, expenditure by area should be shown.

2. If, in any year, actual expenditure varied either from requested or budgeted figures please indicate extent and give reasons.

3. Details of all present plans which are beyond cancellation date (or will be by the date scheduled for completion of this questionnaire).

4. How is promotion allowed for? In costings? As an overhead, etc? Does the method used allow true and accurate statements about brand profitability to be made?

5. Details of any real evidence on the effectiveness or otherwise of advertising and/or specific promotions.

6. Demographic details on your market, frequency of purchase, duplication between brands, etc with notes on where your brands differ significantly (if at all).

7. Please produce all available original consumer research of any kind with notes of what action (if any) was taken.

8. Describe your Brand Management and Research organization (together with supporting services) with details of specific responsibilities and job statements and personal objectives (if used).

Section 7. Sales Force

(Note: This was a long section, for even a cursory examination had shown that sales force performance was bad yet the overhead cost was far too high for the volume generated. It is repeated almost in full as an indication of fruitful areas of examination of the cost and efficiency of a sales force.)

A. Organization, Pay, Conditions

1. Please provide an organization chart in the fullest possible detail showing management levels, spans of control, sales areas, relationships, etc.
2. What is the average number of men per sales team and how was this arrived at?
3. What is company policy with regard to cars? What allowances are made (e.g. personal mileage, garage, car wash, etc)?
4. What other allowances exist (e.g. storage of display material, removal, disturbance, lunches, telephone, trade journals)?
5. What are salary rates and scales?
6. Provide job descriptions for all grades. (What are duties of various levels?)
7. What is the average cost of a salesman (salary, bonus, vehicle, running costs, on-costs, etc)?
8. What special problems does a salesman encounter in your market?
9. What are his working conditions (e.g. working day, evening work, preparation, paper work, number of days worked, holidays, etc)?
10. What is the degree and frequency of contact between a salesman and his first line manager?
11. What incentive/bonus schemes exist or have existed for salesmen/other sales staff? How effective are/were they? If any dropped, why?

B. The Call

1. How many lines does a salesman (nominally) sell (i.e. total list)?

2. Are they always sold in the same order?
3. Are there some lines the salesman always sells first? If so, are these the same everywhere? If not, what are they, by area?
4. Are there regular sales-drive periods? If so, for how long? How far ahead are they planned? What is the current programme? How flexible can you be?
5. What is the total call universe, by channel, by area?
6. What is the frequency of call (actual/believed/desired)? Total calls broken down by frequency.
7. How are call frequencies decided?
8. How many lines are actually sold at that frequency?
9. What have been recent trends in frequency? Why?
10. How does a shop qualify for a call? What is the minimum order? How many outlets still on your books fall below this minimum?
11. What outlet/business information is kept by the salesman, his line manager, head office?
12. Do salesmen ever sell from car stock? If so, how is this controlled? How successful is it and with which lines?
13. What is your call content and timing (by channel)?
14. What is the extent of your journey planning? Who does it? Who reviews it? When were areas last examined? When are they next due to be examined?
15. What call standards are used?
16. What travel standards are used?
17. What is the average geographical area of each journey? What is the range (highest to lowest)?
18. What are total mileage figures, nationally and by area?
19. How is a new territory decided on?
20. How much pioneering is there and who does it? When?
21. What is the procedure for feedback information (competitive activity, new store openings, etc) from salesmen and to whom?

C. Presentation, Merchandising, Training

1. Is there a salesman rating system? Who does the rating? What steps are taken to check the standards used?
2. Are your salesmen used to planned presentations, using stock control and order forms, plan slips, etc? (These terms

may be unfamiliar: we want to get at what the salesman does in the shop, what aids he has in selling, what documentation exists to check what he does.)

3. How frequent is salesman accompaniment and by whom?

4. What formal training arrangements exist and at what levels? Who does it? Do any salesmen receive special pay/allowances for assisting in training?

5. What is the extent of merchandising activity? Do you have separate people or is it part of the salesmen's job? What training do they receive and from whom?

6. To what extent do you have control of stock and fixtures? To what extent is this in the hands of your competitors and how does this affect your activity?

7. Have you established ideal settings, facings, etc for your products? If so, how successful are you in accomplishing them?

8. Objectively, what is your fair share of the fixtures and to what extent do you get it? How does this vary by area/store, etc?

9. What is the display work-load of salesmen? Have they any assistance?

10. What standard promotional material exists (e.g. dump-bins, wire baskets, headboards, etc) and how are they budgeted for (volume and value)?

11. Do you have special materials/special promotions for sectors of the trade and/or individual stores?

12. Are there any special trade attitudes to your market which differ from attitudes to other product areas in the same stores?

13. How is material distributed to salesmen? Where do they store it? About how much at a time?

14. What equipment do salesmen have (e.g. sample case, merchandising kit, binders, etc)?

D. Head Office Selling

1. What is the structure of Head Office selling? How many people are selling to how many accounts?

2. What are your general principles covering contact with all the various kinds of accounts needing Head Office contact?

3. In what form do listings exist (permission to sell to branches) and how frequently are they revised?

4. What are your current listing problems?
5. In which accounts does your share of business exceed your national/area brand share? Why has this happened?
6. Do salesmen have any contact with central delivery accounts? If so, what do they do?
7. List your ten most important accounts and give as full a sales history as possible together with your budgeted sales for next year. (If, in your opinion, ten accounts give an artificial cut-off point – perhaps because there is a very large gap between the ninth and tenth – use whatever number you think appropriate.)
8. What is your attitude towards trade entertainment, membership of trade bodies, participation in their activities? Do you encourage entertainment/participation at local levels? List any expenditure under appropriate headings. Where does the money come from?
9. Does a separate Head Office promotional budget exist? If so, where does it come from and how is expenditure co-ordinated with other brand activity?

Section 8. Sales Administration

1. How are outlet details kept and in how much detail?
2. How many outlets receive a selling call, a merchandising call only, a distribution call only? (Is it fair to assume that an outlet receiving a selling call will receive all three?)
3. How can an order be raised? What sales/ordering history exists at any level?
4. What is the average number of lines sold per call? What is the range? Is there any significant variation in either the average or the range by sales area/account?
5. Please give the same information (as for 4) for the average number of lines stocked.
6. What is the ratio of orders to calls – in total, by frequency of call, by sales area?
7. How do you control uplift of stock? What is the level? What firm instructions are given to salesmen concerning out-of-life stock? At what level do uplifts run?
8. Do any customers receive permanent special prices?
9. What is the form of warranty and conditions of sale on invoices, credit notes, delivery notes?

10. Are differing versions of the same product/packing available in the same distribution area?

(Note: Because of the nature of this business, many questions had to be asked about purchase tax.

Some of these questions duplicate those asked in earlier sections. This was done deliberately as a test of objectivity. In this particular instance, there were considerable differences between the replies from the Sales Director, the Finance Director and the Sales Invoicing Office. The last two had the facts!)

Section 9. Terms and Promotional Payments

1. What discount and prompt-payment terms apply? Do these apply to all brands, all accounts, all areas?
2. Are there any hidden/concealed/disguised/locally negotiated terms? If so, who decides, how is the accounting done, what are the ground-rules?
3. Do any accounts have 'overriding' discounts? If so, how are they paid (cheque, credit note, deduction from invoice), how frequently, from what budget and on whose authority?
4. Do salesmen know of all the terms to all the accounts? If not, what is kept from them?
5. List all accounts receiving terms better than their volume entitles them to. What are the reasons/history?
6. Is prompt-payment allowance automatic. Do some accounts regard it as automatic? Is it calculated on net or gross price? Is it calculated and shown on invoice?
7. Has any attempt been made to remove prompt-payment allowance and commute it into terms or price? Has any competitor ever done so? If the answer is 'yes' in either case, with what degrees of success?
8. How do your terms compare with competitors'?
9. We believe some of your competitors selling in other markets have a common discount system across all products. Does this appear to work to their advantage/disadvantage or your advantage/disadvantage?
10. How much use is made of your discount terms as an aid to increased volume? What procedures are used for advising

salesmen and accounts that they are close to changing levels?

11. What is the extent of your Paid Promotion activity with selected stores? Give expenditure for last two years, budget for next. What types of activity have been used and what seems to be successful/unsuccessful (by brand, if there are significant differences)?

12. How is this expenditure budgeted/controlled? Who is responsible?

13. What formal controls, assessment procedures exist?

14. Are there any long-term agreements with selected customers? If so, with whom and on what basis? If none, why not? Were any attempted – if so, why did they fail?

15. What evidence have you of the success or otherwise of various types of promotion? Quote in full.

Section 10. Distribution

1. What is the value of capital employed? (Please break this down into whatever detail is available.)

2. How is capital expenditure budgeted and what are future plans for replacement capital/new capital expenditure?

3. Total distribution costs and expenses, depot costs, tonnages, deliveries for last two years, budget for next. Give reasons for significant differences.

4. Full details of depots – locations, areas, freehold/leasehold/rented, details of contracts, sub-letting, etc.

5. Numbers of staff involved in various categories.

6. What are your delivery standards and how rigidly are they enforced?

7. How *real* are these standards (i.e. are any of them based on custom or unchallenged assumption)?

8. Do your products involve any special storage/handling conditions and/or contamination problems?

9. How frequently are depots replenished with stock?

10. Have you calculated the risk (and cost) of running out of stock or not supplying a customer within your standard time? (If so, give figures.)

11. To what extent are vehicles and depots currently utilized (by depot and vehicle type)?

12. Average stockholding packed/unpacked, in factory, depots, shops.

(Note: Because it was known that a major reorganization was already under consideration, this particular circumstance required detailed questions about replacement vehicles, palletization plans, mechanical handling, etc. All this was necessary to examine the effect of such plans on future profitability and service.)

Section 11. Production

1. What is the value of capital employed (broken down into as much detail as possible)?
2. How is capital expenditure budgeted and what plans exist for replacement/new capital expenditure?
3. Total factory costs and expenses and production figures (by brand) for last two years, budget for next. Explain any significant variations.
4. What is the average of raw materials, packaging material, etc (including rent allowance for space)? Have any calculations been done on the effects of increasing/reducing such stockholdings – if so, what were the conclusions?
5. Where a production line produces several items please list these by machine.
6. To what extent is the factory under-utilized – in terms of existing machinery, space, labour, hours worked?
7. How many shifts are worked?
8. If optimum factory operating profit were the sole consideration, which lines would you concentrate on and which would you delete? Why?
9. What products generally available in your market are you unable to manufacture? Why?
10. To what extent is the factory automated and to what extent does this prevent individual variations in products?
11. What is the labour situation at each of your factory sites? How quickly could you recruit to respond to changes in total output of, say, one per cent, five per cent, ten per cent, twenty-five per cent?
12. What limitations exist on factory expansion at existing locations? Do any plans exist? What do they cover?

(Note: The remainder of the questions were highly specific to already identified problems or would make it easy to identify the company concerned.)

Section 12. Own-Label Products

1. What is the extent of stores' own-labels in this market? Who are the leading retailers and the leading suppliers? Is it known which manufacturers supply which retailers?
2. What is the extent and trend of your own business? How secure do you regard it? (Turnover, volume, retailers, products: in each case, proportion of total business accounted for.)
3. What criteria are laid down for soliciting own-label business?
4. Give details of retailers who you have solicited unsuccessfully and accounts you have lost. Why?
5. How does your sales trend compare with the market as a whole and other manufacturers—so far as this can be known?
6. How are such products costed?
7. Who handles sales negotiations? Are salesmen involved at store level – generally or with specific accounts?
8. How is production controlled and budgeted?
9. Are any lines produced which are not part of your general home trade range?

Section 13. Export

1. What is your current strategy and policy?
2. What brands, in what packs, are currently sold in which countries?
3. Are any lines/packings available to the export trade only? (Ignore special outer packings.)
4. What is your attitude to such special lines/packs? What are the limitations – if any – on their use and development?
5. What plans exist for new lines, selling existing home trade lines which are new to existing overseas markets, opening new markets?
6. What do you assess as the opportunities/limitations in terms of future development?
7. What are your competitive advantages/disadvantages in terms of product acceptance, compliance with legal restrictions, price, terms, packings, sales contact, etc?
8. Describe sales arrangements by country.
9. What special product/costing variations are entailed in supplying export packs?

10. Give turnover and profit figures (total, by brand, by country by brand) for the last five years, budget for next.

11. Departmental strength and expense figures for last two years, budget for next. Explain any significant differences.

12. To what extent are you restricted by/dependent upon home trade brands and production capacity?

13. How is export promotion financed and budgeted? What reciprocal advertising exists? Give figures, by brand by country, for last five years, budget for next. Who is responsible for budget, control, content?

Section 14. Catering

1. What is your current strategy and policy?

2. What were your turnover and profit figures (by brand) for the last five years? Budget for next.

3. What brands are currently sold in what packs?

4. Are any lines/packings available to the catering trade only?

5. What is your attitude to such special lines/packs? What practical limitations exist on their use and development?

6. What do you assess as the opportunities/limitations in terms of future development?

7. What are your competitive advantages/disadvantages in terms of product acceptance, packings, prices, terms, sales contact, etc?

8. Are any new lines contemplated; if so, when?

9. How is sales contact made and by whom? Does this vary by account, level of buyer, etc?

10. Do retail salesmen do any catering calls?

11. How is delivery effected; how frequently?

12. What special product/costing variations are entailed in supplying catering packs?

General Notes

This questionnaire relates to a food product sold through many outlets and with many problems. In looking for the best solution to its problems all departments had to be subjected to careful, objective management audit. The basic 'self-analysis' approach was discussed both before and after the answers were completed with startlingly different results.

One other thing that was done was to indicate which questions should be answered first and to ask that anything that could be answered quickly should also be supplied immediately. This permits some analysis to be going on all the time and prevents an overload if all the answers to all the questions arrive together.

Whilst the questions relate to a specific kind of business, the kind of question asked should suggest at least the framework of a similar questionnaire for any business that may find itself in need of such detailed analysis.

Appendix B Percentage Sampling Errors on a Single Random Sample

Sample size (N)	1 in 20 level of probability Statistic (x)			1 in 100 level of probability Statistic (x)		
	10% 90%	25% 75%	50% 50%	10% 90%	25% 75%	50% 50%
50	8·3	12·0	13·9	10·9	15·7	18·2
100	5·9	8·5	9·8	7·7	11·1	12·9
150	4·8	6·9	8·0	6·3	9·1	10·5
200	4·2	6·0	6·9	5·3	7·9	9·1
250	3·7	5·4	6·2	4·6	7·0	8·1
300	3·4	4·9	5·7	4·4	6·4	7·4
350	3·1	4·5	5·2	4·1	5·9	6·9
400	2·9	4·3	4·9	3·9	5·6	6·4
450	2·8	4·0	4·5	3·6	5·2	5·9
500*	2·6	3·8*	4·4	3·4	5·0*	5·7
600	2·4	3·5	4·0	3·1	4·5	5·2
700	2·2	3·2	3·7	2·9	4·2	4·8
800	2·2	3·0	3·5	2·7	3·9	4·5
900	2·0	2·8	3·3	2·6	3·7	4·3
1,000	1·8	2·7	3·1	2·4	3·5	4·1
1,500	1·5	2·2	2·5	2·0	2·9	3·3
2,000	1·3	1·9	2·2	1·1	2·5	2·9
5,000	0·8	1·2	1·4	1·1	1·6	1·8
10,000	0·6	0·8	1·0	0·8	1·1	1·3

Formula: $1·96 \sqrt{\dfrac{x(100-x)}{N}}$ (1:20) $\quad 2·57 \sqrt{\dfrac{x(100-x)}{N}}$ (1:100)

*e.g. If 25% of a sample of 500 homes own a refrigerator then the chances are only 1:20 that the true figure for all homes is outside 21·2% and 28·8% (i.e. 25 ± 3·8). The chances are only 1:100 it lies outside 20·0% and 30·0% (i.e. 25 ± 5·0).

INDEX

If you have enjoyed this PAN
Book, you may like to choose
your next book from the titles
listed on the following pages.

Peter Drucker

THE EFFECTIVE EXECUTIVE   50p

'Peter Drucker has done it again: written a clear, readable and useful book about management ... This is a specific and practical book about how to be an executive who *contributes* ...

'The purpose of the book is to induce the executive to concentrate on his own contribution and performance, with his attention directed to improving the performance of the organization by serving outsiders better. I believe Mr Drucker achieves this purpose simply and brilliantly – and in the course of doing so offers many insights on executive work and suggestions for improving executive performance ...

'I can conscientiously recommend that this book be given the very highest priority for executive reading, and even re-reading' – *The Director*

Victor Buell

MARKETING MANAGEMENT IN ACTION
6op

Top management increasingly places the heaviest responsibilities for plans for a company's future upon marketing management. This stimulating book, full of valuable information, case histories, tables and charts, realistically appraises the marketing concept as *managing for profit*.

Always essentially practical, Victor Buell focuses attention on the key issues of marketing, discusses and delineates the inter-related functions of marketing established products and developing new products, describes the four avenues of growth open to any company and provides detailed guidelines to help the marketing manager meet the challenge of the future.

The author has been national vice-president and director of the American Marketing Association.

Henry Deschampsneufs

MARKETING IN THE COMMON
MARKET   50p

Operating successfully in the Common Market
will mean the survival of only the fittest.

Henry Deschampsneufs defines the seven
marketing skills essential to profitable trading
with the European Economic Community,
and shows how to grasp the opportunities
afforded by membership of the EEC to
achieve both personal and commercial advance-
ment.

Chapters include:

Marketing Services in the Market
Manpower in the Market
Marketing plans for the Market
The Market of the Future
The Common Market Today
Manufacturing for the Market
Money and the Market

A PAN Original

Aubrey Wilson
Editor

**THE MARKETING OF INDUSTRIAL
PRODUCTS**   60p

It is in the industrial field where the great
prizes of the future lie.

Industrial marketing practice should be pur-
poseful, dynamic, forward-looking and based
on sound information.

A scientific approach to this subject by management will turn tomorrow's business activities
into a systematic, planned and controlled
process capable of reaping rich rewards.

Sixteen industrial experts, each regarded as
among the leading practitioners in their
particular marketing specialities, show how to
meet the challenge of the future.

'The first major British work in this field' – *The
Times*